THE CLEAR AND SIMPLE
THESAURUS
DICTIONARY

REFERENCE

THE CLEAR AND SIMPLE THESAURUS DICTIONARY

(Originally titled The Young People's Thesaurus Dictionary)

HARRIET WITTELS
JOAN GREISMAN

Edited and with an Introduction by

WILLIAM MORRIS
Editor-in-Chief of the American Heritage Dictionary

GROSSET & DUNLAP • Publishers • New York

Library of Congress Catalog Card Number: 70-158760

ISBN: 0-448-12198-0 (Grosset Paperback)
ISBN: 0-448-04286-X (Library Edition)

1986 PRINTING

THE CLEAR AND SIMPLE
THESAURUS DICTIONARY

INTRODUCTION

"The difference between the right word and the almost right word is the difference between lightning and the lightning bug." — Mark Twain.

Mark Twain is, of course, the author of many of America's most popular books; in fact, some students of our literature consider him our greatest writer. If you haven't already read *Tom Sawyer, Huckleberry Finn, A Connecticut Yankee in King Arthur's Court,* and other Mark Twain novels and stories, then a wonderful treat is in store for you.

Mark Twain spent his life looking for the *right* word, and avoiding the *almost right* word. And that's what this book is all about.

In the pages that follow you will find hundreds of lists of words. Each word in each list means the same thing or nearly the same thing as the other words in that list. Why bother, you may ask, to gather such words together into lists like these? Simply to help you in two ways. First, to give you all the words which are similar in meaning, so that you can choose the word which seems just right for the thought you wish to convey. Second, to introduce to you words you may not already know. Since you know that all words in each group are synonyms (that's the technical name for words similar in meaning), you can easily guess the meanings of unfamiliar words and thereby greatly expand your vocabulary.

You may wonder why in the world the English language has so many words that mean practically the same thing. Wouldn't life be much simpler if we had only one word for each object or idea?

Well, let's look at a word we all use every day — "friend." We all have friends. If we're lucky, we have lots of them. But some of them are closer friends than others. Suppose you are writing a short essay or poem about friends and friendship. You will find it very helpful to look up the word "friend" in this book. There you will find: "acquaintance, intimate, companion, comrade, mate, associate, colleague, partner, crony, playmate," together with such informal or slang words as "chum, buddy, sidekick, pal."

From this group of more than a dozen words, you'll find it easy to pick the *right* word to express exactly the degree of friendship you want to express.

There's another way that this book can help you to choose the right word. Suppose you want to describe a friend who is usually very calm and quiet but suddenly, as the slang expression goes, "loses his cool." So you want a word that is just the opposite of "calm." Look up "calm" and at the very end of the list you will find a word in gray type: "excited." That's the word you are looking for. It's what the word experts call an "antonym" — a word opposite in meaning to another word.

There aren't nearly as many antonyms in English as there are synonyms because one word, in most cases, will serve as the opposite to several other words. However, if "excited" doesn't seem to be exactly the right word to use, look up "excite" and you will find such words as "arouse, stir, stimulate, provoke." Perhaps a better way to describe your friend would be to say that he is "aroused," "stirred," "stimulated," or "provoked." And you don't need to stop here. If you go one step further, you will look up "arouse" and find more than a dozen synonyms there — and one of them may be the *right* word you have been looking for.

This brings us back to the question of why English has so many words that mean the same or nearly the same thing. The answer is that English is the only language which has borrowed words from every other language spoken on the face of the earth.

There are many reasons for this. Back in the times of the Caesars (43 B.C.), Roman legions invaded England and stayed for nearly four hundred years. They didn't contribute much to the development of English, though a few place names still reflect Roman influence. "Winchester," for instance, was once a Roman army camp, and the "chester" comes from the Latin "castra," the word for "camp."

The English language did acquire thousands of words of Latin and Greek origin when the Normans invaded England in 1066, taking over control of the country and, naturally, adding a great many words of French origin to the language. So we had the first examples of two words meaning almost the same thing — one originally French, the other originally English.

But this was just the beginning. The British proved to be masters of the sea for many centuries. As a small island nation, they had to trade with many other countries to get the food and other materials that they needed to live. And along with the supplies that they brought back to England, the traders brought words to enlarge and enrich their language. For example, many of you wear blue jeans, denims, or corduroy jackets and pants. Each of these names came originally to England — and later, of course, to America — from Britain's international trade. The first "jeans" were made of a fabric woven in Genoa, Italy. Originally woven for ships' sails, it is, as you know, a tough, sturdy fabric. Some sailors decided the fabric would make good, long-lasting pants — and blue jeans were born.

"Denim" also is named after the town in which the fabric was originally made — Nimes, a city in southern France. The original name was "serge de Nimes" (serge from Nimes), but it soon was shortened simply to "denim." And that rugged fabric we call "corduroy" was originally made to be used for hunting jackets worn by French kings. So "corduroy" was originally "corde du roi," or "cloth for the king."

But the British didn't only borrow from the French and the Italians. Everywhere their sailors went, they picked up native words and added them to English. The word "thug," for instance, sounds like something invented in New York City to describe the worst kind of gangsters or hoodlums. Actually, it was originally used in India to describe worshippers of the Indian goddess Kali.

In order to maintain the beautiful and elaborate shrines built in honor of Kali, her followers (the "thugs") would waylay, rob, and sometimes kill innocent travelers in India. So infamous were the thugs that the name came into English as a synonym for crook, ruffian, or hoodlum.

More recently, of course, Americans have contributed many thousands of synonyms to that brand of English sometimes called the American Language. We have invented many names for things and ideas that also exist in England but under very different names. For instance, what we call an "elevator," the British call a "lift." Our "cookies" are "biscuits" in England. A "run" in a stocking would be called a "ladder" by an English girl. Our "molasses" is their "treacle." Our "baby carriage" is their "perambulator," or "pram," for short. And so it goes.

In the pages that follow, you will find thousands of words to help you express yourself clearly, effectively, and imaginatively. Remember, you need not stop at the first list you look up. If you don't find precisely the right word, take any one of the other words in the list and look *it* up. That way, you will find the resources of the world's richest language at your fingertips. And always remember what Mark Twain said: make your goal the *right* word, not the *almost right* word.

William Morris

How to Use
The Clear and Simple Thesaurus-Dictionary

Finding Entry Words

The words that have synonyms and antonyms are called entry words.

above overhead, up, aloft, on, upon below

The word **above,** in heavy black type, is the entry word. All entry words are listed in alphabetical order, just like words in a dictionary.

The word in smaller black type at the top of every page is called a guide word. It will help you to find an entry word quickly. The guide word at the top of the left-hand page is actually the first entry word. The guide word at the top of the right-hand page is the last entry word.

A Book of Synonyms and Antonyms

In the *Clear and Simple Thesaurus-Dictionary* you will find synonyms and antonyms for words, *not* the definitions and explanations you can find in a dictionary. Synoyms are words that have the same meaning and can therefore be substituted for one another in a sentence.

expensive costly, high-priced, dear   cheap
The bicycle was too *expensive* for him to buy.
The bicycle was too *costly* for him to buy.
The bicycle was too *high-priced* for him to buy.
The bicycle was too *dear* for him to buy.

If you cannot find a word, it simply does not have synonyms. Its definition will be found in a dictionary. For example, the word *accordion* has no synonyms, but a dictionary will give its meaning as "a musical instrument with keys, metal reeds, and a bellows."

Antonyms are words that have opposite meanings. Many words listed that have synonyms do not have antonyms.

> **army**   legion, forces, troops, military, militia
> **aroma**   fragrance, odor, perfume, scent

Entry Words With Groups of Synonyms

Sometimes an entry word will have synonyms grouped under different numbers. This means that the entry word has more than one meaning, and each meaning has its synonyms.

> **firm**   1. solid, fixed, secure, unyielding, inflexible, stationary, immovable, rigid, 2. company, business, enterprise

With this type of entry word, you must use judgment and common sense in choosing the appropriate group of synonyms. For example, if you wanted to substitute a synonym in the sentence, "His father's **firm** was closed for vacation," you would choose the group of synonyms following the number 2 for the word **firm**.

Entry Words With the Same Spelling

Sometimes an entry word has two different pronunciations, as well as different groups of synonyms. In that case, it will be entered twice, with numbers in front of the entry word itself.

> **1. minute**   instant, moment, twinkling (*Slang* — jiffy, sec, half a shake)
> **2. minute**   small, tiny, miniature, slight, negligible, insignificant

Placement of Antonyms

Antonyms will be listed immediately after the synonyms, in gray. You will find antonyms for an entry word that has many groups of synonyms, right after each group, unless one antonym fits all the groups. In that case, the antonym will be listed on a separate line, under all the groups, in gray.

> **due** 1. proper, rightful, fitting, just, fair, square, equitable unfair, 2. owed paid
> **bright** 1. shining, clear, vivid, 2. smart, alert, intelligent, 3. pleasant, cheerful, lively
> dull

Slang Terms

Occasional slang terms are given in parentheses, listed as synonyms for an entry word. Slang terms are used in common, everyday, informal talk, words that have developed from attempts to find fresh, colorful, or humorous expressions.

> **friend** acquaintance, intimate, companion, comrade, mate, associate, colleague, partner, crony, playmate, chum, buddy (*Slang* — sidekick, pal)

Adapting Forms of the Root Word

Many words are derived from one root word. Ordinarily, in this book, only one of those words will be listed with its synonyms. The other form of the word will simply be mentioned under the chosen entry word, in capital letters. Here again, judgment and common sense will be needed to adapt the synonyms to the form you need.

> **happy** contented, glad, joyful, blissful, cheerful, bright, radiant unhappy, sad
> HAPPILY, HAPPINESS

For example, in the sentence, "He found **happiness** in his work," you would change the synonym *contented* to *contentment* ("He found **contentment** in his work"), the synonym *glad* to *gladness* ("He found **gladness** in his work"), etc.

Adapting Parts of Speech

Similarly, if an entry word can possibly be considered as a verb, adjective, adverb, or noun, but is treated here as a verb, you might need to adapt it for use as one of the other parts of speech.

> **gag**   silence, muzzle, muffle, restrain

In this example, *gag* is treated as a verb, as are all of its synonyms. If you wanted to substitute synonyms for the noun *gag*, as in the sentence, "The robber put a **gag** on his victim's mouth," you would adapt the verb *gag* in this way:

> **gag**   silencer, muzzle, muffler, restraint

A

a   one, any

abandon   desert, forsake, leave, give up entirely, cease, depart, leave undone, discard, relinquish, surrender, discontinue, quit, evacuate, withdraw (*Slang* — throw up, turn one's back on, wash one's hands of, pull out on) keep, fulfill, stay with

abase   bring down, make lower, make humble, demote, degrade, reduce (*Slang* — bump, bust)

abashed   ashamed, embarrassed, confused, bewildered, humiliated, mortified

abate   reduce, lessen, put an end to, stop, do away with, decrease, curtail, moderate   increase

abbey   convent, monastery, nunnery, cloisters

abbot   monk, friar

abbreviate   shorten, curtail, condense, abridge, contract, reduce, cut, compress   lengthen, increase
ABBREVIATION

abdicate   renounce, give up, resign, relinquish, abandon, quit, surrender, vacate   retain

abdomen   belly, paunch, stomach (*Slang* — breadbasket, pot, corporation)   ABDOMINAL

abhor   hate, dislike, detest, loathe, despise, feel disgust for love

abide   1. accept, obey, endure, tolerate, 2. stay, reside, dwell

ability   power, skill, talent, competence, capacity, capability, efficiency, aptitude (*Slang* — know-how)   inability

abject   wretched, miserable, deserving contempt

able   skillful, capable, having power, competent, efficient, qualified   incapable   ABLY

abnormal irregular, eccentric, odd, monstrous, insane, unnatural normal, sane

aboard on board, on (or into) a ship, train or airplane

abode dwelling, residence, home, address, lodging place, quarters, housing (*Slang* — dump, joint, shack)

abolish cancel, exterminate, destroy, put an end to, do away with, wipe out retain ABOLITION

abominable hateful, disgusting, very unpleasant, dreadful, awful, horrible, atrocious, obnoxious, detestable pleasant

abound plentiful, well supplied, filled, teem with, overflow scarce

about 1. concerning, of, upon, 2. nearly, almost, approximately, 3. around, 4. ready to, on the point of

above overhead, up, aloft, on, upon below

abreast alongside, side by side, lined up, beside

abridge make shorter, abbreviate, curtail, condense, contract, reduce, cut, compress lengthen, increase

abroad overseas, away, outside one's country

abrupt sudden, hasty, short, curt, unexpected

abscess sore, inflammation, pustule, wound

absent away, lacking, truant (*Slang* — playing hookey) ABSENCE, ABSENTEE

absolute complete, perfect, thorough, entire, total, essential, positive, supreme partial ABSOLUTELY

absolve forgive, cleanse, discharge, pardon, excuse, acquit blame

absorb take in, soak up, incorporate, integrate, engross, assimilate, sponge, suck up ABSORBENT, ABSORPTION

abstain refrain, withhold, do without pursue

abstract   1. unconcrete, apart from any real thing concrete,   2. difficult, hard to understand clear,   3. remove, take away, deduct   add

absurd   foolish, ridiculous, not true, unbelievable, impossible, ludicrous   meaningful, sensible
ABSURDITY, ABSURDLY

abundance   plenty, large amount, great quantity, profusion, (*Slang* — oodles, gobs, scads)   insufficient, not enough
ABUNDANT, ABUNDANTLY

abuse   mistreat, severely scold, injure, damage, ill-use
appreciate

academy   school, college, educational institution

accelerate   hasten, speed up, quicken, hurry (*Slang* — step on it, hop to it)   slow down, delay
ACCELERATION, ACCELERATOR

accent   emphasis, stress on syllables of a word, tone, pronunciation, inflection

accept   adopt, believe, approve, take what is offered, consent to (*Slang* — buy, swallow)   deny, dissent
ACCEPTABLE, ACCEPTANCE

access   way of approach   ACCESSIBLE

accessory   addition, extra, contributory, assistant, accomplice, supplement

accident   mishap, injury, casualty, chance, event (*Slang* — fluke)   ACCIDENTAL, ACCIDENTALLY

acclaim   applaud, shout welcome, approve (*Slang* — root for)   disapprove, reject

accommodate   oblige, have room for, supply, conform
ACCOMMODATION

accomplice   partner in crime (*Slang* — sidekick)

accomplish do, carry out, finish, complete, fulfill, perform, achieve, realize (*Slang* — knock off, polish off, do the trick) neglect ACCOMPLISHMENT

accord agreement, conformity, harmony disagreement ACCORDANCE, ACCORDINGLY

account 1. story, reason, information, description, tale, statement, 2. list, sum, record

accumulate collect, store up, increase, assemble, gather, compile, amass ACCUMULATION

accurate correct, exactly right, perfect, O.K., all right wrong ACCURACY

accuse blame, charge, impeach, indict, denounce, tattle, (*Slang* — put the finger on, rat on, frame) absolve ACCUSATION

accustom get used to, familiarize, addict, condition

ache continuous pain, hurt, throb

achieve accomplish, carry out, do, finish, complete, fulfill, perform, realize (*Slang* — knock off, polish off, do the trick) fail ACHIEVEMENT

acknowledge admit, recognize, make known, answer, accept, grant, concede dissent ACKNOWLEDGMENT

acme top, highest point, summit, peak, crown, zenith bottom, lowest point

acquaint make familiar, inform, notify, teach, tell, enlighten, (*Slang* — wise-up) ACQUAINTANCE

acquiesce agree, submit, assent, concur, consent, comply, succumb (*Slang* — buy) dissent

acquire gain, obtain, get as one's own, secure, earn (*Slang* — get hold of) lose ACQUISITION

acquit declare not guilty, absolve, forgive, cleanse, discharge, pardon, excuse blame

acrid   sharp, bitter, stinging, nasty, biting, harsh
sweet, pleasant

acrobat   gymnast, athlete, tumbler

act   1. do, perform, behave, 2. pretend, 3. law

action   1. behavior, thing done, performance, way of working, 2. battle

active   lively, working, energetic, vivacious, dynamic, animated, spirited (*Slang* — peppy) idle, lazy

activity   movement, use of power, energy, thing to do, action

actor   stage player, performer, entertainer, trouper

actual   real, factual, true, genuine, concrete, authentic
nonexistent ACTUALLY

acute   sharp and severe, shrewd, discerning, quick, astute, keen, smart (*Slang* — quick on the trigger, smart as a whip, sharp as a tack, nobody's fool) dull

adamant   firm, unyielding, obstinate yielding

adapt   make fit, make suitable, modify, change, alter, vary, adjust ADAPTABLE, ADAPTATION

add   put together, increase, sum up, total, join, unite
subtract ADDITION, ADDITIONAL

address   1. apply oneself, 2. speech, greeting, 3. abode, home

adept   skillful, expert, apt, proficient unskillful

adequate   sufficient, enough, satisfactory, ample, plenty
inadequate, insufficient

adhere   cling, stick fast ADHESIVE

adjacent   near, adjoining, next to, touching, bordering, neighboring

adjoin   be next to, be close to, be side by side, connect, come in contact with

adjourn postpone, end, put off until a later time, discontinue, suspend, recess, dissolve

adjust arrange, set just right, adapt, make fit, make suitable, modify, change, alter, vary ADJUSTMENT

administer 1. manage, execute, preside, 2. apply, give to, contribute

admirable praiseworthy, excellent, very good, commendable, deserving unfavorable, objectionable ADMIRATION, ADMIRE

admit 1. consent, confess, acknowledge (*Slang* — talk, own up, sing, come clean) deny, 2. allow to enter, induct, receive

admonition warning, advice, reminder, caution, word to the wise, tip

ado action, stir, fuss, trouble, commotion, excitement, hubbub, to-do peace, calm

adopt choose, assume, take to oneself, give a home to, accept as one's own reject ADOPTION

adore love and respect, worship, idolize, cherish, admire, revere hate ADORATION, ADORABLE

adorn beautify, decorate, ornament, garnish, glamorize

adroit smart, clever, adept, skillful, expert, apt, proficient unskillful

adult full-grown, grown-up, mature, developed, of age immature

advance move forward, promote, progress, proceed revert ADVANCEMENT

advantage benefit, upper hand, leverage, gain (*Slang* — edge) disadvantage ADVANTAGEOUS

adventure unusual experience, undertaking, enterprise, event, happening, occurrence, exploit, project, incident ADVENTURER, ADVENTUROUS

adverse unfriendly, hostile, unfavorable, contrary, opposite, harmful ADVERSARY

adversity distress, misfortune, hardship, affliction, grief, disaster, trouble prosperity

advertise announce, notify public, call attention to (*Slang* — plug, boost) conceal, hush ADVERTISEMENT

advice counsel, plan, suggestion, recommendation, instruction, direction, tip ADVISE, ADVISABLE

advocate recommend publicly, speak in favor of, defend, support oppose

affable courteous, pleasant, friendly, sociable, gracious, approachable, amiable, communicative
unsociable, unfriendly

affair occasion, occurrence, event, happening, matter, concern, business, party, festivity

affect influence, sway, move, persuade

affection friendly feeling, admiration, love and respect
dislike AFFECTIONATE

affirm assert, confirm, ratify, state, pronounce, declare, endorse, certify veto, deny AFFIRMATIVE

afflict cause pain, trouble, bother, distress greatly, disturb, perturb, agitate soothe AFFLICTION

affluent wealthy, abundant, plentiful, ample, rich, bountiful, well-off, well-to-do, well-fixed (*Slang* — well-heeled, filthy rich) poor

afford 1. have the means, 2. yield, supply, furnish

affront an open insult, offense, provocation (*Slang* — slap in the face)

afraid frightened, fearful, scared, cowardly (*Slang* — chicken) courageous

after 1. later than, following, next, subsequently before,

2. behind, 3. in search of, in pursuit, 4. because of, 5. in spite of, despite AFTERWARD

again another time, once more, anew, afresh, repeatedly

against in opposition to, versus with

age 1. time of life, period in history, 2. grow old, mature, ripen AGED

agency operation, office, management, work

agent doer, performer, actor, worker, operator

aggravate annoy, irritate, provoke, make worse, exasperate, infuriate, irk, vex (*Slang* — miff, peeve, rile) pacify

aggregate total, amount to, add up, accumulate, compile

aggression attack, assault, offense, invasion defense AGGRESSOR

aggressive belligerent, offensive, hostile, militant, combative peaceful

aghast astonished, surprised, amazed, astounded, bewildered, thunderstruck, awed, flabbergasted

agile nimble, fast, alert, quick, spry, athletic dull, slow AGILITY

agitate disturb, incite, instigate, excite, stir up, inflame, provoke calm AGITATION

agony suffering, pain, grief, distress, anguish, torture, torment, heartache, woe peace AGONIZING

agree consent, assent, accept, approve of, comply disagree AGREEABLE

agreement pact, contract, understanding, concord, bargain, treaty, alliance, deal disagreement

agriculture farming, cultivation, husbandry AGRICULTURAL

ahead   in front, before, forward, in advance, leading, winning
behind

aid   help, remedy, relief, assistant, helper, service, benefit
hindrance

ail   1. trouble, bother, disturb, perturb, 2. be ill, suffer, feel
awful, feel sick   AILMENT

aim   1. direct, point, intend, try, 2. purpose, intention,
objective, goal, end, target

airy   light, breezy, fanciful, lighthearted, gay, graceful,
merry grave, gloomy

aisle   passageway, corridor, alley, lane, channel, artery,
opening

ajar   open, gaping closed

akin   related, alike, similar, connected, associated, affiliated,
allied

alarm   1. startle, arouse, frighten, shock, jar, jolt, agitate,
disturb, unnerve calm,   2. signal, call, warning, summons

alcoholic   drunkard, inebriate, sot, tippler (*Slang* — boozer,
wino, lush, drunk, souse)   ALCOHOL

alert   watchful, wide awake, clear-witted, attentive, ready,
prompt, lively, nimble, on the job, on one's toes dull
ALERTNESS

alibi   excuse, story

alien   foreign, different, strange

allay   lessen, check, quiet, relieve, calm, ease, pacify, moderate, restrain, alleviate excite

allege   declare, state

allegiance   loyalty, faithfulness, devotion, fidelity

alley   narrow back-street, path, aisle, passageway, corridor,
lane, opening

alliance   agreement, pact, contract, understanding, bargain, treaty   ALLIED

allot   distribute, share, divide, assign, apportion, allocate, budget (*Slang* — give out, deal out, dole out, mete out, hand out, dish out, shell out, fork out)

allow   1. let, permit, consent, grant, admit, 2. acknowledge, concede, recognize   deny

allowance   allotment, portion, fee, grant, ration, budget

allude   refer indirectly, imply, mention slightly, suggest, hint, infer, intimate

allure   fascinate, attract, charm, tempt, captivate, infatuate

almighty   powerful, great, divine, omnipotent

almost   nearly, close to, just about

alms   charity, dole, contribution, donation (*Slang* — handout)

aloft   high up, overhead

alone   isolated, solitary, solo, lonely, unaccompanied   accompanied

aloof   away, apart, distant, remote, unsociable, reserved, standoffish, cool   friendly

also   too, in addition, as well, besides

alter   make different, change, vary, deviate, modify, diversify   maintain   ALTERATION

alternate   take turns, switch, interchange, spell

alternative   choice, substitute, replacement

altogether   completely, wholly, entirely, thoroughly, totally   partly

always   forever, all the time (*Slang* — for good, for keeps)   never

amass accumulate, collect, heap up, store up, increase, assemble, gather, compile

amateur non-professional, beginner *professional*

amaze surprise, astonish, astound, aghast, bewilder, thunderstruck, flabbergast AMAZEMENT

ambitious aspiring, set on, intent upon *indifferent* AMBITION

amble stroll, saunter, slow pace *rush*

ambush 1. surprise attack, lying in wait, 2. hiding place, trap

amend change, correct, improve, mend AMENDMENT, AMENDS

ammunition powder, shot, bullets, bombs, shells (*Slang* — ammo)

among amid, between, surrounded by, in with

amount sum, quantity, value, measure, price

ample large, abundant, enough, full, sufficient, plenty *insufficient* AMPLY

amuse entertain, divert, delight, tickle, titillate (*Slang* — slay) AMUSEMENT

anchor 1. fasten, secure, fix, attach, 2. ship hook ANCHORAGE

ancient old, aged, antique, archaic, elderly *young, new*

anecdote story, tale, yarn, account, narrative, joke

angelic heavenly, pure, good, lovely, innocent, virtuous, saintly, godly *devilish* ANGEL

anger wrath, ire, rage, fury, annoyance, irritation ANGRILY, ANGRY

anguish   agony, suffering, pain, grief, distress, torture, torment, heartache, woe   peace

animal   creature, beast

animated   lively, gay, vigorous, spry, active, vivacious, snappy, chipper   inactive   ANIMATION

animosity   hatred, dislike, ill will, bitterness love, good will

annex   1. add, attach, join, unite with, 2. something joined, addition, wing, extension   ANNEXATION

annihilate   demolish, destroy, abolish, end, wreck ANNIHILATION

announce   make known, proclaim, report, broadcast, declare, state, notify, tell ANNOUNCEMENT, ANNOUNCER

annoy   tease, vex, disturb, irritate, make angry please, calm   ANNOYANCE

anoint   oil, grease

answer   reply, respond

antagonize   oppose, cross, go against, counter, provoke, embitter   soothe ANTAGONISM, ANTAGONIST, ANTAGONISTIC

anticipate   expect, await, hope for, foresee ANTICIPATION

antics   capers, pranks, funny gestures, practical jokes, tricks (*Slang* — shenanigans)

antipathy   hatred, strong dislike   love

antique   ancient, old, aged, archaic   new ANTIQUATED, ANTIQUITY

anxious   1. uneasy, concerned, fearful, troubled, bothered, perturbed, agitated, worried   relaxed,   2. eager, desirous, keen   ANXIETY, ANXIOUSLY

apartment flat, suite, dormitory

apathy indifference, unconcern, lethargy feeling, interest

aperture opening, hole, gap

apex tip, acme, highest point, summit, top, peak, crown, zenith lowest point

apologize beg pardon, ask forgiveness, express regret, offer an excuse APOLOGETIC, APOLOGY

appall horrify, shock, dismay, terrify, stun (*Slang* — scare stiff)

apparatus equipment, gear, rig, tackle, furnishings

apparel clothing, dress, garments, garb, attire

apparent plain, seeming, obvious, evident, clear hidden, mysterious APPARENTLY

apparition ghost, illusion, vision, phantom, dream, fantasy

appeal ask earnestly, beg, plead, implore, entreat

appear seem, look APPEARANCE

appease calm, satisfy, quiet, allay, lessen, check, relieve, ease, pacify, moderate, restrain, alleviate irritate

appendage something attached, addition, supplement, tail

appetite hunger, desire, craving

applaud approve, praise, cheer, hail, acclaim, clap (*Slang* — root for) disapprove, reject APPLAUSE

appliance tool, machine, device, instrument, implement, utensil

apply 1. request, ask, petition, 2. put on, administer APPLICANT, APPLICATION

appoint elect, choose, name, vote for, assign, nominate APPOINTMENT

appreciate value, enjoy, think highly of, respect, admire, be grateful repel
APPRECIABLE, APPRECIATION, APPRECIATIVE

apprehend 1. fear, dread, 2. seize, arrest, capture, take prisoner (*Slang* — pinch, run in, nab) release
APPREHENSION

apprehensive afraid, worried, anxious, uneasy, concerned, fearful, troubled, bothered, agitated, perturbed relaxed

apprentice beginner, learner, novice, amateur experienced APPRENTICESHIP

approach 1. come near, advance retreat, 2. entrance, inlet, passageway, access

appropriate 1. suitable, proper, fitting, becoming inappropriate, 2. allot, distribute, share, divide, assign, apportion, allocate, budget (*Slang* — give out, deal out, dole out, mete out, hand out, dish out, shell out, fork out)
APPROPRIATION

approve like, think well of, accept, ratify, endorse, O.K. disapprove, frown on APPROVAL

approximate approach, near, close, roughly correct
APPROXIMATELY

apt 1. likely, suitable, appropriate, proper, fitting unlikely, 2. quick to learn, bright, clever, acute, sharp, shrewd, discerning, astute, keen, smart (*Slang* — quick on the trigger, smart as a whip, sharp as a tack, nobody's fool)

aqueduct waterway, gully, canal, channel, pipe

arbitrary unreasonable, willful fair, reasonable

arbitrate settle, referee, umpire, negotiate, mediate
ARBITRATION

architecture building, structure, construction
ARCHITECT

ardent   enthusiastic, eager, zealous, earnest, sincere, fervent, passionate, warm   apathetic, cool

arduous   difficult, strenuous, hard, laborious (*Slang* — tough, rough)   easy

area   1. extent, space, region, expanse, zone, territory, district, section, neighborhood, 2. size

argue   reason, object, persuade, bicker (*Slang* — hassle) ARGUMENT

arid   1. dry, waterless   wet, fertile,   2. dull, stuffy, flat, unimaginative   colorful

aristocrat   gentleman, nobleman (*Slang* — swell, blueblood) ARISTOCRACY, ARISTOCRATIC

arm   1. part of a body, 2. weapon. 3. equip, defend, fortify, empower

armistice   peace, truce, treaty, agreement, pact, contract, understanding, concord, alliance, deal

army   legion, forces, troops, military, militia

aroma   fragrance, odor, perfume, scent AROMATIC

arouse   stir, excite, awaken, move, provoke, pique, kindle, inflame, foment, stimulate, agitate, disturb, shake

arrange   settle, put in order, adapt, fit, classify, catalog, organize, systematize   confuse, muddle
ARRANGEMENT

array   1. order, 2. display, 3. dress, adorn

arrest   stop, check, seize, catch, apprehend, capture, take prisoner (*Slang* — pinch, run in, nab)   release

arrive   come, reach, get to (*Slang* — show up)   leave
ARRIVAL

arrogant   too proud, haughty, insolent, cavalier (*Slang* — stuck-up, uppish)   humble, modest ARROGANCE

art   1. drawing, painting, sculpture, design, work, composition, masterpiece, 2. skill, knack, craft, technique

artery   1. blood vessel, 2. main road, aqueduct, channel, pipe

artful   1. crafty, sly, deceitful, 2. skillful, clever, cunning, shrewd, knowing (*Slang* — shifty, cagey, slick)   artless

article   1. composition, story, essay, report, treatise, 2. object, thing

artifice   clever device, trick, ruse, foul play, scheme

artificial   false, pretended, substitute, ungenuine, unreal, fake, synthetic, imitation, counterfeit   real, authentic

artisan   craftsman, worker, mechanic

artless   1. natural, simple, without trickery, 2. without art, unskilled, ignorant   artful

ascend   go up, rise, climb, mount   descend

ascertain   find out, learn, solve, answer, clear up

ascribe   assign, attribute

ashamed   embarrassed, humiliated, abashed, mortified   proud

ask   question, find out, inquire, request, invite   answer

askance   1. with suspicion, with disapproval, 2. sideways

askew   crooked, disorderly, twisted, awry   straight

aspect   view, look, appearance

aspire   seek, desire, be ambitious, aim, strive
ASPIRANT, ASPIRATION

ass   1. donkey, mule, burro, 2. dunce, stupid, stubborn, silly, fool (*Slang* — dope, dumbbell, dumb-bunny)

assail   attack, assault (*Slang* — go for, sail into)

assassinate kill, murder, purge
ASSASSIN, ASSASSINATION

assault attack, offense, onslaught, charge (*Slang* — drive, push)

assemble meet, gather together, congregate, collect, crowd, throng, cluster, group scatter, disperse ASSEMBLY

assent agree, consent, accept, approve of, comply dissent

assert declare, state, insist on, affirm, pronounce
ASSERTION

asset valuable things, property, funds, wealth, accounts, resources, goods, capital

assign appoint, elect, allot, choose, name, distribute, apportion, allocate (*Slang* — give out, deal out, dole out, mete out, hand out, dish out, shell out, fork out)
ASSIGNMENT

assimilate absorb, digest, soak up, blot up

assist help, aid, support, lend a hand
ASSISTANCE, ASSISTANT

associate 1. join, connect, combine, unite disconnect, 2. companion, partner, ally ASSOCIATION

assorted various, different, classified, grouped, several
ASSORTMENT

assuage quiet, calm, allay, lessen, check, ease, relieve, pacify, moderate, restrain, alleviate excite

assume 1. suppose, take for granted, presume, suspect, understand, believe, think, 2. put on, adopt
ASSUMPTION

assure convince, make certain, promise, guarantee, pledge
ASSURANCE, ASSUREDLY

astonish surprise, astound, amaze ASTONISHMENT

astound   amaze, surprise, astonish

asunder   apart, separate, divided   together

asylum   refuge, shelter, institution, home, madhouse (*Slang* — booby hatch)

athletic   active, strong, muscular, brawny, able-bodied, well-built, sporting, gymnastic   ATHLETE

atone   make up, make amends, repay   ATONEMENT

atrocious   wicked, cruel, savage, brutal, ruthless, terrible, horrible, dreadful, awful, vile, wretched, contemptible kind, good

attach   fasten, join, connect, affix, add, put together, increase, unite   detach   ATTACHMENT

attack   raid, siege, bombardment, assault, offense, onslaught, charge, drive, push

attain   1. reach, arrive, come, get to, 2. gain, accomplish, finish, complete, fulfill, achieve, realize   ATTAINMENT

attempt   try, endeavor, make an effort (*Slang* — take a fling at, have a go at)

attend   1. be present, visit, go to   be absent,   2. serve, help, work for, administer to, care for
ATTENDANCE, ATTENDANT

attention   care, courtesy, consideration, concern, thoughtfulness, politeness   ATTENTIVE

attest   give proof, testify, certify, give evidence, swear, vouch

attire   dress, array, adorn

attitude   viewpoint, standpoint, position, opinion

attract   pull, interest, draw, fascinate, allure, charm, tempt, captivate, infatuate   ATTRACTION

attractive   pleasing, winning, charming, desirable, beautiful   unattractive

attribute   1. assign, ascribe, give, place, apply, 2. characteristic, quality, trait, nature, feature

audacious   bold, daring, foolhardy, arrogant, haughty, insolent, cavalier   shy, humble   AUDACITY

audible   hearable, distinct, clear, plain   inaudible

augment   increase, enlarge, expand, raise, extend, broaden, magnify   decrease

auspicious   favorable, fortunate, lucky, promising, timely unfortunate, untimely

austere   harsh, stern, strict, severe (*Slang* — tough, hard-boiled)   soft, lenient

authentic   real, reliable, genuine, legitimate, actual, factual, true (*Slang* — straight, sure enough, honest to goodness) false, artificial

authoritative   commanding, powerful, influential, official AUTHORITY

authorize   give power to, legalize, enable, assign

autocrat   ruler, monarch, dictator, tyrant

autograph   sign, endorse, approve

automatic   self-acting, spontaneous, self-working   manual AUTOMATICALLY, AUTOMATION

auxiliary   helping, assisting, aiding

avail   use, help, benefit, profit, advantage, value, worth, serve

available   handy, convenient, ready, at hand, obtainable unavailable, unobtainable

avarice   greed, lust, desire for money   AVARICIOUS

average   1. usual, ordinary, passable, fair unusual, extraordinary, 2. middle, medium   extreme

averse   opposed, unwilling, against, forced, involuntary willing

aversion   strong dislike, hatred, loathing   love

avert   prevent, avoid, turn away, prohibit   invite

avid   eager, greedy

avocation   hobby, minor occupation, sideline

avoid   keep away from, shun, evade, snub   seek
AVOIDANCE

award   prize, grant, gift, trophy, reward, medal

aware   knowing, realizing, conscious, cognizant
ignorant, unaware

awe   fear and wonder, astonishment, surprise, dread, respect, alarm

awful   unpleasant, atrocious, wicked, cruel, savage, brutal, ruthless, terrible, horrible, dreadful, vile, wretched
pleasant   AWFULLY

awkward   clumsy, ungraceful, cumbersome, ungainly
graceful   AWKWARDLY, AWKWARDNESS

awry   wrong, askew, crooked, disorderly, twisted
right, straight

B

babble   baby talk, foolish talk, chatter, prattle, gabble

background   experience, knowledge, training, practice,

bad   evil, wrong, unfavorable   good   BADLY

badger   1. question, tease, annoy, torment, bother, pester, harass, bait (*Slang* — pick on, ride), 2. small hairy animal

baffle   puzzle, perplex, confound, mystify, bewilder (*Slang* — stump, stick, flaw, get, beat)

bait   1. badger, question, tease, annoy, torment, bother, pester, harass (*Slang* — pick on, ride), 2. trap, lure, tempt

balance 1. equalize, weigh, measure, stabilize, steady, 2. scale

bald hairless, bare, simple, open, nude, uncovered hairy, covered

baleful harmful, damaging, injurious harmless

balk be unwilling, be stubborn, be obstinate be willing

ballad song, poem, ditty

ballot vote, choice, poll

balmy mild, soft, gentle, fragrant

ban prohibit, forbid, outlaw, bar, block, obstruct, exclude, shut out allow

bandit highwayman, robber, thief, gangster, brigand

bang strike, hit, slam

banish exile, expel, force away, drive away, deport, outlaw BANISHMENT

bank 1. shore, barrier, slope, 2. treasury, storage, 3. series, row, string

banquet feast, formal dinner, affair

banter tease, joke, jest (*Slang* — rib, kid)

bar 1. block, obstruct, exclude, shut out, forbid, ban, prohibit allow, 2. pole, rod, stick, 3. lawyers as a group, 4. saloon, tavern, counter, 5. music staff

barbarian uncivilized, cruel, coarse, savage, uncouth, brutal, uncultured, primitive civilized BARBARIC, BARBAROUS

bare naked, nude, bald, open, uncovered covered

barely scarcely, hardly, just

bargain 1. agree, contract, 2. sale (*Slang* — a buy, a steal)

barren unproductive, childless, unfertile, sterile, blank fertile, productive

barricade obstruction, barrier, fortification

barrier barricade, obstruction, fortification

barter trade, deal, exchange, swap

base 1. found, establish, set, settle, fix, 2. low, mean, selfish, cowardly, inferior, 3. bottom, foundation, groundwork, 4. station, headquarters

bashful awkward, uneasy, shy, timid, coy aggressive

basic essential, fundamental, underlying

bat hit, knock, strike, crack, clout (*Slang* — clobber, belt, slug)

bathe 1. swim, 2. launder, rinse, 3. pour over, drench, cover, soak, saturate, medicate

batter 1. beat, pound, smash, thrash, 2. mixture, 3. baseball player

battery set, series

battle struggle, fight, combat, war, contest, conflict peace

bauble toy, plaything, trinket

bawl shout, cry, wail, weep, sob, howl

beach shore, coast, waterfront, seaside

beacon watchtower, signal, alarm, flare

beam 1. shine, smile, glow, 2. timber, bar, shaft

bear 1. carry, endure, withstand, hold, support, produce, yield, 2. animal

bearing 1. manner, air, 2. reference, relation, connection, 3. direction, way, course

beast animal, creature BEASTLY

beat 1. strike, blow, bat, hit, knock, crack, clout (*Slang —* clobber, belt, slug), 2. mix, stir, 3. accent in music, 4. outdo, surpass, win, defeat, triumph (*Slang —* lick) BEATEN

beautiful pretty, handsome, attractive, lovely ugly BEAUTEOUS, BEAUTIFY, BEAUTY

beckon gesture, motion, invite, signal

bedlam uproar, confusion, racket, tumult, rumpus peace, calm

bedraggled sloppy, shabby, wet and limp

beefy strong, solid, heavy, stocky, muscular weak

before earlier, prior, previously, formerly, in advance after

beg ask, beseech, appeal, plead, implore, entreat

begin start, commence, take off (*Slang —* dig in, get the show on the road) end, finish BEGINNER

beguile 1. deceive, cheat, trick, dupe, bamboozle, 2. amuse, entertain, charm

behalf interest, good, benefit, welfare

behavior conduct, action, acts, manner BEHAVE

behest command, order, bidding

behind 1. after, later than, 2. retarded, backward ahead

behold see, look, notice, view, perceive, observe, sight

belated delayed, late, tardy, overdue early

belie 1. misrepresent, distort, twist, 2. disappoint

believe trust, suppose, think, surmise (*Slang —* swallow) doubt BELIEF

belittle minimize, underrate, underestimate overrate

belligerent warlike, aggressive, offensive, hostile, militant, combative peaceful

bellow roar, yell, shout

belly abdomen, stomach, paunch (*Slang* — breadbasket, pot, corporation)

belongings possessions, property BELONG

below under, lower, less above

bend 1. curve, turn, 2. bow, stoop, kneel, 3. yield, submit

beneath below, under above

benediction blessing, thanks, prayer

beneficial favorable, helpful, profitable, useful, advantageous harmful BENEFIT

benevolence kindness, generosity, good will, charity ill will BENEVOLENT

bent determined, inclined

berate scold, yell at

beseech beg, ask, appeal, plead, implore, entreat

beset attack, surround

besides moreover, also, too, in addition, as well

besiege attack, assault, raid, siege, bombard, charge

bespeak 1. reserve, engage, 2. show, indicate, express, signify

best prime, choice, select worst

bestial beastly, brutal, cruel, savage

bestow give, put, place, present, award

bet wager, gamble

betray mislead, deceive, trick (*Slang* — double-cross)

betrothal engagement, marriage contract BETROTH

better superior, preferable, improved worse BETTERMENT

between   betwixt, among

beware   be careful, guard against, take care, look out, watch out, look sharp (*Slang* — keep one's eyes peeled, watch one's step)

bewilder   confuse, baffle, puzzle, perplex, confound, mystify (*Slang* — stump, stick, get, beat)   clarify
BEWILDERMENT

bewitch   1. put under a spell, hex, 2. charm, delight, enchant

beyond   farther, past, exceeding

bias   1. slanting, oblique, diagonal, 2. prejudice, prejudgment, sway

bid   command, order, direct, instruct, ask, invite, enjoin

big   large, important, great, grand, considerable, grown-up, adult, mature   little, small

bind   1. tie, fasten, restrain, wrap, weld, 2. oblige, require

birth   beginning, origin, inception, infancy   end, death

bit   1. small amount, piece, 2. harness, restraint

bite   cut with teeth, nip, pierce   BITTEN

biting   sharp, cutting, sneering, sarcastic, acid

bitter   distasteful, unpleasant   pleasant   BITTERLY

blade   sword, knife

blame   accuse, charge, impeach, indict, denounce, tattle (*Slang* — hang on, put the finger on, rat on, frame)   absolve

blameless   innocent, faultless (*Slang* — clean)   guilty

bland   1. smooth, mild, soft, gentle   harsh,   2. agreeable, polite   disagreeable

blank   empty, void, vacant

blast   explosion, blowout, burst, discharge

blaze 1. fire, flame, flare, 2. notch, marking

bleak bare, chilly, cold, dreary, dismal cheerful

bleed 1. to lose blood, 2. grieve, pity, sorrow

blemish stain, scar, injury, defect

blend mix, combine, beat, join, stir separate

bless praise, thank, glorify curse BLESSED

blight 1. spoil, ruin, destroy, decay, wither, 2. decaying, disease

blind 1. sightless, visionless, 2. without thought, without judgment BLINDLY, BLINDNESS

bliss happiness, joy, delight, glee, elation sadness BLISSFUL

blithe airy, light, breezy, fanciful, lighthearted, gay, graceful, merry gloomy BLITHESOME

bloat swell, puff up, inflate deflate

blob bulge, bubble, globule

block 1. clog, obstruct, hinder clear, 2. lump, solid, mass

blockade obstruction, barrier, barricade, fortification

bloodthirsty cruel, murderous

bloom flourish, thrive, flower, glow, blossom

blossom develop, flower, bloom

blot erase, wipe out, obliterate

blow 1. puff, breeze, 2. knock, stroke, whack, rap

blowout burst, explosion, blast

bluff 1. deceive, trick, delude, 2. steep cliff, bank

blunder stumble, mistake, flounder (*Slang* — goof, put one's foot in one's mouth)

blunt 1. dull, unsharp sharp, 2. outspoken, candid, frank, straightforward, direct

blur   dim, smear, cloud

board   1. mount, embark, get on, 2. committee, cabinet, 3. wood, lumber, 4. food, meals (*Slang* — grub)

boast   brag, pat oneself on the back   BOASTFUL

body   1. substance, firmness, 2. the main part, mass, bulk, 3. group, collection, throng, crowd

boil   1. fume, seethe, rage, 2. cook, bubble, 3. swelling, pimple

boisterous   violent, rough, noisy, rowdy, tumultuous
serene

bold   1. defiant, impudent, brazen, arrogant, haughty, insolent, cavalier   modest,   2. vigorous, free, clear
BOLDNESS

bolt   1. flee, break away, take flight (*Slang* — make a break for it, clear out), 2. lock, fastener

bombard   attack, fire upon, shell, torpedo, open fire
BOMBARDMENT

bonus   extra, more, premium

boom   1. progress, increase, advance, gain, grow, swell, thrive, flourish, 2. thunder, roar, rumble, 3. pole, beam

boon   1. blessing, godsend, gift, windfall, 2. pleasant, jolly, merry, jovial

boost   lift, push, shove, help, thrust, hoist

boot   1. kick, 2. shoe

bootless   useless, purposeless   useful

booty   plunder, prize, loot, stolen goods

bore   1. drill, pierce, puncture, 2. make weary, irk (*Slang* — put to sleep)

born   brought forth, hatched, produced

borrow   take (*Slang* — touch)   lend

boss 1. supervise, oversee, look after, direct, 2. foreman, manager

bother worry, fuss, trouble, concern, annoy

bottom base, foundation, lowest part top

bound 1. enclosed, surround, 2. spring back, leap, jump, 3. going, on the way, 4. boundary, limit

boundary bound, limit, border, division, barrier

boundless unlimited, endless, infinite limited

bounteous generous, plentiful, abundant, liberal scarce

bountiful fertile, bounteous, generous, plentiful, abundant scarce

bout 1. test, contest, trial, struggle, battle, 2. spell, length of time, turn, round

bow bend, stoop, kneel

box 1. fight, hit, 2. container, crate

boy lad, youth, fellow, male, buddy

boycott strike, revolt, picket, blackball, ban

brace 1. support, strengthen, tighten, tie, 2. a support, prop

bracket 1. couple, join, relate, enclose, 2. support, brace

brag boast, pat oneself on the back

brake stop, slow down, decelerate, curb accelerate

branch 1. spread, divide, expand, 2. part of a tree

brand 1. mark, burn, label, tag, 2. kind, sort, type, stamp

brave courageous, bold, valiant, gallant, heroic cowardly BRAVERY

brawl quarrel, riot, racket, fracas

brawn muscle, strength weakness BRAWNY

brazen shameless, immodest, bold, forward modest

breach break, gap, falling-out, quarrel

break 1. fracture, rupture, crack, burst heal, mend, 2. violation, 3. interruption, interval, pause, rest, letup

breed raise, produce, train, race, develop, bring up, cultivate

breezy brisk, lively, jolly, carefree, spry, energetic, active, spirited (*Slang* — peppy) gloomy

brevity shortness, conciseness, briefness length

brew 1. plan, plot, scheme (*Slang* — cook up), 2. cook, prepare, ferment

bribe buy off (*Slang* — grease the palm) BRIBERY

bridle 1. restrain, control, check, hold back, 2. harness

brief short, concise, terse, curt long

brigand robber, bandit, thief

bright 1. shining, clear, vivid, 2. smart, alert, intelligent, 3. pleasant, cheerful, lively dull BRIGHTNESS

brilliant 1. sparkling, bright, shining, clear, vivid, 2. smart, alert, intelligent BRILLIANCE

brisk 1. breezy, 2. spirited, lively, jolly, spry, energetic, active, quick dull

brittle fragile, crisp, breakable, frail strong, sturdy

broad wide, large, expansive, roomy narrow BROADEN

broadcast publish, distribute, scatter, announce, circulate

broken burst, ruptured, shattered repaired BROKE

brood 1. ponder, contemplate, study, reflect, consider, meditate, 2. family group

brotherhood bond, kinship, relationship, fraternity, fellowship

browse 1. read, scan, 2. feed, graze

bruise   injure, hurt, wound   heal

brush   1. clean, rub, remove, wipe, 2. shrubs, bushes

brusque   abrupt, blunt, gruff, curt, harsh, surly   courteous

brutal   coarse, barbarian, cruel, savage   kind
BRUTALITY

buccaneer   pirate, sea robber, privateer

buck   1. jump, leap, spring, vault, 2. male animal

buckle   1. fasten, clasp, hook, clip, 2. bend, distort, wrinkle, 3. belt, strap, catch, clip

bud   1. sprout, flourish, develop, 2. baby plant

buddy   friend, pal, companion, partner, comrade, chum (*Slang* — sidekick, crony)

budge   move, stir

budget   ration, allowance, schedule

buff   polish, rub, shine, wax, burnish

buffet   blow, beat, bat, hit, knock, strike, crack, clout (*Slang* — clobber, belt, slug)

build   construct, make, create   BUILDER, BUILDING

bulk   lump, mass, majority

bulletin   message, circular, news, statement, flash, newsletter

bully   tease, pester, annoy, badger, torment, bother, harass

bump   push, collide, shake, hit

bunch   group, set, batch, cluster

bundle   parcel, package, bale, packet

bungle   botch, tumble, blunder (*Slang* — goof)

buoyant   1. light, floating, elastic, springy   heavy, 2.

cheerful, lighthearted, carefree gloomy, sad
BUOYANCY

burden load, charge, task, hard work BURDENSOME

burglar robber, thief, housebreaker BURGLARY

burly strong, sturdy, brawny weak

burn blaze, fire, flame, flare

burnish buff, polish, rub, shine, wax

burrow 1. dig, tunnel, excavate, 2. search, hunt, seek

burst broken, ruptured, exploded

bury cover, conceal, hide, immerse, cache uncover
BURIAL

business work, occupation, profession, trade, affair, job

bustle fuss, noise, activity, flurry, ado, action, stir, trouble, commotion, excitement, hubbub, to-do calm

busy working, active, occupied, engaged, on the job
idle, inactive

busybody meddler, gossip, tattletale, kibitzer

button fasten, clasp, hook, close unbutton, open

buxom 1. plump, 2. cheerful, healthy, merry, jolly

buy purchase, shop, market sell BUYER

by near, beside, at

byway path, passage, detour, back street

C

cab taxi, carriage, coach, car

cabin house, cottage, bungalow, hut

cable   1. telegraph, wire, 2. rope, cord, wire

cache   store, bury, cover, conceal, hide

cackle   shrill laugh, babble, chatter, prattle

cafeteria   restaurant, cafe, snack bar, diner

calamity   1. misfortune, mishap, accident, 2. disaster, catastrophe, tragedy

calculate   1. count, compute, figure, estimate, reckon, 2. plan, reason, think, suppose
CALCULATION, CALCULATOR

call   1. cry, shout, yell, 2. speak, ask, command, invite, telephone   CALLER

calling   profession, occupation, trade, vocation

callous   hard, unfeeling, insensitive, heartless, cold
sensitive

calm   quiet, still, peaceful, serene, tranquil   excited

camouflage   disguise, masquerade

campaign   crusade, drive, cause, movement

can   container, tin, receptacle

canal   waterway, aqueduct, gully, duct, tube

cancel   wipe out, erase, obliterate, repeal

candid   sincere, blunt, outspoken, frank, straightforward, direct

candidate   applicant, seeker, nominee

candor   frankness, sincerity, fairness

canine   dog, pooch, puppy

canny   1. shrewd, artful, crafty, skillful, clever, cunning (*Slang* — slick)   artless,   2. cautious, prudent, careful

canopy   cover, awning, shelter, screen

cantankerous quarrelsome, cranky, cross, irritable, mean

cap 1. cover, top, crown, lid, 2. excel, beat

capability ability, power, fitness, capacity, skill, talent, competency, efficiency (*Slang* — know-how, what it takes) inability

capacity 1. size, volume, content, 2. intelligence, mentality, power, fitness, 3. position, function, duty, role

caper 1. leap, jump, hop, skip, romp, cavort (*Slang* — cut up, horse around), 2. frolic, prank, trick, play, antic (*Slang* — monkeyshine, shenanigan)

capital 1. important, leading, top, chief, 2. money, funds, stock, 3. city, government seat, 4. large letter

caprice whim, fancy, fad, unreasonable desire
CAPRICIOUS

capsize upset, overturn, overthrow, tip over

caption title, heading, headline

captivate charm, fascinate, delight, bewitch

capture arrest, seize, imprison, apprehend (*Slang* — pinch) free CAPTIVE, CAPTIVITY

car automobile, vehicle (*Slang* — buggy, jalopy, wreck, heap, crate, wheels)

caravan 1. group, procession, parade, 2. wagon, van

carcass animal corpse, body

care 1. thought, worry, attention, concern, 2. protection, charge, supervision, keeping, custody neglect

career profession, occupation, vocation, calling, trade

carefree happy, gay, lighthearted, breezy, lively, jolly, spry, energetic, spirited, active unhappy

careful cautious, watchful, prudent careless
CAREFULLY

careless reckless, slovenly, sloppy careful

caress stroke, touch, fondle, pet

cargo load, freight, shipment

carnival fair, festival, fete, jamboree

carol song, hymn, ballad

carp 1. complain, find fault, pick, tear to pieces praise, 2. fresh-water fish

carpet rug, mat, floor covering

carriage 1. vehicle, conveyance, 2. posture, position, bearing

carry hold, transport, take

carve cut, slice

case 1. condition, state, circumstance, 2. covering, box, receptacle, 3. lawsuit, legal action

cash money, currency (*Slang* — dough, jack, cabbage, wampum) CASHIER

casket box, coffin, crate

cast 1. throw, fling, pitch, toss, 2. mold, form, shape, 3. company, troupe, actors, 4. sort, kind, type, variety, 5. color, tint, shade

castle palace, mansion, chateau

casual accidental, chance, informal, unexpected, natural planned

casualty misfortune, accident, mishap, injury, fluke

catalog 1. list, classify, record, group, sort, 2. file

catastrophe calamity, misfortune, tragedy, disaster, accident

catch 1. take, arrest, seize, apprehend, capture, 2. surprise, discover CATCHER

catchy 1. attractive, 2. tricky, deceptive, misleading

cater 1. pamper, coddle, spoil, oblige, indulge, 2. serve, provide

cause motive, reason, interest, basis, grounds

caution warn, advise, alert, admonish, remind, tip
CAUTIOUS

cavalcade procession, column, parade

cavalier 1. haughty, contemptuous, arrogant, insolent, 2. gentleman, horseman, knight, escort

cave cavern, shelter, den, lair

cavity hole, pit, crater

cavort prance about, caper, frolic, leap, jump, hop, skip, romp (*Slang* — horse around, cut up)

cease stop, end, halt, quit, discontinue (*Slang* — drop it) continue

cede give up, surrender, yield, relinquish acquire

celebrate 1. proclaim, observe, commemorate, 2. make merry, revel (*Slang* — make whoopee) CELEBRATION

celebrity notable, well-known person, somebody unknown

celestial heavenly, divine, godly, angelic

cement fasten, solidify, secure, weld

cemetery graveyard, burial ground

censure blame, reproach, denounce, criticize, condemn (*Slang* — pan, knock) approve

center middle, heart, core, nucleus

central main, chief, principal, leading

ceremonious 1. formal, ritualistic, stately, pompous informal, 2. courteous, polite, gracious CEREMONY

certain 1. sure, positive, definite uncertain, 2. some, particular, special CERTAINLY, CERTAINTY

certify guarantee, testify, vouch, affirm, confirm
CERTIFICATE

cessation end, discontinuation, close continuation

chafe 1. rub, heat, warm, 2. anger, annoy, vex, disturb, irritate

chagrin embarrassment, mortification, humiliation, disappointment

chain bind, restrain, fasten, shackle

chair seat, bench

chairman speaker, presiding officer

challenge confront, question, defy, dare, dispute, doubt
CHALLENGER

chamber room, compartment

champion 1. winner, victor, best, choice, select, conqueror
loser, 2. defender, upholder, protector, advocate
CHAMPIONSHIP

chance 1. opportunity, occasion, opening, 2. possibility, probability, likelihood, prospect, 3. fate, luck, lot (*Slang* — the breaks)

change 1. alter, vary, deviate, substitute, replace, 2. cash, money, coins

channel 1. waterway, strait, passageway, corridor, artery, 2. TV station

chant song, psalm, prayer, ballad

chaos confusion, disorder, muddle, mix-up (*Slang* — snafu, hassle, foul-up) order CHAOTIC

chap 1. crack, break, split, become rough, 2. fellow, man, boy

chapter section, part, division

char burn, scorch, sear, singe

character 1. nature, makeup, constitution, temperament, disposition, 2. actor, performer, player, 3. letter, sign, symbol, 4. eccentric (*Slang* — crackpot, oddball, nut, screwball)

characterize describe, distinguish, represent, portray, picture, depict CHARACTERISTIC

charge 1. load, fill, stuff, 2. order, command, direct, bid, 3. blame, accuse, complain, denounce, impeach, indict (*Slang* — put the finger on, rat on, frame), 4. rate, ask as a price, 5. attack, rush at

charitable generous, kindly, giving, big-hearted selfish CHARITY

charming pleasing, delightful, fascinating, appealing, enchanting, alluring obnoxious CHARM

charter 1. hire, lease, rent, 2. treaty, alliance

chase 1. follow, pursue, run after, 2. drive away, repulse, reject

chaste pure, clean, virtuous, modest, decent impure

chasten punish, chastise, discipline, restrain

chastise chasten, punish, discipline, restrain

chat talk, converse, gossip

chatter 1. babble, foolish talk, prattle, gabble, 2. shiver, rattle, chill, quiver

cheap 1. inexpensive, low-priced dear, 2. common, plentiful, abundant scarce CHEAPEN

cheat defraud, swindle, beguile, deceive, trick, dupe, bamboozle

check 1. stop, control, restrain, curb, 2. prove, mark, verify, 3. bill, certificate, money

checkup examination, physical

cheer 1. comfort, praise, gladden, 2. hope, good spirits, gladness, happiness sadness CHEERFUL

cherish adore, worship, hold dear, protect, treasure

chest 1. box, locker, safe, dresser, 2. breast, thorax

chew bite, grind, nibble, munch

chicken-hearted cowardly, timid, lily-livered (*Slang —* yellow) brave

chide reproach, blame, scold, reprimand, lecture (*Slang —* bawl out, chew out, give what-for)

chief leader, head, authority (*Slang —* big cheese, big wheel)

chiefly mainly, mostly, above all, especially

child youngster, baby, tot, juvenile, youth, young boy or girl, offspring (*Slang —* kid)

chilly cold, cool, brisk, nippy, wintery, snappy warm

chime 1. ring, jingle, peal, 2. agree, harmonize

chip 1. break, crack, 2. piece, bit, crumb

chisel 1. make, sculpture, carve, 2. engrave, inscribe, 3. tool, point

chivalrous courteous, gallant, knightly, polite, noble CHIVALRY

choice 1. selection, pick, decision, option, alternative, preference, 2. best, cream

choke smother, suffocate, strangle, muffle

chop cut, cleave, sever (*Slang —* hack, whack)

chore task, job, work, assignment, duty, function

chorus 1. choir, group, unison, 2. verse, stanza, refrain

chronic constant, established, fixed, set, lasting, continuing

chronicle history, story, account, journal, narrative

chubby   plump, round, stout, fat, fleshy, corpulent, pudgy, stocky, tubby, chunky   skinny

chuck   1. pat, tap, flick, 2. throw, toss, pitch, fling

chuckle   laugh, giggle, titter

chum   friend, mate, buddy, pal, companion, partner, comrade (*Slang* — sidekick, crony)

chunk   lump, wad, bulk, mass (*Slang* — hunk)

cinch   grip, bind, hold, wrap, tie, fasten

circulate   go around, publish, broadcast, distribute, scatter, announce   CIRCULATION, CIRCULATORY

circumstance   condition, situation, state

citadel   fortress, stronghold

citation   1. honorable mention, decoration, medal, 2. summons, subpoena, 3. quotation

cite   quote, name, refer, mention, illustrate

citizen   inhabitant, occupant, resident
CITIZENRY, CITIZENSHIP

city   metropolis, municipality

civil   1. public, common, social, 2. ceremonious, courteous, polite   uncivil

civilization   culture   CIVILIZE

clad   clothed, dressed, attired (*Slang* — dolled up, fixed up, spruced up)

claim   1. demand, require, 2. right, due, interest, title

clammy   cold and damp, sweaty

clamor   cry out, demand, complain

clamp   fasten, clasp, brace

clan   group, crowd, clique, tribe, folk, family

clap   strike, bang, applaud

clarify   explain, refine, make clear, simplify   confuse

clash   1. contradict, oppose, disagree, differ, conflict   agree, 2. collide, bump, bang, hit

clasp   grasp, buckle, fasten, hook, clip

class   1. rank, grade, quality, 2. group, category, division

classify   organize, group, categorize, sort

clatter   noise, rattle, racket, din

clean   cleanse, purify, wash, tidy   dirty   CLEANLINESS

clear   1. remove, eliminate, get rid of   retain, 2. free, acquit   apprehend, 3. clean, cleanse, purify, wash, tidy   CLARITY, CLEARLY

cleavage   split, division, break

cleft   space, opening, crack, crevice, notch, indentation

clemency   mercy, pity, sympathy, compassion, lenience, mildness   harshness, severity

clench   grasp, grip, clutch, hold   release

clever   skillful, cunning, bright, smart, alert, intelligent   dull

client   customer, prospect, patron

climate   weather, elements, atmospheric conditions

climax   1. result, end, conclusion (*Slang* — payoff), 2. turning point

climb   mount, ascend, rise

clinch   1. seize, grip, cinch, bind, hold, wrap, tie, fasten, 2. establish, insure, make certain

cling   hold, grasp, adhere, stick

clip   1. cut, shear, crop, 2. fasten, attach, 3. pace

clique   set, clan, group, crowd, folk, family

cloak 1. hide, conceal, cover, protect, 2. robe, wrap, coat

clod 1. lump, hunk, chunk, 2. stupid person, oaf, lout

clog stuff, block, obstruct, choke

close 1. shut, fasten, lock open, 2. end, finish, stop, conclude, terminate start

close 1. near, approaching, imminent far, 2. stuffy, airless, stifling, suffocating CLOSELY

clothe dress, cover, wrap, attire

cloudy dark, unclear, overcast, gloomy, dismal

clout rap, bat, hit, knock, strike (*Slang* — crack, clobber, belt, slug)

clown 1. fool, play (*Slang* — horse around), 2. comic performer, prankster

club 1. hit, beat, strike, blow, bat, knock (*Slang* — crack, clout, clobber, belt, slug), 2. bat, stick, 3. group, society, clique

clue hint, evidence, proof, sign, key, lead

clump cluster, lump

clumsy awkward, ungraceful, ungainly, cumbersome

cluster bunch, group, set, batch

clutch cling, hold, grasp, adhere, stick

clutter 1. rubbish, trash, debris, 2. confusion, disorder, jumble

coach 1. train, teach, tutor, 2. carriage, car

coagulate thicken, clot, set

coarse 1. rough, choppy, bumpy fine, smooth, 2. common, poor, inferior, 3. crude, vulgar refined

coast 1. slide, glide, ride, 2. seashore, seaside, waterfront, beach COASTAL, COASTLINE

coat   wrap, cloak, robe

coax   persuade, influence, urge, pressure, push

cocky   conceited, impudent, swaggering, saucy

coddle   pamper, cater to, spoil, oblige, indulge

code   laws, rules, arrangement, system, signal

coerce   compel, force (*Slang* — strong-arm)

coin   1. invent, make up, devise, originate, 2. money, silver
COINAGE

collapse   break down, fail, crash, topple (*Slang* — fizzle out)

collar   1. seize, nab, capture, 2. neckband

colleague   associate, buddy, friend, companion, partner, comrade

collect   assemble, gather, accumulate, store up
COLLECTION, COLLECTOR

collide   conflict, bump, clash, bang

colony   settlement, community
COLONIAL, COLONIZATION

colorful   vivid, picturesque, bright, gay, rich   colorless

colorless   dull, uninteresting, flat, dreary   colorful

colossal   huge, gigantic, vast, enormous, immense, mammoth
insignificant

column   1. division, section, part, 2. tower, pillar, cylinder, monument

combat   battle, struggle, fight, contest, conflict, war

combine   join, unite, mix, connect, couple, blend, fuse
separate   COMBINATION

combustible   flammable, burnable, fiery
COMBUSTION

comedian comic, gagman, funnyman COMEDY

comely attractive, fair, good-looking, pleasing, personable

comfort console, ease, assure, relieve, cheer, gladden
COMFORTABLE

comical amusing, funny, humorous tragic COMIC

command 1. bid, order, direct, instruct, enjoin, 2. power,
control COMMANDER

commemorate honor, celebrate, observe, proclaim

commence begin, start, take off, fire away
COMMENCEMENT

commend 1. praise, compliment, approve (*Slang* — boost,
plug) criticize, disapprove, 2. commit, assign, trust
COMMENDATION

comment remark, note, observe, mention

commerce trade, business, dealings COMMERCIAL

commit 1. entrust, promise, pledge, 2. perform, do

committee council, group, delegation

commodious roomy, spacious, comfortable close

commodity product, ware, article

common 1. public, general private, 2. usual, familiar,
ordinary, everyday odd, 3. low, crude, coarse, vulgar,
poor, inferior refined COMMONLY

commotion disturbance, tumult, confusion, rumpus, ado,
action, stir, fuss, trouble, excitement, row, stir, hubbub,
to-do order

communicable contagious, catching, transferable, infectious

communicate inform, tell, enlighten, report, convey (*Slang*
— wise up) COMMUNICATION

community 1. society, people, colony, district, town, 2. ownership together

commute 1. exchange, substitute, replace, switch, 2. travel, move COMMUTER

compact 1. concise, short, brief lengthy, 2. agreement, contract, pact, understanding, concord, bargain, treaty, alliance, deal

companion partner, accompanist, buddy, friend, pal, comrade, chum (*Slang* — sidekick, crony) COMPANIONSHIP

company 1. group, association, 2. business, firm, enterprise, 3. guest, visitors, companions

compare match, liken, contrast, measure COMPARABLE, COMPARATIVE, COMPARISON

compassion clemency, mercy, pity, sympathy, leniency, mildness harshness, severity COMPASSIONATE

compatible agreeing, harmonious incompatible, differing

compel force, make, require

compensate pay, reward, atone for, balance, make up for COMPENSATION

compete rival, vie with COMPETITION, COMPETITIVE, COMPETITOR

competent able, effective, adequate, capable, qualified, fit incompetent

compile gather, collect, assemble, accumulate, store up

complacent self-satisfied, contented dissatisfied COMPLACENCY

complain grumble, squawk, find fault, fret (*Slang* — crab, bellyache, kick, grouch) COMPLAINT

complement supply, complete, supplement

complete 1. finish, conclude, terminate, end, clean up, wind up, close up (*Slang* — put the lid on it, button up, call it a day) start, begin, 2. whole, entire, thorough incomplete COMPLETELY, COMPLETION

complex 1. complicated, confused, involved, mixed simple 2. prejudice, bias, leaning, inclination COMPLEXITY

complexion appearance, look, color, pigment

complicate confuse, confound, involve, complex, mix up (*Slang* — foul up) simplify COMPLICATION

compliment commend, flatter, praise, congratulate COMPLIMENTARY

comply conform, agree, assent, submit, obey dissent

compose 1. make up, devise, put together, construct, build, create, make, 2. calm, pacify, soothe, quiet COMPOSER, COMPOSITE

composition 1. writing, work, paper, document, script, 2. composite, combination, mixture, blend

composure calmness, quiet, self-control, peace, rest, serenity tranquility excitement, agitation

comprehend 1. understand, realize, know (*Slang* — catch on, get the drift), 2. include, contain, cover exclude COMPREHENSION, COMPREHENSIVE

compress squeeze, press, reduce, condense, concentrate, crush expand, spread COMPRESSOR

comprise include, consist of, contain, involve exclude

compromise settle, yield, concede, adjust, meet halfway (*Slang* — go 50-50)

compulsory compelled, required, necessary

compute calculate, count, figure, estimate, reckon COMPUTATION

comrade buddy, friend, pal, companion, partner, chum (*Slang* — sidekick, crony)

conceal hide, cover, cloak, veil, camouflage disclose CONCEALMENT

concede admit, allow, grant, confess refuse, deny

conceited vain, boastful, proud, cocky, saucy CONCEIT

conceivable imaginable, thinkable, possible, likely, plausible inconceivable, doubtful CONCEIVE

concentrate 1. think about, focus wander (in thought), 2. strengthen, intensify, make stronger weaken CONCENTRATION

concept thought, notion, idea, opinion CONCEPTION

concern 1. interest, affect, trouble, involve, 2. business, company, firm, enterprise

concert 1. music, recital, 2. agreement, harmony, unison, teamwork

conciliate soothe, allay, quiet, calm, pacify, moderate, restrain, alleviate irritate CONCILIATORY

concise brief, short, terse, curt lengthy

conclude 1. close, end, finish, stop, terminate begin, 2. reason, suppose, assume, presume, infer, gather CONCLUSION

concoct make, invent, prepare, devise, create, manufacture (*Slang* — cook up)

concord peace, harmony, agreement

concrete 1. real, solid, substantial, tangible abstract, flimsy, 2. cement, pavement

concur agree, cooperate (*Slang* — play ball) disagree

concussion shock, head injury

condemn disapprove, doom, censure, blame, reproach,

denounce, criticize (*Slang* — pan, knock) approve
CONDEMNATION

condense compress, squeeze, reduce, concentrate
enlarge, expand CONDENSATION

condition 1. circumstance, situation, state, 2. provision,
specification CONDITIONAL

conduct 1. manage, direct, guide, lead, 2. behavior, action,
manner CONDUCTOR

confederation league, alliance, association, union
CONFEDERATE

confer consult, discuss, talk over (*Slang* — go into a huddle)
CONFERENCE

confess admit, acknowledge, consent (*Slang* — talk, sing,
come clean) deny CONFESSION

confide trust in, rely, depend, tell a secret, disclose

confident certain, sure, convinced, believing doubtful
CONFIDENCE

confidential secret, unpublishable, off the record (*Slang*
— inside)

confine enclose, surround, contain, keep in, coop up, imprison, restrain free, release

confirm establish, verify, substantiate, prove, O.K.
CONFIRMATION

confiscate seize, take

conflagration fire, blaze

conflict 1. clash, oppose, disagree, differ agree, 2. fight,
struggle, opposition, contest, battle peace

conform comply, agree, assent, submit, obey dissent

confound confuse, perplex, baffle, puzzle, mystify, bewilder,
stump (*Slang* — stick, floor, get, beat) clarify

confront   oppose, face, meet squarely, encounter

confuse   complicate, mix up, mistake, muddle, jumble (*Slang* — ball up, foul up) clarify   CONFUSION

congeal   freeze, thicken, stiffen, clot, solidify melt, soften

congenial   agreeable, pleasing, compatible, harmonious, like-minded conflicting

congested   overcrowded, overloaded, stuffed, full (*Slang* — jam-packed) empty

congratulate   bless, compliment, flatter, commend, praise CONGRATULATION

congregate   crowd, mass, gather, meet, assemble (*Slang* — gang around) disperse, scatter

conjecture   guess, suppose

conjure   entreat, appeal, plead, implore

connect   join, unite, combine, link, attach disconnect, separate CONNECTION

conquer   overtake, vanquish, defeat, crush, win, triumph CONQUEROR, CONQUEST

conscientious   exacting, particular, faithful, scrupulous neglectful

conscious   1. alive, awake unconscious, 2. knowing, realizing, sensitive, sensible, aware, cognizant unaware

consecutive   following, successive, continuous interrupted

consent   permit, agree, assent, accept, approve of, comply refuse

consequently   therefore, as a result, accordingly, hence CONSEQUENCE

conservative   cautious, opposed to change, unextreme, protective changing

conserve   preserve, save, keep, guard, protect, maintain CONSERVATION

consider 1. think, study, ponder, reflect, contemplate, deliberate (*Slang* — mull over), 2. think of, regard, look upon

considerable important, much, great, significant, powerful insignificant, unimportant

considerate thoughtful, mindful of others, kind, sympathetic inconsiderate, thoughtless CONSIDERATION

consign hand over, deliver, transfer, entrust, send, convey

consist comprise, make up, include

consistency 1. firmness, stiffness, 2. steadiness, uniformity, keeping changing CONSISTENT

console comfort, cheer, solace, sympathize CONSOLATION

consolidate unite, combine, condense, concentrate, merge, compress, squeeze, reduce

consort 1. husband or wife, spouse, mate, 2. associate, companion, buddy, friend, pal, partner, comrade

conspicuous noticeable, distinct, clear, obvious, prominent, outstanding inconspicuous

conspire plot, scheme (*Slang* — cook up) CONSPIRACY, CONSPIRATOR

constantly always, often, without stopping, continual seldom, scarcely

consternation dismay, alarm, terror, fright, scare, dread

constitute organize, form, set up, establish, compose CONSTITUTION, CONSTITUENT

constrain force, compel, urge, press

constrict contract, compress, squeeze, press, crush expand, spread

construct manufacture, form, build, make, create CONSTRUCTION

constructive helpful, useful, worthwhile destructive

construe explain, interpret, infer misconstrue, misunderstand

consult confer, discuss, talk over (*Slang* — go into a huddle)

consume 1. use up, spend, eat up, drink up, 2. waste, destroy, exhaust CONSUMER, CONSUMPTION

contact touch, connect, reach, join, approach

contagious catching, spreading, infectious, epidemic CONTAGION

contain 1. hold, include, comprise, consist of, involve exclude, 2. control, restrain, curb (*Slang* — keep under wraps) CONTAINER

contaminate pollute, corrupt, defile, infect purify

contemplate 1. consider, think, study, ponder, reflect, deliberate, 2. plan, intend, expect CONTEMPLATION

contemptible mean, atrocious, wicked, cruel, brutal, ruthless, terrible, horrible, dreadful, awful, vile, wretched good, angelic CONTEMPTUOUS

contend fight, struggle, argue, quarrel

contented satisfied, pleased, delighted dissatisfied CONTENTMENT

contest 1. contend, fight, struggle, argue, quarrel, 2. game, sport, tournament CONTESTANT

continue last, endure, go on, keep on, persist discontinue, stop CONTINUITY, CONTINUOUS

contortion twist, distortion, crookedness

contour outline, profile, form

contraband prohibited, forbidden, illegal, smuggled, outlawed legal

1. contract   1. form, start, enter into, 2. agreement, pact, understanding, bargain, treaty, alliance, deal
CONTRACTOR

2. contract   shrink, reduce, compress   expand
CONTRACTION

contradict   deny, oppose, dispute   agree
CONTRADICTION, CONTRADICTORY

contrary   opposed, opposite, different, clashing, conflicting
agreeable

contrast   compare, match, liken, measure

contribute   give, donate, participate, provide
CONTRIBUTION

contrite   regretful, sorry, penitent

contrive   invent, scheme, plan, plot, devise, conspire
CONTRIVANCE

control   1. command, influence, master, 2. restrain, check, contain, curb (*Slang* — keep under wraps)

controversy   dispute, argument, quarrel (*Slang* — hassle)

convalesce   recover, rally, heal, recuperate, improve
relapse   CONVALESCENT

convene   gather, meet, assemble   disperse

convenient   handy, suitable, timely, nearby   inconvenient
CONVENIENCE

conventional   customary, usual, traditional, accepted, established, formal   unusual   CONVENTION

converse   talk, speak with, discuss, communicate with (*Slang* — chew the rag, shoot the breeze)   CONVERSATION

convert   change, transform
CONVERSION, CONVERTIBLE

convey   1. carry, transport, take, 2. communicate, inform, tell, enlighten, report, 3. transfer, consign, hand over, deliver, entrust, send   CONVEYANCE

convict   condemn, doom, sentence   acquit
CONVICTION

convince   persuade, assure, make certain, promise, guarantee, pledge

convoy   accompany, escort, protect, conduct, guide, lead

convulsion   fit, tantrum, seizure, spasm, attack
CONVULSE

cook   prepare

cool   1. chilly, fresh   warm,   2. calm, unexcited   excited

cooperate   work together, collaborate (*Slang* — play ball)
COOPERATION, COOPERATIVE

coordinate   arrange, organize, harmonize

cope   struggle, put up, face

copious   plentiful, abundant, ample   scarce

copy   imitate, repeat, duplicate, reproduce

cordial   sincere, hearty, warm, friendly, hospitable
unfriendly   CORDIALITY

corporation   industry, company, business, firm, enterprise

corpulent   fat, stout, chubby, plump, round, fleshy, pudgy, stocky, tubby, chunky   thin

corral   hem in, surround, capture, herd, round up, enclose, fence in   release, free

correct   1. mark, change, remedy, adjust, 2. true, right, proper, accurate   incorrect, wrong   CORRECTION

correspond   1. write, communicate with, 2. agree, harmonize, resemble   CORRESPONDENCE, CORRESPONDENT

corridor   hallway, passageway, aisle

corroborate confirm, establish, verify, substantiate, prove, O.K.

corrode deteriorate, eat away, rot, rust

corrupt wicked, evil, rotten, dishonest, crooked, shady
CORRUPTION

cost 1. price, charge, rate, amount (*Slang* — damage, score, tab), 2. loss, sacrifice, expense COSTLY

costume outfit, dress, equip, fit, suit

council conference, assembly, committee, group, delegation

counsel advise, recommend, instruct, suggest, confer
COUNSELOR

count 1. add, total, number, 2. depend, rely (*Slang* — bank on), 3. consider, regard, judge

countenance appearance, expression, face, looks (*Slang* — mug, kisser, puss)

counteract 1. offset, balance, neutralize, 2. act against, oppose, contradict, cross agree

counterfeit copied, imitation, fake, artificial (*Slang* — phony) authentic, real

countersign password, secret signal, watchword

countless many, endless, unlimited, innumerable limited

country land, region, nation, territory

couple join, pair, team

courage bravery, boldness, valor, gallantry cowardice
COURAGEOUS

courier messenger, runner

course direction, line, way, track, channel

court 1. please, pursue, chase, woo (*Slang* — run after, play up to), 2. yard, enclosure, 3. playground, field, 4. tribunal

courteous polite, civil, gracious, obliging, respectful rude
COURTESY

courtly elegant, courteous, polite, civil, gracious, obliging, respectful ill-bred

covenant agreement, pact, contract, understanding, concord, bargain, treaty, alliance

cover 1. hide, protect, shelter, conceal uncover, 2. include, consist of, comprise, contain, involve exclude

covert 1. secret, hidden, disguised, covered, veiled, concealed open, 2. shelter, hiding place, hideaway, refuge

covet desire, crave, lust, want, envy

coward weakling (*Slang* — weak sister, chicken, scaredy-cat) hero, brave person COWARDICE, COWARDLY

cower crouch, squat, cringe

coy shy, modest, bashful, timid, demure bold

cozy comfortable, snug, relaxing, homey uncomfortable
COZILY

crack 1. break, split, open, slit, 2. blow, shot, bang, noise

crack-up 1. crash, smash, collide, 2. collapse, breakdown

cradle 1. support, hold, carry, 2. rocker, bed

craft skill, trade, art, handicraft

crafty sly, scheming, calculating, plotting, cunning

cram stuff, fill, load, pack, gorge, saturate

cramp 1. confine, box in, limit, restrict, 2. pain, twinge

cranky cross, irritable, churlish good-humored

crash strike, shatter, break, smash

crate box, container

crave covet, desire, lust, want, envy

crazy   insane, mad, lunatic, daft, unbalanced (*Slang* — cracked) sane   CRAZE

crease   fold, ridge, wrinkle, crinkle

create   1. make, form, invent, originate, manufacture, 2. cause, produce, bring about
CREATION, CREATIVE, CREATOR

credit   belief, trust, faith, honor

credulous   undoubting, believing, trusting, gullible doubting

crest   1. decoration, insignia, 2. tuft, feathers, plume, 3. peak, ridge, summit, top, crown   base

crestfallen   dejected, depressed, discouraged, downcast (*Slang* — down in the mouth)   cheerful, merry

crevice   cleft, rift, gap, break

crew   staff, force, gang

crime   wrongdoing, sin, vice, evil   CRIMINAL

cringe   crouch, cower, squat

crinkle   wrinkle, ripple, crease

cripple   damage, weaken, disable, injure

crisis   emergency, critical point, crucial period, turning point

crisp   1. brittle, fragile, frail, breakable   strong, 2. fresh, sharp, clear, bracing

critical   1. disapproving, faultfinding   approving, 2. crucial, decisive, urgent, pressing   unimportant   CRITIC

crony   friend, pal, buddy, companion, partner, comrade, chum

crook   1. hook, bend, curve, 2. criminal, gangster, lawbreaker, thief

croon   hum, sing, vocalize

crop 1. cut, clip, shear, 2. produce, growth, yield, harvest

cross 1. pass, step over, 2. mate, interbreed, 3. oppose, go against, 4. cranky, irritable, churlish good-humored

crouch cower, squat, cringe

crowd group, mass, throng, mob

crown 1. honor, reward, glorify, decorate, 2. head (*Slang* — noodle), 3. crest, peak, ridge, summit, top base, 4. head ornament, tiara

crucial important, critical, urgent, decisive, pressing unimportant

crucify torture, torment, punish, execute
CRUCIFIXION

crude rough, unrefined, raw, vulgar refined

cruel mean, heartless, brutal, ruthless kind
CRUELTY

crumble break up, disintegrate

crumple crush, crinkle, wrinkle, crease, ripple

crusade cause, movement, drive, campaign
CRUSADER

crush 1. subdue, conquer, 2. compress, squeeze, press, reduce expand

crutch support, prop, brace

cry wail, sob, weep, bawl laugh

cuddle snuggle, nestle, fondle

cudgel beat, club, whip

cue hint, signal, clue, key, lead

cull select, pick out, separate

culminate top, crown, end, terminate

culpable guilty, faulty, blamable innocent

culprit offender, sinner, wrongdoer

cultivate condition, prepare, train, develop, improve CULTIVATION

cultured refined, learned, polished, well-bred uncouth CULTURE, CULTURAL

cumbersome bulky, clumsy, awkward, unmanageable, burdensome, troublesome manageable

cunning skillful, clever, crafty, sly, scheming, calculating, plotting

curb 1. check, stop, control, restrain, 2. pavement

cure restore, remedy, heal

curious 1. strange, odd, unusual, queer, peculiar, 2. inquisitive CURIOSITY

currency money, cash, legal tender

current 1. flow, stream, 2. prevalent, present, happening past

curse 1. swear, 2. affliction, trouble, burden

curt abrupt, sudden, short, unexpected

curtail shorten, abbreviate, condense, abridge, contract, reduce, cut, compress lengthen

curve bend, turn, wind, twist, curl

cushion 1. soften, support, 2. pillow

custodian guardian, keeper, caretaker CUSTODY

custom tradition, use, habit, practice, way, manner CUSTOMARY

cut 1. reduce, contract, abbreviate, shorten, curtail, condense, abridge, compress increase, 2. sever, split

cute 1. pretty, dainty unattractive, 2. clever, shrewd, smart, cunning dull

cycle series, circle

D

dab pat, smear, coat

dabble splash, splatter, putter, toy, fiddle

daft 1. silly, foolish, 2. crazy, insane (*Slang* — loony, goofy, wacky, balmy, batty, nutty, screwy, bugs, cuckoo) sane

daily regularly, day by day

dainty fresh, delicate, small, pretty, cute gross
DAINTILY

dally loiter, dawdle, lag, linger, delay rush

damage harm, hurt, impair, spoil, ruin, upset (*Slang* — mess up, foul up, gum up the works) remedy

dame lady, woman

damn condemn, doom, denounce, censure, curse

dampen 1. moisten, wet, sprinkle, 2. depressed, discouraged, 3. muffle, mute, dull, deaden, smother, suppress encourage
DAMP

dangerous unsafe, hazardous, risky, perilous, chancy safe
DANGER

dangle hang, droop, sag, swing, flap

dank wet, moist, damp, humid, muggy dry

dapper neat, trim, smart, chic, well-dressed, natty, sporty, dressy, swanky (*Slang* — sharp, spiffy, classy, nifty, sprucy, swell)

daring bold, fearless, audacious, foolhardy, adventurous cautious DARE

dark 1. black, obscure light, 2. gloomy, dismal, somber, solemn, grave, dreary cheerful, 3. hidden, secret, concealed, obscured open DARKEN, DARKNESS

darling   beloved, dear, precious, adored, cherished

darn   mend, repair, fix, patch up

dart   1. dash, rush, scurry, scoot, hurry, 2. throw, fling, toss, cast

dash   1. hurry, rush, dart, scamper, hasten, 2. drop, trace, touch, pinch

data   facts, information, evidence, proof, grounds

date   1. time, day, 2. appointment, engagement, 3. fruit

daub   1. grease, lubricate, coat, cover, 2. soil, dirty, stain, spot, smear, 3. scribble, scrawl, paint badly

daunt   frighten, discourage, deter, dishearten   encourage

dauntless   brave, fearless, unafraid   fearful

dawdle   idle, loiter, linger, delay, tarry, dillydally (*Slang* — stick around)   rush

dawn   1. daybreak, sunrise, 2. beginning, start, commencement, outset   ending

daze   confuse, bewilder, muddle, upset, ruffle

dazzle   shine, glow, flash, glaze, glare, blind

dead   1. lifeless, deceased, gone, 2. dull, inactive, flat, dreary   alive   DEADEN, DEADLY, DEATH

deal   1. allot, grant, give, 2. trade, buy, sell, 3. act, behave, 4. bargain, compact, agreement, understanding, transaction DEALER

dear   1. precious, darling, beloved, adored, admired, idoiized, 2. expensive, costly, high-priced (*Slang* — stiff, steep)   inexpensive

dearth   lack, scarcity, shortage   abundance

debase   lower, discredit, degrade, demote, run down   lift

debate   discuss, argue, reason, dispute

debris   ruins, rubbish, trash, scrap, litter, residue, junk

debt   obligation, amount due   DEBTOR

decay   rot, spoil, crumble, disintegrate   flourish, bloom

decease   die, perish, depart, expire (*Slang* — croak, kick the bucket, pop off)

deceive   beguile, trick, hoax, dupe, betray, mislead, lie   DECEIT, DECEITFUL, DECEPTION

decent   1. respectable, proper, correct, right   improper, 2. adequate, good enough, suitable, fit   inadequate   DECENCY

decide   settle, determine, resolve, judge   DECIDEDLY, DECISION

decipher   solve, explain, figure out

declare   state, assert, announce, affirm, say, pronounce   DECLARATION

decline   1. refuse, reject (*Slang* — turn down, not buy) accept, 2. sink, fail, run down, fall, weaken   strengthen, 3. slope, descent, slant, hill   DECLIVITY

decompose   decay, rot, crumble, disintegrate

decorate   adorn, trim, beautify, ornament, fix up (*Slang* — doll up)   DECORATIVE, DECORATION

decorum   decency, etiquette, manners, social graces, formality

decoy   bait, lure (*Slang* — come-on)

decrease   lessen, diminish, reduce, curtail, cut, shorten, compress   increase

decree   pronounce, order, rule, pass judgment, command, dictate

dedicate   inscribe, devote, address, assign   DEDICATION

deduct   subtract, remove, withdraw, take away, discount
add   DEDUCTION

deed   1. act, action, performance, doing, fete, 2. contract, policy

deem   think, believe, consider, judge, regard, suppose, assume

deface   mar, blemish, disfigure, deform   improve

defeat   overcome, win, triumph (*Slang* — lick, do in)

defect   fault, flaw, weakness, failing, shortcoming, blemish, imperfection, deficiency   perfection   DEFECTIVE

defend   protect, safeguard, shield, support   attack
DEFENSE, DEFENSIVE

defenseless   helpless, unprotected   protected

defer   1. put off, delay, postpone, 2. yield, submit, bow to, respect, accept, acknowledge   DEFERENCE

deficient   lacking, incomplete, wanting, needing, missing (*Slang* — shy on)   complete   DEFICIENCY

defile   1. dirty, pollute, contaminate   purify,   2. march, parade, file

define   1. explain, describe, clarify, 2. fix, set, establish, outline   DEFINITION

definite   clear, precise, distinct, plain, obvious, evident, clear-cut, exact   indefinite, unclear   DEFINITELY

deform   disfigure, blemish, mar, spoil, make ugly
improve, beautify   DEFORMITY

defraud   cheat, swindle, gyp (*Slang* — beat, cook, stick, shortchange, chisel)

deft   skillful, nimble, clever, adept, expert, proficient, apt, handy, ingenious (*Slang* — crackerjack)   unskillful

defy   resist, confront, challenge, disobey, ignore, disregard
obey   DEFIANT, DEFIANCE

degrade   demote, reduce, lower, downgrade (*Slang* — take down a peg, run down, knock, bump, bust)

degree   1. step, grade, notch, amount, extent, measure, period, 2. rank, title, honor

deign   stoop, lower oneself, yield, concede, give in

deity   divinity, god

dejected   sad, depressed, discouraged, downcast, disheartened, despondent, blue (*Slang* — down in the mouth) cheerful

delay   detain, put off, postpone, hold up

delegate   1. assign, authorize, entrust, appoint, charge, 2. representative, envoy, agent, deputy   DELEGATION

deliberate   1. ponder, consider, think over, study, meditate, reflect, mull over, 2. slow, leisurely, easy, unhurried   hasty   DELIBERATELY, DELIBERATION

delicate   mild, soft, fine, dainty, frail, light, fragile, sensitive, tender   gross   DELICACY

delicious   tasty, savory, luscious (*Slang* — scrumptious, yummy)

delightful   pleasant, lovely, charming, appealing, pleasing (*Slang* — out of this world)   unpleasant   DELIGHT

delirious   giddy, raving, frantic, mad, violent, hysterical (*Slang* — out of one's head)   DELIRIUM

deliver   1. transfer, pass, hand over, consign, give, 2. say, voice, express, communicate, recite, relate, 3. free, rescue, release, liberate   DELIVERANCE, DELIVERY

delude   mislead, deceive, beguile, hoax, dupe, fool, betray (*Slang* — slip one over on, double-cross)   DELUSION

deluge   1. flood, overflow, run over, overwhelm, 2. rain, flood, torrent, storm

delve   search, dig, scoop, hunt, look, explore

demand 1. ask, inquire, want to know, 2. require, need, call for, want

demeanor behavior, manner, conduct, way, actions

demolish destroy, wreck, tear apart, dismantle, shatter
restore

demon devil, fiend, evil spirit, monster, ogre

demonstrate display, show, illustrate, clarify
DEMONSTRATION

demote degrade, reduce, lower (*Slang* — bump, bust)
promote

demure coy, timid, bashful, prim, overmodest bold

denomination group, sect, class, kind, brand, sort, name

denote indicate, mean, say, signify, imply, show, mark, express

denounce blame, censure, reproach, condemn, accuse, charge, indict, damn (*Slang* — knock, pan, slam)
commend

dense 1. crowded, packed, compact, thick, heavy, close, solid, compressed empty, 2. stupid, dull (*Slang* — dumb, thick) bright, smart DENSITY

dent pit, notch, nick, impress

deny refute, contradict, dispute, renounce, reject admit
DENIAL

depart 1. leave, go away, exit, 2. die, decease, perish, pass on
arrive DEPARTURE

depend rely, trust, confide
DEPENDENCE, DEPENDENT

depict represent, portray, describe, picture, illustrate, characterize

deplore regret, be sorry for, lament

deportment　behavior, conduct, manners, action

deposit　1. put down, lay, place, leave, store　withdraw, 2. pledge, stake　DEPOSITOR

depot　1. station, stand, post, 2. storehouse, depository, warehouse

depress　1. sadden, deject, discourage, dishearten　cheer, 2. lower, sink　raise, 3. weaken, reduce, lessen　increase DEPRESSION

deprive　take away, take from　give

deputy　agent, representative, delegate

deride　ridicule, laugh at, make fun of (*Slang* — ride, pan, razz)　DERISION, DERISIVE

derive　get, obtain, acquire, gain, secure, receive

derogatory　belittling, unfavorable, slanderous　flattering

descend　decline, fall, drop, plunge　ascend　DESCENT

descendant　child, offspring

describe　define, characterize, portray, picture, depict, represent, paint, tell　DESCRIPTION, DESCRIPTIVE

desert　leave, forsake, abandon (*Slang* — walk out on, pull out, sell out)　DESERTER

deserve　merit, earn, be worthy of (*Slang* — rate)

design　1. sketch, draw, paint, picture, portray, depict, 2. intend, plan, propose　DESIGNING

designate　1. show, indicate, point out, specify, 2. name, nominate, appoint

desire　wish, want, fancy, lust
DESIRABILITY, DESIRABLE, DESIROUS

desist　stop, cease, end, halt, discontinue, abandon　continue

desolate　1. empty, vacant, void, barren　dense, 2. gloomy, dismal, dreary　cheerful　DESOLATION

despair   lose hope, give up

desperate   frantic, wild, reckless, mad   DESPERATION

despise   hate, scorn, loathe, disdain   love

despoil   rob, plunder, loot

despondent   depressed, dejected, downhearted, downcast, discouraged (*Slang* — down in the mouth)   cheerful

despot   ruler, tyrant, dictator, oppressor, slave driver

destination   1. end, goal, objective, 2. lot, fortune, fate   DESTINE, DESTINY

destitute   poor, penniless, bankrupt, down-and-out (*Slang* — broke, flat, strapped)   wealthy

destroy   1. spoil, ruin, wreck, devastate   restore, 2. kill, slay, exterminate, finish   DESTROYER, DESTRUCTION, DESTRUCTIVE

detach   1. separate, unfasten, disconnect   join, attach, assign, delegate, draft   DETACHMENT

detail   1. itemize, elaborate, dwell on, tell fully, 2. commission, assign, delegate, 3. part, portion, fraction, division, segment, fragment

detain   delay, retard, hold up, slow up   hurry

detect   discover, spot, spy, recognize, perceive, catch   DETECTIVE

deter   discourage, hinder, prevent, prohibit   encourage

determined   firm, sure, convinced, resolute, resolved, serious   doubtful   DETERMINE, DETERMINATION

detest   hate, dislike, loathe, abhor, despise, scorn   love   DETESTABLE

dethrone   remove, dismiss, overthrow

detour   shift, go around, bypass

devastate   destroy, ruin, wreck

develop 1. grow, flourish, mature, 2. progress, advance
DEVELOPMENT

device 1. machine, apparatus, tool, instrument, implement, 2. plan, scheme, trick

devil demon, fiend, ogre, monster

devise plan, invent, contrive, arrange, create, make up

devoid empty, vacant, bare, blank full

devote dedicate, assign, apply, attend to

devotion 1. affection, love, fondness, liking hatred, 2. loyalty, dedication infidelity

devour 1. eat, consume, swallow, 2. waste, destroy, ruin

devout 1. religious, pious, 2. earnest, sincere, hearty, devoted, serious, zealous indifferent

dexterity skill, cleverness, competence

diagnose interpret, gather, deduce, analyze DIAGNOSIS

diagram draw, sketch, portray, design, depict

dial tune in, call, ring

dialogue conversation, talk, speech, words

diary record book, memo, journal, account, chronicle

dice 1. cube, cut, 2. cubes (*Slang* — ivories)

dictate 1. order, demand, direct, instruct, rule, charge, 2. advise, recommend, suggest
DICTATION, DICTATORSHIP

die decease, perish, expire, pass away (*Slang* — croak, kick the bucket, pop off) live DYING, DEAD

different unlike, distinct, opposite, contrary, reverse, dissimilar, varied, assorted same, alike
DIFFER, DIFFERENCE

difficult hard, rough, rugged, arduous (*Slang* — tough, wicked, mean) easy DIFFICULTY

dig scoop, excavate, gouge, tunnel DUG

digest 1. absorb, 2. understand, comprehend, grasp, catch on (*Slang* — get the drift), 3. brief, summary DIGESTION, DIGESTIVE

digit 1. number, numeral, figure, 2. finger or toe

dignified noble, worthy, stately, majestic, grand undignified DIGNIFY, DIGNITY, DIGNITARY

dilapidated decayed, ruined, battered, broken-down, run-down (*Slang* — beat-up)

dilate expand, enlarge, widen, broaden, magnify, increase contract, reduce

diligent hard-working, industrious, energetic lazy DILIGENCE

dillydally loiter, delay, tarry, linger, dawdle (*Slang* — hang around, take one's sweet time, stick around) hurry, speed

dilute weaken, reduce, thin, cut, water down strengthen

dim faint, weak, pale, indistinct, vague, darkish bright

dimension measurement, size, expanse, proportions

diminish decrease, reduce, lessen, curtail, cut increase, enlarge

din noise, racket, clamor, uproar, tumult quiet

dine 1. eat, sup, 2. feed, nourish DINER, DINNER

dingy dirty, dull, grimy, dark, gray bright

dip sink, ladle, immerse, dunk

diplomat politician, envoy, ambassador, emissary, a tactful person DIPLOMATIC

dire bad, terrible, dreadful, horrible, awful, wretched, disastrous, tragic, black

direct 1. manage, control, conduct, handle, head, govern, rule, regulate, 2. order, command, dictate, instruct, charge, 3. show, point, aim, 4. address, inscribe
DIRECTION, DIRECTLY, DIRECTOR, DIRECTORY

dirty grimy, soiled, muddy, untidy, dingy, messy, sloppy clean DIRT, DIRTINESS

disable cripple, make useless, put out of order, weaken enable DISABILITY

disadvantage drawback, handicap, liability, inconvenience advantage

disagree differ, quarrel, conflict, dispute (*Slang* — row, scrap, hassle) agree
DISAGREEABLE, DISAGREEMENT

disappear vanish, go away, fade out appear
DISAPPEARANCE

disappoint dissatisfy, let down, displease satisfy
DISAPPOINTMENT

disapprove disfavor, frown upon, object to, oppose (*Slang* — turn one's thumbs down on, take a dim view of) approve

disarm demilitarize, paralyze, make powerless strengthen

disaster casualty, calamity, misfortune, mishap, catastrophe, tragedy, accident fortune DISASTROUS

disband separate, scatter, disperse, split, break up, dismiss, dissolve assemble

discard reject, throw away, get rid of, dispose of, scrap, cast off (*Slang* — junk) keep

discern see, behold, observe, view, perceive, recognize, know, realize, understand, detect, spot, spy

discharge unload, release, dismiss, expel, dump, fire, let go

disciple   believer, follower, convert

discipline   1. train, drill, exercise, practice, prepare, condition, groom (*Slang* — lick into shape), 2. punish, chastise, correct, penalize (*Slang* — give what-for)

disclaim   deny, refuse, withhold, reject   accept

disclose   uncover, open, reveal, show, expose, unmask   hide, conceal

discolor   fade, dull, tarnish, bleach

discomfort   distress, trouble, bother, disturb, perturb, upset   comfort, please

discord   1. disagreement, difference, dispute, conflict, friction   agreement, 2. noise, racket, din, clamor   quiet

discount   1. deduct, subtract, remove   add, 2. allow for, consider, take into account

discourage   deter, prevent, hinder, disapprove, keep from, deject, daunt   encourage   DISCOURAGEMENT

discourse   talk, converse, lecture, preach, expound, address

discover   reveal, learn, observe, see, notice, perceive, find, disclose, expose   DISCOVERY

discredit   1. doubt, disbelieve   believe, 2. disgrace, dishonor, shame, humiliate (*Slang* — knock)

discreet   careful, prudent, considerate, thoughtful, cautious   indiscreet   DISCRETION

discriminate   separate, segregate, distinguish, set apart   DISCRIMINATION

discuss   debate, talk over, reason, consider, confer (*Slang* — kick around, chew the rag)   DISCUSSION

disdain   scorn, despise, reject, spurn   respect   DISDAINFUL

disease   sickness, illness, ailment, malady, infirmity   health   DISEASED

disfigure   deform, deface, blemish, mar, injure, scar, spoil

disgrace   shame, dishonor, discredit, humiliate, embarrass
DISGRACEFUL

disguise   conceal, hide, cover, camouflage, misrepresent

disgust   sicken, offend, repel, revolt, nauseate

dish   1. give, serve, 2. receptacle, container

dishearten   discourage, depress, sadden, deject   cheer

disheveled   rumpled, mussed, untidy, sloppy   neat

disintegrate   break up, separate, decompose, crumble, decay, rot

dismal   dark, gloomy, dreary, miserable, bleak, depressing
bright, cheerful

dismantle   disassemble, take apart, demolish, wreck

dismay   bewilder, disturb, embarrass, bother, confuse, alarm, frighten

dismiss   discharge, expel, send away (*Slang* — fire, can, sack, bump, give the gate, show the door)   enlist
DISMISSAL

dispatch   1. send, transmit, forward, discharge, 2. hurry, hasten, speed, rush

dispel   scatter, disperse, drive away   assemble

dispense   distribute, give out, deal out, issue, allot, grant, dole out, mete out (*Slang* — hand out, dish out, fork out, shell out)

disperse   scatter, distribute, spread

display   demonstrate, illustrate, exhibit, present, parade, flaunt   conceal

disposal   1. removal, elimination, release, 2. arrangement, settlement, adjustment, administration

disposition   1. nature, temperament, character, inclination, 2. arrangement, settlement, order, adjustment, administration

dispute   argue, debate, quarrel, oppose, resist, fight, bicker, contest   agree

dissect   cut, examine, analyze

dissent   disagree, differ, take exception   agree
DISSENSION

dissipate   1. scatter, spread, dispel, disperse, 2. squander, waste, spend foolishly   save

dissolve   1. melt, liquefy, 2. cease, end, fade, pass away, disappear

dissuade   discourage, talk out of

distance   1. space, length, extent, reach, 2. far away
nearness   DISTANT

distend   expand, swell, stretch, widen, enlarge, magnify, increase, blow out, bulge   contract, decrease

distinct   1. different, dissimilar, diverse, separate   similar, 2. clear, plain, obvious, precise, exact, clear-cut, definite, unmistakable   indefinite
DISTINCTION, DISTINCTIVE

distinguish   1. tell apart, define, see, detect, 2. honor, dignify, make famous

distinguished   important, great, outstanding, famous, well-known, noted, popular, celebrated, honored

distort   twist, contort, misrepresent, falsify

distract   divert, confuse, disturb

distress   pain, hurt, afflict, torment, torture, agonize, trouble, bother, disturb, upset   please

distribute scatter, disperse, spread, dispense, allot, dole out, mete out (*Slang* — hand out, dish out, fork out, shell out) collect DISTRIBUTION

district region, area, zone, territory, place, section, neighborhood

disturb 1. annoy, irk, vex, bother, irritate, 2. trouble, perturb, concern, agitate, upset, excite, alarm DISTURBANCE

dive plunge, drop, fall DIVER

diverse 1. different, unlike, distinct, 2. various, several same DIVERSITY

divert 1. distract, detract, confuse, 2. amuse, entertain, delight, tickle DIVERSION

divide separate, portion, partition, split, share, sort unite DIVISIBLE, DIVISION, DIVISOR

divine 1. heavenly, sacred, holy, 2. superb, delightful, excellent, great, beautiful, 3. foretell, predict, guess, forecast, prophesy, anticipate DIVINITY

divorce separate, disjoin, divide, disconnect

divulge reveal, tell, make known, publish, broadcast, circulate, let out, come out with

dizzy giddy, staggering, spinning, unsteady, confused steady DIZZINESS

do perform, act, behave, produce DOINGS

docile obedient, willing, receptive, responsive, yielding, gentle, tame, mild stubborn

dock 1. anchor, moor, tie, 2. clip, cut off

doctor 1. treat, remedy, heal, cure, 2. physician, medic

doctrine belief, teachings, creed

document writing, paper, certificate, statements

dodge   avoid, duck, recoil

doff   remove, take off, undo   don, put on

dogged   stubborn, willful, headstrong, obstinate   yielding

doldrums   blues, low spirits, gloom (*Slang* — dumps) cheerfulness

dole   give, donate, allot, dispense, grant, deal out, mete out (*Slang* — hand out, fork out, shell out)

doleful   sad, mournful, dreary, dismal

dolt   dunce, blockhead, numskull (*Slang* — dope)

domain   sphere, realm, province, field, property

domestic   1. household, family, internal, 2. tame, 3. servant, maid   DOMESTICATE

dominate   control, rule, command, lead DOMINANT, DOMINATION

domineering   arrogant, overbearing, high-handed, bossy

dominion   1. rule, control, command, power, hold, grasp, 2. lands, sphere, country, domain

don   put on, slip on, dress in, wear

donate   give, contribute, present, bestow, award, allot, grant   DONATION, DONOR

done   finished, complete, ended, concluded, terminated, over, wound up, through with (*Slang* — fini, washed up)

donkey   1. dolt, stubborn person, 2. ass, mule, burro

doom   condemn, damn, censure, convict, sentence

dormant   sleeping, inactive   active, awake

dose   amount, quantity, portion (*Slang* — slug)

double   1. duplicate, copy, 2. fold, turn over, 3. twice as much   DOUBLY

doubt mistrust, suspect, question, challenge, dispute
believe DOUBTFUL

douse 1. dip, immerse, dunk, 2. extinguish, quench

dowdy shabby, untidy, messy, mussy, sloppy, seedy tidy

downcast dejected, sad, discouraged, disheartened, depressed, gloomy, melancholy, glum (*Slang* — down in the mouth) cheerful

downfall 1. ruin, failure, defeat, upset, overthrow success, 2. rainstorm, cloudburst, flood, downpour

downhearted discouraged, dejected, depressed, downcast, sad, glum, melancholy (*Slang* — down in the mouth)

downpour rainstorm, cloudburst, flood, downfall

downright thorough, complete, plain, positive, utter, absolute, entire, total

dowry 1. settlement, endowment, 2. talent, gift, ability, genius

drab dull, unattractive, flat, lifeless bright

draft 1. wind, air, 2. sketch, drawing, rough copy, outline, 3. enlistment, enrollment, induction, call-up, recruitment, 4. note, bill, check

drag 1. pull, heave, haul, draw, tug, tow, 2. crawl, creep, linger on, tarry, lag, dillydally, delay speed

drain 1. dry, empty, draw off, 2. deprive, filter, use, spend, exhaust replenish DRAINAGE

dramatize stage, produce, present, feature, put on
DRAMA, DRAMATIC, DRAMATICALLY, DRAMATIZATION

drape cover, hang, flow DRAPERY

drastic extreme, severe, intense, rough, violent, fierce, tough mild

draw   1. pull, drag, haul, 2. attract, lure, magnetize, interest repel, 3. sketch, portray, picture, design, 4. tie, equal, match

drawback   disadvantage, handicap, fault, obstacle, objection, failing, shortcoming, flaw, catch (*Slang* — bug) advantage

dread   fear, be afraid

dreadful   bad, terrible, awful, unpleasant, horrible, vile, wretched, detestable, ghastly splendid

dream   imagine, vision, muse   DREAMER, DREAMY

dreary   gloomy, dull, dismal, somber, depressing, discouraging, disheartening   pleasant

dredge   dig, excavate, scoop, pick up

drench   soak, wet, saturate, flood

dress   clothe, adorn, decorate, attire, outfit   DRESSER

dressing   1. medicine, bandage, 2. sauce, seasoning

dribble   drip, trickle, leak

drift   wander, roam, stray, meander, ramble, float, cruise, glide

drill   1. practice, instruct, teach, train, exercise, prepare, condition, discipline (*Slang* — lick into shape), 2. tool

drink   swallow, sip, guzzle

drive   1. steer, ride, handle, operate, work, run, conduct, manage, 2. move, thrust, compel, force, make, impel
DRIVER, DRIVEN, DROVE

drizzle   rain, shower, sprinkle

droll   amusing, humorous, laughable, funny, witty dull

drone   1. hum, buzz, 2. male bee, 3. loafer, nonworker, unemployed, idler

drool   salivate, dribble, trickle

droop 1. hang, dangle, drag, 2. weaken, sink, fade, fail, decline, 3. despond, despair, lose heart, give up

drop 1. fall, dive, plunge, descend rise, 2. end, cease, stop start, 3. dismiss, let go, give up, abandon, 4. hardly anything, small amount much

drown submerge, sink, immerse, inundate

drowsy sleepy, dreamy, heavy-eyed awake, alert
DROWSE

drudge work away, plod (*Slang* — grind, plug away)
DRUDGERY

drug 1. numb, deaden, put to sleep, knock out (*Slang* — dope), 2. medicine, potion, narcotic (*Slang* — dope)
DRUGGIST

drum 1. beat, tap, strike, pound, 2. repeat, drill, 3. musical instrument DRUMMER

drunk intoxicated, tipsy, dizzy (*Slang* — soused, pickled, crocked, tight, high, lit up, stiff)
DRUNKARD, DRUNKEN

dry waterless, arid, parched, thirsty wet DRYER

dual twofold, double, duplicate

dub name, call, title, label, tag, christen

dubious doubtful, uncertain, questionable certain

duck 1. plunge, dip, submerge, sink, immerse, dunk, 2. sidestep, 3. web-footed bird

due 1. proper, rightful, fitting, just, fair, square, equitable unfair, 2. owed paid DULY

duel fight, contest, contend, struggle

dull 1. blunt, unsharp sharp, 2. gray, dingy, dreary bright, 3. stupid, slow clever, 4. boring, uninteresting, dry, flat interesting, 5. slow, inactive, sluggish busy

dumb 1. silent, mute, speechless, 2. stupid, dull, dense (*Slang* — numskulled) smart

dummy 1. imitation, copy, model, figure, doll, fake, 2. dolt, dunce (*Slang* — dope)

dump empty, unload, discharge, discard, throw away, scrap

dunce dolt, dummy, fool (*Slang* — dope)

dupe deceive, trick, beguile, betray, hoax, bamboozle

duplicate copy, repeat, reproduce, double

durable longlasting, enduring, permanent, endless, sturdy, solid, strong perishable

duration time, period, term (*Slang* — hitch)

dusk 1. sundown, sunset, twilight, evening, nightfall dawn, 2. shade, dark, gloom DUSKY

dust 1. clean, wipe off, 2. sprinkle, powder, 3. fine powder DUSTY

duty 1. task, work, job, chore, assignment, charge, function, obligation, responsibility, 2. tax, toll, tariff DUTIFUL

dwarf midget, runt, shrimp

dwell live, reside, inhabit, occupy (*Slang* — hang out) DWELLER, DWELLING

dwindle shrink, decrease, diminish, lessen, decline, subside, waste away increase

dye color, stain, tint

dynamic active, energetic, forceful, strong, lively, intense, animated, spirited (*Slang* — peppy) weak

E

eager wanting, wishing, desirous, anxious, keen, ready, willing unconcerned

early 1. beforetime, in advance late, 2. long ago, in the past, back EARLIER, EARLIEST

earn get, gain, obtain, require, secure, make, deserve, merit, be in line for (*Slang* — rate) EARNINGS

earnest determined, sincere, serious, decided, resolute, devoted insincere

earth 1. world, globe, 2. ground, dirt, soil, land, sod EARTHEN, EARTHLY

ease 1. relieve, reduce, soothe, allay, comfort, lighten, relax, loosen aggravate, 2. help, aid, facilitate

easy 1. simple, effortless, plain, not hard hard, 2. comfortable, restful, relaxing, cozy, snug uncomfortable, 3. kindly, mild, gentle, lenient strict, 4. pleasant, smooth, natural, informal formal EASIER, EASIEST, EASILY

eat 1. dine, consume, chew, swallow, 2. corrode, erode, waste away EATABLE, EATEN, EDIBLE

ebb decrease, diminish, lessen, decline, subside, recede, retreat, withdraw increase

eccentric unusual, peculiar, odd, abnormal, irregular, queer (*Slang* — screwy, wacky, nutty) normal

echo repeat, duplicate, imitate

eclipse hide, conceal, cover, screen, veil, obscure, darken, shadow, overcast

economy thrift, frugality, saving ECONOMIC, ECONOMICS, ECONOMIZE

ecstasy joy, rapture, happiness, delight, glee, elation sadness

edge border, bound, fringe EDGEWAYS, EDGEWISE

edict decree, order, law, ruling, proclamation

edifice building, structure, construction, establishment

edit correct, check, rewrite, revise, amend
EDITION, EDITOR, EDITORIAL

educate teach, instruct, school, train, tutor, enlighten,
direct, guide, show EDUCATION, EDUCATIONAL

eerie strange, weird, spooky, deathlike, ghastly, ghostly
EERIER, EERIEST

efface erase, destroy, rub out, obliterate

effect cause, influence, produce, bring about, evoke, determine, achieve, make, accomplish, execute, complete
EFFECTIVE

efficacy ability, capacity, competence, proficiency
inability EFFICIENCY, EFFICIENT

effort attempt, try, endeavor, undertaking, fling (*Slang* —
crack, whack, stab, whirl)

egg 1. ovum, embryo, 2. urge, stir, agitate, incite, provoke,
arouse (*Slang* — put up to)

eject remove, eliminate, drive out, expel, oust (*Slang* —
bounce, kick out, give the bum's rush, give the old heave-
ho, give the 1-2-3, throw out on one's ear) receive, include

elaborate dwell on, develop, work out, detail

elapse pass, expire, run out, slip away

elastic 1. flexible, pliable, yielding, adaptable inflexible, 2.
rubber band ELASTICITY

elated overjoyed, enchanted, delighted, jubilant, rejoicing
unhappy ELATION

elder older, senior younger ELDERLY, ELDEST

elect choose, pick, select, vote for, appoint ELECTION

electrify 1. charge, generate, shock, 2. excite, thrill, jolt, agitate, stir, ruffle, shake, upset
ELECTRIC, ELECTRICAL, ELECTRICIAN, ELECTRICITY, ELECTROMAGNET, ELECTRON

elegant refined, superior, tasteful, polished, cultured, fine vulgar ELEGANCE

elementary fundamental, basic, primary, essential, simple, beginning, introductory, initial, underlying advanced
ELEMENTARY SCHOOL

elevate lift, raise, boost ELEVATION, ELEVATOR

elf mischief-maker, devil, imp, fairy ELVES

elicit draw forth, summon, secure, get from

eligible qualified, fit, desirable, suitable ineligible

eliminate remove, discard, reject, throw out, get rid of, exclude, dispose of include ELIMINATION

elongate lengthen, extend, stretch, prolong shorten

elope flee, run, escape

eloquent fluent, well-spoken, expressive, meaningful
ELOQUENCE

else other, different, instead, another

elude avoid, escape, evade, miss, dodge (*Slang* — duck)
ELUSIVE

emaciated thin, undernourished, wasted, starved, haggard

emancipate free, release, liberate, deliver, rescue, save enslave, restrain EMANCIPATION

embalm preserve, keep

embankment bank, buttress, shore, barrier, dam, fortification

embark depart, start, board disembark

embarrass fluster, confuse, bewilder, humiliate, shame, mortify EMBARRASSMENT

embed enclose, fix, root, plant, lodge, wedge, inset, inlay EMBEDDED

embezzle steal, thieve, take, rob

embitter anger, provoke, incense, arouse, inflame, antagonize, alienate, set against

emblem symbol, sign, token, badge, mark

embody include, comprise, contain, cover, take in, embrace, incorporate exclude

embrace 1. grasp, hug, clasp, enfold, press, hold, clutch, 2. include, contain, comprise, cover, involve, 3. accept, adopt, take up

embroider 1. stitch, decorate, ornament, adorn, trim, embellish, 2. exaggerate, overstate, overdo, stretch, magnify EMBROIDERY

emerge appear, come out, come into view

emergency crisis, crucial period, pinch (*Slang* — squeeze, clutch)

emigrate leave, migrate EMIGRANT, EMIGRATION

eminent high, great, prominent, noble, distinguished, superior, important, outstanding, famous unknown EMINENCE

emissary delegate, messenger, envoy, agent, diplomat, minister, ambassador, spy

emit give off, discharge, ooze, send out receive

emotion feeling, sentiment, sensitivity, excitement EMOTIONAL

emphasis stress, importance, accent, insistence EMPHASIZE, EMPHATIC, EMPHATICALLY

employ hire, engage, contract, sign, retain, occupy, busy, use EMPLOYEE, EMPLOYER, EMPLOYMENT

empower permit, enable, authorize, sanction, license, warrant, commission, delegate, assign, entrust

empty 1. discharge, let out, eliminate, evacuate, 2. flow out, drain, run out, 3. vacant, void, barren, blank full EMPTINESS

emulate imitate, follow, copy, rival, vie with, compete with EMULATION

enable empower, qualify, authorize, sanction, license forbid

enact 1. pass, legislate, 2. portray, represent, act out, perform, stage

enchant delight, charm, thrill, enthrall, titillate, fascinate, captivate (*Slang* — tickle to death, tickle pink, knock dead, slay) ENCHANTMENT

encircle include, take in, comprise, enclose, surround, encompass, bound

enclose surround, fence, contain, include, encircle, envelop, shut in ENCLOSURE

encompass encircle, include, surround, enclose

encore 1. again, 2. repetition, curtain call

encounter 1. meet, come across, 2. battle, confront, collide, oppose

encourage support, urge, invite, promote, sponsor, cheer, inspire discourage ENCOURAGEMENT

encroach intrude, interfere, infringe, trespass, break in upon (*Slang* — barge in, bust in, butt in)

encumber burden, load, weigh down, hamper, saddle with relieve ENCUMBRANCE

end finish, stop, terminate, close, conclude, cease, quit, discontinue, halt, result, complete, wind up, clean up (*Slang* — put the lid on it, call it a day) ENDING

endanger risk, imperil, jeopardize, hazard

endear charm, captivate, allure embitter

endeavor try, effort, strive, attempt, labor, struggle (*Slang* — take a fling at, have a go at, give it a whirl, make a stab at, take a crack at)

endless continuous, constant, ceaseless, incessant, uninterrupted, nonstop, eternal, infinite, perpetual, everlasting

endorse sign, approve, support, accept, ratify, certify, confirm, O.K., validate, pass

endow give, invest, bequeath, provide, supply, furnish, contribute ENDOWMENT

endure 1. last, continue, persist, remain, stay vanish, 2. stand, undergo, bear, experience, feel, suffer, tolerate ENDURANCE

enemy opponent, foe, opposition friend, ally

energy force, strength, vigor, potency, vim, drive, might, power, vitality, stamina (*Slang* — pep, guts) weakness ENERGETIC, ENERGETICALLY

enfold embrace, clasp, wrap, hug, surround, envelop

enforce compel, force, make, oblige, drive, execute ENFORCEMENT

engage 1. involve, entangle, absorb, engross, occupy, hold, grip, 2. employ, busy, hire, contract for, 3. promise, agree, commit ENGAGEMENT

engaging interesting, absorbing, fascinating, engrossing, enthralling, spellbinding, charming, enchanting, captivating, appealing, tempting, enticing, delightful, lovely, exquisite dull, boring

engender cause, produce, develop, generate, breed

engineer guide, manage, direct, regulate, conduct, run, lead, maneuver ENGINE, ENGINEERING

engrave carve, cut, fix, print, inscribe, stamp, sketch, impress ENGRAVING

engross occupy, absorb, engage, fascinate, enthrall

engulf swallow, devour, flood, inundate

enhance improve, better, enrich, uplift (*Slang* — step up, soup up, jazz up) impair

enigma riddle, puzzle, mystery, problem, stumper (*Slang* — brain twister)

enjoy like, appreciate, savor, relish (*Slang* — get a kick out of) disgust ENJOYABLE, ENJOYMENT

enlarge increase, expand, broaden, magnify reduce, shrink ENLARGEMENT

enlighten clarify, inform, instruct, illuminate, explain, simplify, acquaint, teach, educate

enlist 1. join, enroll, sign up, 2. induce, prompt, move, influence, sway, persuade

enliven stimulate, inspire, cheer, brighten (*Slang* — pep up) calm

enmity hate, dislike, loathing, unfriendliness love

enormous large, great, vast, immense, huge, colossal, giant (*Slang* — whopping) tiny

enough sufficient, ample, plenty, satisfactory, adequate insufficient

enrage madden, infuriate, anger, inflame, provoke

enrich improve, enhance, better, uplift

enroll 1. list, register, write, record, join, 2. enlist, draft, induct, recruit ENROLLMENT

enshrine   entomb, inter, bury

ensign   1. flag, banner, pennant, standard, colors, 2. officer

enslave   subject, capture, hold down   free

ensue   follow, succeed, result

ensure   1. assure, make certain, guarantee (*Slang* — clinch),
2. protect, guard, defend, shelter, cover, shield, screen

entangle   involve, complicate, confuse, trap, snare
ENTANGLEMENT

enter   go into, set foot in, join   exit
ENTRANCE, ENTRY

enterprise   ambition, project, fete, undertaking, business,
venture, deed, exploit, achievement, adventure
ENTERPRISING

entertain   1. amuse, delight, interest, excite, fascinate,
give a party, 2. consider, contemplate, have in mind
ENTERTAINMENT

enthrall   fascinate, charm, captivate, intrigue, enchant,
delight, titillate, thrill (*Slang* — send)

enthrone   crown, glorify, exalt, install, instate, inaugurate
impeach

enthusiastic   interested, attracted, eager, keen about (*Slang*
— wild about, crazy about, mad about)
unconcerned, disinterested
ENTHUSIASM, ENTHUSIAST, ENTHUSIASTICALLY

entice   attract, tempt, lure, seduce (*Slang* — give the come-
on, rope in)

entirely   wholly, fully, altogether, completely, thoroughly,
totally, exclusively, solely   partly
ENTIRE, ENTIRETY

entitle   name, call, designate, tag, label, title, identify,
authorize, empower, enable, license   forbid

entrance 1. fascinate, charm, intrigue, enthrall, enchant, delight, thrill, 2. hypnotize, spellbind

entreat beg, ask, implore, plead ENTREATY

entrust delegate, assign, charge, commission

enumerate list, count, tally, number

enunciate speak, pronounce, announce, state, express ENUNCIATION

envelop wrap, cover, embrace, surround, encompass, hide, conceal

environment surroundings, neighborhood, vicinity, setting

envoy messenger, delegate, agent, diplomat

envy covet, be jealous of ENVIABLE, ENVIOUS

epidemic widespread, prevalent, contagious, infectious, catching

episode occurrence, happening, experience, event, incident, affair

epoch era, period, age

equal match, rival, tie, parallel (*Slang* — break even) unequal EQUALITY, EQUALIZE, EQUALLY

equilibrium balance, stability, firmness, soundness, steadiness instability

equip provide, furnish, fit, prepare, rig, costume EQUIPMENT

equitable fair, just, square, even, rightful, due, fit, proper EQUITY

equivalent equal, match, like, rival, substitute, replacement (*Slang* — ringer)

era epoch, period, age

eradicate eliminate, get rid of, remove, exterminate

erase cancel, wipe out, obliterate, cross off ERASER

erect 1. build, construct, make rise, 2. upright, vertical, straight bent ERECTION

erode disintegrate, break up, corrode, wear away, rust EROSION

err misjudge, go wrong, slip, sin

errand task, job, chore, assignment, duty, exercise

errant wandering, roving, roaming, rambling, meandering, drifting, straying, vagrant

erratic uncertain, irregular, queer, abnormal, unusual, changeable, unstable constant

erroneous mistaken, incorrect, untrue, wrong, false true ERROR

erupt burst forth, vomit, discharge, pour out ERUPTION

escape evade, get away, flee (*Slang* — jump, skip, fly the coop, ditch, shake, skip, duck)

escort accompany, conduct, guide, lead, usher, attend, squire, chaperon

especially particularly, principally, chiefly, mainly, mostly, primarily

espionage spying

essay 1. try, attempt, test, experiment, undertake (*Slang* — take a fling at, have a go at, give it a whirl), 2. composition, article, study, paper, thesis

essence 1. meaning, significance, substance, 2. perfume, scent, smell, odor, fragrance

essential needed, necessary, important, vital, fundamental, required, basic ESSENTIALLY

establish 1. fix, set, settle, found, organize, 2. prove, demonstrate, show ESTABLISHMENT

estate property, land

esteem 1. think, consider, judge, regard, 2. prize, value, appreciate, treasure, rate highly

estimate judge, calculate, evaluate, rate, value, figure, compute, gauge ESTIMATION

etch engrave, imprint, stamp, impress ETCHING

eternal always, forever, endless, perpetual, everlasting, permanent, infinite, continual, constant, ceaseless temporary ETERNITY

ethereal light, airy, delicate dense

etiquette manners, social code, formalities

evacuate leave, withdraw, remove, depart, quit, empty, abandon, vacate arrive EVACUATION

evade avoid, escape, miss, bypass (*Slang* — ditch, shake, dodge, duck) EVASION

evaporate vanish, disappear, fade away EVAPORATION

even 1. level, flat, smooth uneven, 2. same, uniform, equal, identical, 3. still, yet

evening nightfall, sunset, sundown

event happening, occurrence, incident, episode, experience

eventually finally, ultimately, in time EVENTUAL

everlasting perpetual, permanent, eternal, infinite, endless, continual, constant, ceaseless temporary

evermore forever, always temporarily

every each, all

evict expel, oust, turn out EVICTION

evidence facts, proof, grounds, data, indication, sign, clue

evident clear, plain, apparent, obvious, clear-cut doubtful, vague

evil   bad, wrong, sinful, wicked   good

evoke   bring forth, summon, induce, prompt

evolve   unfold, develop, grow, progress, advance
EVOLUTION

exact   detailed, precise, correct, accurate   vague
EXACTING, EXACTLY

exaggerate   overstate, stretch, overdo, magnify, enlarge
(*Slang* — talk big, lay it on thick)   minimize
EXAGGERATION

exalt   honor, praise, laud, extol, glorify, compliment, elevate
condemn, disapprove

examine   1. inspect, observe, study, consider, review, analyze, 2. test, quiz, question   EXAMINATION

example   1. sample, model, pattern, representative, symbol,
2. arithmetic problem

exasperate   irritate, aggravate, annoy, anger, infuriate, madden (*Slang* — give one a pain, get one's goat, burn one up,
get under one's skin, get in one's hair)   EXASPERATION

excavate   dig, scoop, pull up, unearth, burrow
EXCAVATION

exceed   surpass, better, excel, top, cap, beat
EXCEEDINGLY

excel   surpass, better, top, cap, beat, exceed
EXCELLENCE, EXCELLENT

except   1. excluding, omitting, leaving out, barring, besides,
save, outside of, aside from   including, 2. reject, exclude,
deny   accept, include   EXCEPTING, EXCEPTION

exceptional   unusual, extraordinary, remarkable, notable,
outstanding   ordinary

excess   left over, addition, extra, surplus, remaining   lack
EXCESSIVE

exchange change, substitute, switch, trade, swap

excite arouse, stir, stimulate, provoke, incite, move, affect
compose, calm
EXCITABLE, EXCITED, EXCITEMENT

exclaim cry out, clamor, shout
EXCLAMATION, EXCLAMATORY

exclude bar, shut out, outlaw, keep out, reject, forbid,
prohibit include
EXCLUSION, EXCLUSIVE, EXCLUSIVELY

excursion trip, journey, outing, tour

excuse 1. pardon, forgive, absolve, 2. reason, alibi

execute 1. do, perform, complete, carry out, put into effect,
accomplish, 2. put to death, kill
EXECUTION, EXECUTIONER

executive directing, managing, administrative

exemplify illustrate, demonstrate, show

exempt free, release, excuse, except, let off liable

exercise practice, use, train, drill, prepare, condition, perform (*Slang* — lick into shape)

exert use, employ, put forth, utilize EXERTION

exhale breathe out, give off, expel, blow inhale

exhaust 1. empty, drain, use up, consume, finish, spend
save, 2. tire, fatigue, wear out, knock out (*Slang* — poop,
bush)

exhibit show, demonstrate, display, present, flaunt (*Slang* —
flash, sport) EXHIBITION

exhilarate cheer, gladden, enliven, encourage, inspire,
stimulate, refresh, excite (*Slang* — give a lift, pep up)
sadden, deject EXHILARATION

exhort urge, advise, press, coax, prompt (*Slang* — twist
one's arm)

exile banish, expel, cast out, deport, ban, exclude admit

exist 1. be, live, 2. occur, prevail, stand EXISTENCE

exit depart, go out, leave enter

exodus departure, leaving, going, parting, exit entrance

exorbitant excessive, unreasonable, outrageous, overpriced cheap

exotic 1. foreign, strange native 2. colorful, bright, rich, vivid, gay dull

expand spread, swell, unfold, grow, enlarge, extend, broaden, increase, magnify contract, reduce
EXPANSE, EXPANSION

expect anticipate, look for, await, think, suppose, hope
EXPECTANT, EXPECTATION

expedient useful, helpful, fitting, desirable, appropriate, wise, sensible unwise, absurd

expedition 1. journey, trip, trek, pilgrimage, 2. speed, promptness, swiftness, haste, hurry delay

expel remove, get rid of, eliminate, eject, dispose of, dismiss, discharge, oust, banish, outlaw (*Slang* — bounce, give the hook, kick out, give the bum's rush, give the old heave-ho, give the 1-2-3) admit

expend spend, use up, consume, exhaust, waste store
EXPENDITURE

expensive costly, high-priced, dear (*Slang* — stiff, steep) cheap EXPENSE

experience 1. happening, occurrence, incident, episode, adventure, 2. sensation, feeling, emotion, 3. practice, knowledge, know-how inexperience EXPERIENCED

experiment try, test, prove, verify (*Slang* — play around with, fool around with, try it for size)
EXPERIMENTAL, EXPERIMENTATION

expert skillful, adept, apt, handy, clever, proficient, masterful, ingenious (*Slang* — crack, crackerjack) incompetent

expire end, cease, perish, die, pass away, vanish, disappear continue, commence EXPIRATION

explain solve, answer, clarify, simplify, illustrate, show, demonstrate EXPLANATION, EXPLANATORY

explicit clear, distinct, definite, direct, candid, express, positive, unmistakable indefinite, unclear

explode blow up, burst, erupt EXPLOSION, EXPLOSIVE

exploit 1. use unfairly, take advantage of (*Slang* — play for a sucker), 2. deed, feat, adventure, bold act

explore search, hunt, look, research, examine, investigate, delve into, probe EXPLORATION, EXPLORER

export send abroad, ship import

expose open, uncover, show, display, reveal, disclose, unmask hide, conceal EXPOSITION, EXPOSURE

expound explain, clarify, illuminate, demonstrate, teach, lecture, present

express 1. say, voice, present, tell, describe, 2. show, indicate, imply, 3. send, dispatch, ship, 4. fast, quick, speedy, rapid, swift slow EXPRESSION, EXPRESSIVE

expressly plainly, definitely

expulsion removal, ejection, elimination, discharge admittance

exquisite 1. lovely, delicate, beautiful, superb, magnificent, marvelous, wonderful, delightful, charming, appealing, enchanting, heavenly, attractive ugly, 2. sharp, intense, acute dull

extend 1. stretch, reach out, lengthen, increase, enlarge,

expand, broaden, magnify decrease, shorten, 2. give, grant, donate, present, allot, contribute, supply, provide, furnish take
EXTENSION, EXTENSIVE, EXTENT

exterior outside, outer, external, surface interior

exterminate destroy, get rid of, eliminate, kill, dispose of, wipe out

external outside, outer, exterior, surface internal

extinct dead, gone, past, obsolete EXTINCTION

extinguish put out, smother, quench, suppress, crush (*Slang* — crack down on, shut down, squelch, sit on, put the lid on)

extol praise, glorify, laud, compliment, exalt

extra additional, supplementary, surplus, more, spare

extraordinary special, unusual, remarkable, exceptional, wonderful, marvelous, noteworthy, memorable ordinary
EXTRAORDINARILY

extravagant extreme, excessive, overdone, exaggerated, unreasonable, luxurious, grand meager
EXTRAVAGANCE

extreme 1. extravagant, excessive, exaggerated, overdone, drastic, radical moderate, 2. final, last, conclusive, terminal, endmost first, beginning
EXTREMELY, EXTREMITY

extricate release, free, liberate, rescue, clear capture

exult rejoice, delight, be glad lament, grieve
EXULTANT, EXULTATION

eye look, glance, watch, observe, regard, view, inspect, stare (*Slang* — size up, give the once-over)

F

fable story, legend, myth, fairy tale, fiction truth

fabric cloth, textile, goods, material

fabulous unbelievable, amazing, remarkable, striking, notable, marvelous

facade front, face

face 1. confront, oppose, meet, encounter, brave avoid, 2. features, looks, countenance (*Slang* — mug, kisser, puss), 3. look, expression FACIAL

facet side, aspect, view, phase

facilitate ease, help, assist, speed, smooth the way FACILITY

fact detail, item, point, truth, certainty, evidence, data, clue lie FACTUAL

factor cause, element, part, ingredient, basis

factory plant, works

faculty 1. talent, gift, power, ability, capacity, qualification, aptitude, 2. teachers, staff

fad fashion, craze, rage

fade 1. dim, lose color, pale, dull, bleach, 2. weaken, sink, fail, droop, decline (*Slang* — cave in, fizzle out, peter out, hit the skids, conk out, give out, poop out)

fag tire, fatigue, weary, exhaust

fagot sticks, twigs, firewood

fail 1. flunk, be unsuccessful, lose out (*Slang* — flop, lay an egg) succeed, 2. neglect, fall short, 3. weaken, fade, decline (*Slang* — cave in, fizzle out, peter out, hit the skids, conk out, give out, poop out) FAILING, FAILURE

faint 1. swoon, black out, weaken, keel over (*Slang* — pass out), 2. weak, dim, pale, indistinct, vague, hazy, blurred clear, strong

fair 1. light, pale, whitish dark, 2. clear, sunny, bright, pleasant cloudy, 3. average, mediocre outstanding, 4.

honest, just, square, right, impartial unfair, unjust, 5. festival, fete, affair, bazaar, exposition, market FAIRLY

fairy sprite, elf, goblin, pixie, sylph

faith 1. trust, belief, confidence, hope, 2. religion, teaching FAITHFUL, FAITHLESS

fake 1. pretend, deceive, falsify, disguise, distort, feign (*Slang* — go through the motions, put on an act, put up a false front), 2. false, mock, make-believe, imitation, counterfeit, artificial, fraudulent (*Slang* — phony) real, genuine

fall 1. drop, plunge, descend, tumble ascend, 2. lapse, slip, 3. ruin, destruction, defeat, overthrow, 4. autumn, 5. wig, hairpiece

fallow unprepared, uncultivated, idle, unproductive cultivated

false 1. untrue, incorrect, lying, wrong true, 2. deceitful, disloyal, two-faced loyal, 3. artificial, fake, counterfeit, mock, imitation real, genuine FALSEHOOD

falter hesitate, stumble, stagger, waver, flounder

fame reputation, name, renown, glory, popularity, notoriety FAMED, FAMOUS

familiar 1. well-known, popular unknown, 2. friendly, close, personal, intimate distant, 3. well acquainted, informed in, versed in, knowledgeable unfamiliar FAMILIARITY

family group, household, kin, relatives, folks

famine starvation, lack, need, want, shortage, deficiency, absence sufficiency, plenty

famish hunger, starve

fan 1. stir, arouse, whip, stimulate, spread, flare soothe, calm, 2. blower, 3. admirer, follower, devotee, fancier (*Slang* — hound, rooter)

fanatic enthusiast, zealot (*Slang* — bug, nut)

fancy   1. imagine, visualize, picture, dream, suppose, think, 2. like, care for, love (*Slang* — go for, have eyes for)   dislike, 3. elaborate, ornate, flowery, fussy, frilly   (*Slang* — classy)   simple   FANCIFUL

fang   tooth, tusk

fantastic   odd, unreal, strange, wild, unusual, incredible, outrageous   ordinary, usual

fantasy   1. imagination, vision, illusion, fancy, 2. fiction, myth, fable, legend, story, fairy tale

far   1. distant, remote, removed   near, 2. much, a great deal   FAR OFF, FARTHER

fare   1. eat, be fed, 2. prosper, get on, progress, thrive, 3. charge, toll, fee, 4. passenger

farewell   1. good-by, good luck, good day, so long, cheerio, see you later   hello, 2. departing, leaving, parting, taking leave   arriving

farm   1. cultivate, grow, raise, ranch, harvest, 2. hire, let, rent, lease, charter, 3. plantation, ranch, homestead   FARMER

far-reaching   broad, wide, extensive, sweeping, widespread   limited

fascinate   interest, excite, attract, enthrall, captivate, charm, intrigue, enchant, thrill, delight   bore   FASCINATION

fashion   1. make, shape, form, create, mold, 2. style, mode, vogue, custom   FASHIONABLE

fast   1. go hungry, starve   eat, 2. speedy, swift, rapid, quick, hasty   slow, 3. firm, stable, sure, dependable, solid, steady   changing

fasten   tie, lock, attach, secure, close, bind, connect   untie, separate, open

fastidious   particular, selective, critical, choosy

fat   1. stout, fleshy, plump, chubby, tubby, chunky   thin, 2. oil, lubrication, grease   FATTEN

fatal   1. deadly, destructive, killing, mortal, disastrous, 2. important, fateful, serious, significant   unimportant

fate   fortune, destiny, lot, end   FATED, FATEFUL

father   1. originate, cause, produce, bring about, breed, 2. priest, 3. male parent, daddy, sire   FATHERLY

fathom   1. understand, follow, grasp, comprehend (*Slang —* dig, get the picture, get the drift, get), 2. measure, gauge

fatigue   tire, exhaust, wear out

fault   mistake, error, defect, flaw, shortcoming, wrongdoing, misdeed, catch (*Slang —* bug)   FAULTY

favor   1. prefer, rather, like better, 2. resemble, look like, 3. kindness, service, good deed, benefit, courtesy FAVORABLE

favorite   choice, cherished, prized, beloved, precious, pet, adored, treasured

fealty   loyalty, faithfulness, allegiance, devotion, faith, attachment   disloyalty

fear   dread, be afraid   FEARFUL, FEARLESS

feasible   possible, practical, workable, attainable impossible

feast   1. enjoy, like, love, delight in, rejoice in, appreciate (*Slang —* get a kick out of), 2. banquet, treat, feed, spread

feat   deed, act, action, exploit, achievement, accomplishment, stunt

feature   1. show, headline, star, 2. part, characteristic, trait, mark

fee   charge, dues, toll, fare

feeble weak, powerless, frail strong

feed 1. nourish, supply, nurture, 2. eat, dine FED

feel 1. touch, finger, handle, 2. be, seem, look, appear, 3. experience, know, encounter, meet, undergo, endure, suffer, sense FEELER, FEELING

feign pretend, fake, act, bluff, assume, affect, play FEINT

felicity 1. happiness, bliss, gladness, delight, joy, cheer, glee, enchantment, 2. blessing, good fortune, luck

fellow 1. lad, boy, man, chap, guy, 2. companion, counterpart, mate, partner, comrade, associate FELLOWSHIP

female ladylike, womanly, feminine male FEMININE

fen marsh, swamp

fence 1. enclose, wall, fortify, blockade, 2. fight, joust, duel, 3. sell illegally, black-market, bootleg
FENCER, FENCING

ferment 1. change chemically, sour, 2. excite, agitate, disturb, stir, trouble, ruffle calm, pacify

ferocious fierce, savage, vicious, brutal, wild, cruel, ruthless, bloodthirsty gentle, tame FEROCITY

ferret 1. hunt, search, 2. weasel

ferry 1. carry, transport, haul, cart, 2. boat

fertile productive, fruitful, enriched, abundant, creative
unproductive, barren
FERTILITY, FERTILIZATION, FERTILIZE
FERTILIZER

fervent sincere, devoted, ardent, zealous, passionate, intense, enthusiastic FERVOR

festive merry, gay, jolly, jovial, joyous, gala
FESTAL, FESTIVAL, FESTIVITY

fetch bring, go get

fetching enchanting, appealing, interesting, enticing, inviting, alluring, fascinating, captivating, delightful, exquisite,
lovely displeasing

fete festival, party, gala affair

fetter bind, tie, chain, shackle, restrain

feud quarrel, dispute, controversy, fight, squabble, animosity, bitterness peace

fever heat, flush, sickness, high body temperature
FEVERISH

few not many, small number, very little many

fib lie, falsehood, untruth, tale, story, yarn truth

fickle changing, unstable, not constant, flighty, uncertain,
unreliable, unfaithful constant

fiction fantasy, untruth, invention, legend, myth, fable,
fairy tale truth

fidelity 1. loyalty, faithfulness, allegiance, devotion, faith,
attachment, fealty disloyalty, 2. accuracy, exactness, cor-
rectness, precision

fidget fuss, twitch, jerk, wriggle, squirm, twist, wiggle

field 1. land, space, region, tract, plot, ground, pasture, 2.
sphere, range, realm, area

fiend 1. devil, monster, demon, ogre, 2. addict FIENDISH

fierce savage, raging, wild, violent, vicious, brutal, ferocious,
cruel calm, kind

fiery 1. hot, burning, flaming, 2. aroused, excited, violent,
heated, ardent, feverish, fervent unemotional

fiesta festival, holiday, festivity, fete

fight quarrel, struggle, combat, contest, battle, contend,
oppose, attack, row (*Slang* — scrap)

figure **100**

figure 1. symbol, number, numeral, digit, 2. price, cost, charge, amount, 3. shape, form, physique, build, structure, 4. person, individual, 5. picture, drawing, diagram, illustration, design, pattern, outline, chart, sketch

filch steal, take, pilfer, thieve (*Slang* — lift, swipe, cop, pinch)

file 1. sort, classify, group, categorize, catalog, store, 2. march, parade, 3. smooth, grind, sand, sharpen, edge

fill 1. load, pack, stuff, cram empty, 2. supply, provide, furnish FILLING

filly mare, female colt

film 1. photograph, take a picture (*Slang* — shoot), 2. coat, coating, layer, covering FILMY

filter strain, percolate, screen, sift, refine, purify, cleanse, drain, separate

filth dirt, muck, foul matter, rot FILTHY

final last, deciding, closing, terminal, conclusive beginning FINALLY

finale end, finish, conclusion, termination beginning, opening

finance sponsor, back, support, aid, assist, subsidize, stake (*Slang* — bankroll) FINANCIAL, FINANCIER

find 1. discover, disclose, come upon lose, 2. learn, get, gain knowledge, gather, 3. decide, declare, determine

fine 1. penalize, tax, charge, 2. delicate, minute coarse, 3. refined, tasteful, polished, 4. excellent, good, nice, splendid (*Slang* — great, grand, dandy, swell, keen, nifty)

finery clothes, frillery, ornaments (*Slang* — glad rags)

finger 1. touch, handle, feel, manipulate, 2. digit

finish 1. end, complete, close, terminate, conclude, stop, cease (*Slang* — wind up, clean up, button up, put the lid on it, call it a day)   begin, 2. perfect, polish, refine

fire   1. ignite, heat, kindle, 2. dismiss, discharge, expel, lay off, release (*Slang* — sack, can, bounce, boot, give the ax, give the gate)   hire, 3. arouse, excite, inflame, stir, provoke, agitate   calm, soothe, 4. shoot, discharge, blast

firearms   guns, artillery, ammunition

firebrand   1. lighter, 2. troublemaker, agitator, provoker, instigator, rabble-rouser

firm   1. solid, fixed, secure, unyielding, inflexible, stationary, immovable, rigid   flexible, 2. company, business, enterprise

first   1. principal, main, chief, leading, primary, dominant, 2. beginning, foremost, before, ahead, in front   last, 3. rather, sooner, preferably

fissure   split, crack, opening, break, crevice, gap

fit   1. suit, adapt, adjust, 2. proper, right, suitable, qualified   improper, 3. strong, healthy, well   unfit, 4. attack, seizure, spell, spasm, convulsion, frenzy, rage   FITTING

fitful   irregular, sporadic, choppy, disconnected, broken   regular, constant

fix   1. mend, repair, adjust, regulate, doctor   break, impair, 2. settle, establish, stabilize, solidify, 3. dilemma, quandary

fixture   appliance, attachment, accessory

flag   1. signal, wave, 2. weaken, droop, wilt, fade, 3. pennant, banner, standard, colors

flair   talent, perception, insight

flamboyant   flaming, brilliant, striking, ornate, vivid, dazzling, fancy   simple

flame   blaze, burn   FLAMMABLE

flank   1. side, border, 2. attack, strike

flare 1. flame, blaze, glow, burn, 2. spread, expand, open up, unfold

flash 1. flame, flare, blaze, 2. telegraph, wire, cable, radio FLASHY

flat 1. level, even, horizontal, smooth uneven, 2. dull, lifeless exciting, 3. off-key, unmusical, 4. apartment, suite FLATTEN

flatter praise, compliment (*Slang* — soft-soap, butter up) FLATTERY

flaunt display, exhibit, parade (*Slang* — flash, sport) hide, conceal

flavor season, spice, give taste FLAVORING

flaw damage, defect, crack, fault, weakness, blemish perfection FLAWLESS

flay 1. peel, skin, strip, 2. criticize, attack, assail (*Slang* — roast, pitch into, sail into)

fleck spot, mark, speckle, dot

flee run away, disappear (*Slang* — beat it, blow, scram, clear out, make off, skip) FLED

fleece 1. rob, cheat, swindle (*Slang* — rook, beat, con), 2. wool

fleet 1. rapid, swift, fast, quick, nimble slow, 2. ships, 3. group, band, company

flesh 1. meat, body, 2. skin, 3. family FLESHY

flex bend, arch, curve stiffen, straighten FLEXIBLE

flick strike, snap, crack, jerk, flip

flicker 1. flutter, waver, 2. woodpecker

flimsy slight, frail, weak, delicate, dainty, fragile strong, sturdy

flinch shrink, cringe, recoil, draw back

fling   1. throw, sling, pitch, toss, cast, hurl (*Slang* — peg, fire), 2. celebration, spree, escapade, lark

flip   1. toss, throw, fling, sling, pitch, cast, hurl (*Slang* — peg, fire), 2. jerk, snap, flick

flippant   rude, disrespectful, saucy, pert, impudent, cocky, flip, cheeky, smart, smart-alecky (*Slang* — fresh, nervy) polite

flit   fly, glide, flutter

float   1. buoy up, sustain, hold up   sink, 2. raft, 3. parade car

flock   group, crowd, throng, mob, bunch, pack, multitude

flog   beat, whip, lash, spank, thrash

flood   overfill, drench, overflow, inundate, oversupply, deluge

floor   1. defeat, overcome, upset, overthrow, 2. ground, pavement, 3. level, story

flop   1. drop, fall, sink, go down, droop, slump, sag   rise, 2. fail, lose (*Slang* — lay an egg, fold up, strike out) succeed

flounder   1. struggle, have trouble, stumble, 2. fish

flourish   1. thrive, prosper, grow, develop, sprout, bloom fade, 2. wave, flaunt, display, parade, exhibit, show

flout   sneer, insult, mock, ridicule, jeer, taunt

flow   glide, stream, pour, run, gush

flower   blossom, bloom, develop, flourish, thrive
FLOWERING, FLOWERY

fluffy   soft, downy, feathery, woolly, furry

fluid   liquid, flowing, watery   solid

flurry   1. fluster, excite, agitate, confuse, ruffle, 2. commotion, confusion, disturbance, 3. light snowstorm

flush   1. blush, redden, color, 2. rush, chase, 3. level, flat, even, 4. full, stuffed, packed

fluster   excite, confuse

flutter   wave, flap, flourish, tremble, move

fly   1. glide, coast, sail, wing, 2. flee, run away (*Slang* — take to one's heels, make off, clear out), 3. insect   FLIGHT

foam   bubble, lather, froth

focus   adjust, concentrate

foe   enemy, adversary, opponent   friend

fog   cloud, blur, dim, confuse   clarify   FOGGY

foil   1. outwit, frustrate, thwart, spoil, ruin, 2. metal, 3. sword

fold   1. bend, double over   unfold, 2. pen, enclosure, 3. church   FOLDER

folk   1. people, persons, society, public, 2. tribe, nation, race, clan, breed

follow   1. come next, succeed, ensue, trail   lead, precede, 2. pursue, trace, 3. use, obey, act according to   ignore FOLLOWER, FOLLOWING

folly   foolishness, silliness, stupidity (*Slang* — dumb thing to do)   cleverness

fond   loving, liking, affectionate, adoring, romantic, sentimental, tender   disliking

fondle   pet, caress, cuddle

font   1. fountain, spring, 2. basin

food   edibles, provisions, nutriment, nourishment (*Slang* — grub, eats, chow)

fool   1. play, joke, 2. deceive, trick, mislead (*Slang* — kid, spoof), 3. ninny, ignoramus, know-nothing, dunce, blockhead, scatterbrain, simpleton (*Slang* — chump, numskull, silly, jerk, dope, dumbbell, simp)   FOOLISH

foolhardy   bold, rash, daring, audacious, reckless   cautious

foolproof   safe, tight, resistant

foot   1. walk, hoof it, march, hike, 2. part of body, sole (*Slang* — dog, kicker, tootsy), 3. base, lowest part, foundation top

footing   1. support, toehold, standing, 2. relationship, position

forage   1. hunt, search, look, explore, 2. animal food, fodder, feed, grain

foray   plunder, pillage, raid, invade

forbear   refrain, hold back, abstain, avoid, control oneself indulge   FORBEARANCE

forbid   prohibit, disallow, bar, ban, taboo, prevent, deter encourage   FORBIDDEN

force   1. compel, make, drive, oblige, pressure, motivate, 2. thrust, push, shove, ram, break through, 3. power, strength, might, vigor, energy weakness, 4. group, body, staff, personnel, crew, gang   FORCEFUL, FORCIBLE

fore   front, forward, foremost, first, chief, head, primary

foreboding   warning, prediction, foretelling, forecast, promise, omen, prophecy, premonition

forecast   prophecy, prediction, foretelling, promise, omen

forefather   ancestor, predecessor, forebear

foreign   alien, external   FOREIGNER

foreman   supervisor, superintendent, overseer, boss

foremost   first, chief, leading, head, main, principal, dominant, primary

foresee   anticipate, predict, forecast, foretell, prophesy FORESEEN, FORESIGHT

forest   wood, timberland   FORESTRY

foretell   predict, prophesy, forecast, promise

forever   always, evermore, eternity

forfeit lose, sacrifice, let slip retain

forge 1. make, shape, form, create, mold, 2. counterfeit, falsify, make up, 3. progress, push onward, 4. blacksmith's shop, smelter

forget not remember, escape one, lose sight of remember
FORGETFUL, FORGOT

forgive pardon, excuse, absolve, quit blame
FORGIVEN, FORGIVENESS

forgo give up, sacrifice, surrender, yield, relinquish, do without, waive retain, keep

fork 1. silverware, 2. branch, offshoot

forlorn hopeless, miserable, desperate, despondent, forsaken, abandoned, deserted, defenseless, helpless

form 1. develop, compose, make, create, fashion, construct, shape, mold, 2. kind, sort, class, grade, type, variety, species, make, 3. manner, method, fashion, style, way, procedure
FORMATION

formal orderly, regular, systematic, businesslike, stiff, arranged, structural, correct, proper, customary informal
FORMALITY

former earlier, past, previous, preceding, prior, first latter
FORMERLY

formidable difficult, hard, rough, rugged, tough (*Slang* — wicked, mean) easy, simple

formulate define, describe, express, voice, put

forsake leave, give up, abandon, quit
FORSAKEN, FORSOOK

forth forward, onward, on, ahead back

forthcoming approaching, imminent, coming, near, close (*Slang* — in the cards)

forthwith immediately, promptly, without delay, instantly, at once, quickly, swiftly (*Slang* — pronto)

fortify strengthen, brace, invigorate, reinforce weaken
FORTIFICATION

fortitude courage, strength, vigor, vitality, stamina, spunk
(*Slang* — guts) weakness

fortunate lucky, auspicious unlucky

fortune 1. riches, wealth, prosperity, treasure poverty, 2.
luck, chance, fate, lot, destiny

forum 1. square, plaza, 2. discussion, debate, deliberation,
consideration, study, 3. tribunal, law court

forward 1. send, dispatch, deliver, pass, 2. onward, ahead,
frontward, advanced backward, 3. pert, bold, aggressive,
insolent, presumptuous, brazen, immodest (*Slang* — crusty,
nervy, cocky, cheeky, smart-alecky) shy

fossil remains, trace, vestige, relic

foster nourish, nurture, feed, cultivate, nurse, care for,
support, mind, tend, rear

foul 1. dirty, nasty, smelly, stinking, offensive, disgusting,
vile savory, 2. wicked, vicious, evil, bad, wrong, sinful,
base, low good, 3. unfair fair

foundation 1. base, ground, 2. establishment, institution,
organization

founder 1. fall, stumble, tumble, topple, 2. break down,
collapse, sink, fail, 3. producer, creator, maker, author,
originator, inventor, builder

foundling orphan, waif

foundry forge, smelter, blacksmith's shop

fountain 1. spring, spout, spray, 2. source

fowl bird, poultry

foxy crafty, shrewd, artful, cunning, knowing, sly, clever,
canny artless

fraction part, portion, division, segment, section whole

fracture break, crack, burst, rupture, chip

fragile delicate, frail, slight, dainty, breakable, flimsy, brittle sturdy, strong

fragment part, portion, segment, section, fraction, division whole

fragrant sweet-smelling, perfumed, odorous, aromatic foul FRAGRANCE

frail weak, slight, delicate, dainty, fragile strong FRAILTY.

frame 1. make, plan, put together, build, construct, form, design, devise, arrange, 2. border, edge, bound, trim, 3. body, figure, form, 4. support, skeleton FRAMEWORK

frank open, candid, sincere, straightforward, forthright, outspoken, blunt deceitful

frantic excited, frenzied, wild, violent, delirious, hysterical calm, unexcited FRANTICALLY

fraternal brotherly, kind, sympathetic, friendly, congenial, sociable unfriendly, antisocial FRATERNITY

fraud cheating, trickery, dishonesty, swindle (*Slang* — gyp)

fraught loaded, filled lacking

fray 1. wear away, rub, tatter, 2. fight, quarrel, battle, conflict, clash, brush, tussle, skirmish, scuffle, struggle, melee (*Slang* — scrap, run-in)

freak unusual, queer, incredible, grotesque, bizarre

free 1. clear, acquit, dismiss, release, discharge, relieve, reprieve, deliver, liberate, emancipate enslave, 2. loose, unfastened, untied restrained, 3. independent, open, unrestrained, at liberty restricted, 4. complimentary, gratis, untaxed, without charge taxed FREEDOM

freeze   1. chill, refrigerate   defrost, 2. stiffen, remain motionless   FREEZER, FROZE, FROZEN

freight   load, cargo, burden, shipment, goods
FREIGHTER

frenzy   fury, madness, excitement, passion, rage, agitation,
fit, delirium   serenity, calmness   FRENZIED

frequent   1. visit often, haunt   (*Slang* — hang out at), 2.
many, recurrent, common, prevalent, regular, habitual
infrequent   FREQUENCY, FREQUENTLY

fresh   1. new, unused, firsthand, original   old, stale, 2.
unsalty, 3. bright, alert, unfaded, brisk, vigorous, energetic,
refreshed   dull   FRESHEN

fret   worry, fuss   (*Slang* — stew)   FRETFUL

friction   resistance, clash, conflict, grinding, scraping
harmony

friend   acquaintance, intimate, companion, comrade, mate,
associate, colleague, partner, crony, playmate, chum, buddy
(*Slang* — sidekick, pal)   enemy
FRIENDLINESS, FRIENDLY, FRIENDSHIP

fright   1. fear, terror, alarm, dismay, dread, awe, horror,
phobia, panic   fearlessness, 2. eyesore, mess   beauty
FRIGHTEN, FRIGHTFUL

frigid   1. cold, stiff, chilling, icy, reserved, unfeeling, restrained, aloof, distant   warm, friendly, 2. freezing, wintry,
crisp, brisk, nippy, raw, sharp, frosty   warm

frill   ornament, ruffle, flounce, embellishment, luxury

fringe   border, trimming, edge, brim, rim

frisk   frolic, play, romp, caper   FRISKY

frivolous   silly, shallow, unimportant, light, trivial, foolish,
inane   serious, important

frock   gown, dress, garment, robe

frolic play, frisk, romp, caper FROLICSOME

front fore, first part, face, head back

frontier back country, border, outskirt

frost freezing, cold FROSTY

frosting icing, topping

froth 1. foam, lather, 2. trivia, rubbish, unimportant important

frown scowl, pout, look sullen, look displeased smile

frugal economical, thrifty, saving, prudent wasteful FRUGALITY

fruit 1. plant product, 2. yield, result FRUITFUL, FRUITLESS

frustrate foil, thwart, defeat, spoil, ruin aid, help FRUSTRATION

fry cook, sauté

fuel kindling, combustible

fugitive 1. runaway, escaping (*Slang* — hot), 2. temporary, passing, transient lasting, permanent

fulfill perform, do, carry out, execute, finish, complete, transact, discharge, satisfy FULFILLMENT

full 1. complete, entire, stuffed, packed, crammed empty, 2. plump, round, fat thin, 3. broad, wide, expansive, roomy skimpy FULLNESS, FULLY

fumble bungle, blunder, muff, grope awkwardly

fume 1. be angry, burn, seethe, rage, storm, rave, 2. smoke, vapor, gas

fumigate disinfect, sterilize, sanitize

fun amusement, playfulness, joking, sport, good time, pleasure, entertainment, enjoyment (*Slang* — picnic) FUNNY

function 1. work, be used, act, operate, perform, serve, 2. ceremony, gathering, service, rite, ritual, exercise

fund stock, supply, resources, assets

fundamental essential, basic, underlying, primary, elementary

funeral burial, last rites

funnel channel, siphon, pipe

fur pelt, hide, skin FURRY

furious raging, violent, angry, mad, rabid, overwrought, upset, enraged, infuriated (*Slang* — hopping mad, fit to be tied) calm, placid FURY

furl roll up, fold unfold

furlough vacation, leave of absence, sabbatical

furnace stove, heater, oven, kiln, forge

furnish supply, provide, give, equip, outfit FURNITURE

furrow wrinkle, crease, groove

further 1. help, aid, advance, promote hinder, 2. farther, beyond, past, over FURTHEST

furthermore in addition, then, again, also, too, besides, similarly, likewise, by the same token

furtive secret, sly, stealthy, sneaky, underhanded open, honest

fuse 1. join, blend, melt, unite, combine, stick together, weld, solder, glue separate, 2. exploder, blaster FUSION

fuss worry, bother, fret (*Slang* — stew) FUSSY

futile useless, vain, unsuccessful, ineffective useful

future coming, hereafter, tomorrow past

fuzz fluff, fur, down FUZZY

G

gadget   device, tool, instrument, implement, utensil, apparatus, appliance, contraption (*Slang* — gimmick)

gag   1. silence, muzzle, muffle, stop one's mouth, restrain, 2. joke, jest

gain   1. get, obtain, secure, acquire, earn, receive   lose, 2. benefit, 3. advance, make progress, improve, look up, pick up, come along   deteriorate

gait   pace, walk, step, stride

gala   festive, merry, gay, jolly, joyous, joyful

gale   1. wind, windstorm, tempest, squall, 2. noisy outburst, shout

gall   1. bitterness, impudence, nerve, 2. bile

gallant   1. brave, courageous, valiant, bold, heroic cowardly, 2. noble, chivalrous, courteous, knightly, manly, fine, grand, stately   ungentlemanly, ill-mannered GALLANTRY

gallery   1. passage, corridor, hallway, arcade, 2. balcony, grandstand (*Slang* — peanut gallery)

gallop   run, ride, sprint, bound, trot

gallows   hanging, execution, rope, noose

galosh   rubber, overshoe, boot

gamble   speculate, risk, bet, wager, try one's luck GAMBLER

gambol   frolic, run, play, sport, romp, caper, cavort, carry on (*Slang* — cut up, horse around)

game   1. brave, plucky, spirited, daring (*Slang* — spunky) unwilling, 2. contest, match, play, fun, 3. scheme, plan, plot, 4. hunted animals, wildlife, quarry, prey

gang group, crew, ring, band, party, company, pack, troop, bunch, crowd (*Slang* — mob)

gangway passageway, bridge

gap 1. break, opening, pass, cleft, crevice, rift, gulf, hole, 2. blank, unfilled space

gape 1. yawn, open mouth wide, 2. gap, gulf, hole, opening

garage carport, auto repair shop

garb clothing, apparel, dress, attire, garments (*Slang* — duds)

garbage waste, scraps, refuse, rubbish, trash, debris, litter, junk

garden grow, raise, cultivate, plant   GARDENER

gargle mouthwash, antiseptic

gargoyle waterspout

garland wreath, spray, bouquet, lei

garment robe, frock, article of clothing, togs (*Slang* — duds)

garner store, collect, save up, accumulate, amass, stockpile, hoard

garnish decorate, trim, adorn, beautify, embellish, dress up, spruce up, fix up (*Slang* — doll up)

garret attic, loft

garrison 1. fort, stronghold, 2. military unit, regiment, battalion, company, troop

gas 1. vapor, fume, 2. gasoline, petroleum   GASEOUS

gash cut, wound, laceration

gasoline petroleum

gasp pant, puff, choke

gate fence, barrier

gateway door, portal, entry, opening

gather 1. collect, bring together, assemble, accumulate, amass, bunch, group, cluster, compile scatter, 2. fold, tuck, pleat GATHERING

gaudy showy, tasteless, garish, vulgar (*Slang* — loud) tasteful

gauge measure, estimate, judge, rate, appraise, assess, size up

gaunt 1. thin, lean, skinny, scrawny, lanky, bony, 2. desolate, blank, bleak, empty

gavel mallet

gay 1. happy, merry, spirited, lively, animated, vivacious, playful, joyful, joyous, jolly, jovial, cheerful, pleasant unhappy, solemn, 2. colorful, bright, vivid, rich dull GAIETY, GAILY

gaze stare, gape, gawk

gear 1. equip, furnish, outfit, rig, 2. wheel mechanism

gem 1. jewel, precious stone, 2. treasure, good thing, joy, first-rater

general 1. common, widespread, indefinite, vague, broad, 2. officer, commander GENERALLY

generate produce, cause, bring about, create, originate GENERATOR

generous 1. unselfish, giving, kind, liberal, openhanded, bighearted selfish, 2. large, plentiful, ample small GENEROSITY

genial pleasant, cheerful, friendly, kindly, warm, comforting, cordial, agreeable, amiable, good-natured disagreeable, unpleasant

genius 1. intelligence, inspiration, talent, creative thought, gift, 2. prodigy, master, wizard

genocide slaughter, massacre, killing, butchery, carnage

gentle 1. mild, soft, moderate, tender rough, 2. kindly, friendly, good-natured, cordial, genial, amiable, sympathetic, humane harsh, mean, 3. refined, well-bred, cultured, polished, genteel, noble ill-bred
GENTILITY, GENTLY

genuine real, true, authentic, pure, legitimate, bona fide, sincere fake

germ 1. seed, origin, beginning, 2. microorganism

germinate grow, develop, sprout, flourish, thrive

gesture signal, sign, motion, movement

get 1. obtain, receive, gain, fetch, bring, retrieve, acquire, secure give, 2. become, turn, grow, 3. persuade, influence, induce, 4. incur, bring about

geyser spring, steam, volcanic water, jet, gush, fountain

ghastly 1. horrible, terrible, dreadful, deplorable, outrageous, vile, wretched, detestable, contemptible, frightful, shocking, appalling, repulsive (*Slang* — awful, atrocious) lovely, beautiful, 2. pale, sallow, deathlike ruddy

ghost spirit, specter, phantom, spook GHOSTLY

giant huge, immense, vast, enormous, tremendous, colossal, monumental, mammoth, gigantic tiny, minute

gibe jeer, sneer, scoff, mock, taunt, boo, hiss, hoot approve

giddy 1. dizzy, reeling, 2. silly, flighty, scatterbrained serious

gift 1. present, offering, 2. ability, talent, endowment, power, aptitude GIFTED

gigantic huge, immense, vast, enormous, tremendous, colossal, monumental, mammoth tiny, minute

giggle laugh, chuckle, titter, snicker

gild 1. coat, paint, cover, 2. sweeten, embellish GILT

gird 1. bind, belt, tie, wrap untie, 2. surround, encircle, 3. prepare, ready, get set GIRT

girl lass, female, maiden, damsel, miss GIRLISH

girth size, dimensions, measure, proportions, width, expanse

give 1. present, offer, hand over, bestow, donate, contribute, grant, award, furnish, provide, supply, allot, deliver, deal out, dole out, mete out (*Slang* — hand out, dish out, fork out, shell out, fork over, come across with, kick in) take, 2. yield, bend

given 1. presented, handed over, 2. stated, supposed, assumed, 3. inclined, disposed, addicted, bent

glacier iceberg GLACIAL

glad happy, pleased, bright, gay, delighted, charmed, thrilled, tickled, gratified, satisfied, joyful, joyous, cheerful sad GLADDEN

glade clearing, open space

gladiator fighter, battler, combatant, contestant, contender, competitor

glamorous fascinating, charming, entrancing, enchanting, bewitching, spellbinding, alluring, captivating, enthralling, attractive, interesting, appealing, enticing unattractive GLAMOUR

glance look, glimpse, skim

glare 1. stare, scowl, glower, 2. shine, glow, burn, glaze, flash, flare, dazzle, blind

glass 1. goblet, cup, tumbler, 2. crystal, pane GLASSY

glaze gloss, polish, luster, buff, wax, coat, cover

gleam shine, glow, beam, glare, radiate, burn, glimmer, glisten, twinkle, sparkle

glean gather, harvest, reap, pick, separate, select

glee   joy, delight, mirth, happiness, gladness, cheer, enchantment, elation, bliss, merriment   sadness GLEEFUL

glen   valley, ravine

glide   cruise, coast, skim, slide, sweep, flow, sail, fly, move easily GLIDER

glimmer   1. shimmer, blink, flicker, 2. hint, indication, suggestion, inkling, clue

glimpse   glance, see, notice, catch sight of

glint   gleam, flash, glimpse, glance, peek

glisten   sparkle, glitter, shine, glimmer, twinkle

glitter   sparkle, glimmer, twinkle, shine, glisten

gloat   exult, triumph, glory (*Slang* — crow over)

globe   1. sphere, ball, 2. earth, world, universe, 3. map GLOBAL

gloomy   1. dark, dim, dismal, dreary, somber, bleak, depressing, discouraging, 2. sad, melancholy, glum cheerful GLOOM, GLOOMILY

glorify   worship, praise, laud, exalt, extol, honor, ennoble belittle GLORY

glorious   magnificent, splendid, grand, superb, fine, impressive, proud, stately, majestic, elegant, luxurious, extravagant (*Slang* — wonderful, divine, terrific, sensational, colossal, tremendous, swell, plush, super) terrible

gloss   shine, luster, sheen, glow, gleam GLOSSY

glossary   dictionary, wordbook, thesaurus

glow   1. burn, blaze, flame, flare, flicker, shine, radiate, glare, dazzle, 2. redden, blush, flush, 3. tingle, tremble, shiver, quiver, quake, thrill

glower   stare, scowl, glare, frown

glue   fasten, stick together, bind, paste, cement

glum   sad, gloomy, dismal, sullen, moody   cheerful

glutton   greedy eater (*Slang* — hog, pig)

gnarled   knotted, twisted, rugged   GNARL

gnash   crunch, gnaw, grind

gnaw   grind, gnash, chew

go   1. move, leave, travel, pass, proceed, advance   come, 2. act, work, 3. become, get to be, turn, grow into, 4. operate, function, 5. be given, aim, point, head for, 6. belong, have place   GONE

goad   urge, drive, pride, push, shove, poke, jab, spur

goal   1. end, finish, destination, objective, aim, object, target, 2. score, point

gobble   1. eat fast, devour, gulp, gorge, stuff, 2. turkey talk

goblet   glass, cup

goblin   spirit, elf, troll, dwarf

God   Lord, the Maker, the Creator, the Supreme Being, the Almighty

godly   religious, pious, obeying, loving, holy, righteous, spiritual, pure, saintly, divine

golden   1. metallic, 2. shining, bright   dull, 3. very good, superior, excellent, fine, nice, splendid, valuable   inferior GOLD

gong   bell, chimes

good   1. excellent, fine, nice, splendid (*Slang* — dandy, swell, keen, nifty, hunky-dory), 2. well-behaved, proper   bad, 3. desirable, right, appropriate, fitting, suitable, becoming, satisfying, seemly, nice, decent   undesirable, 4. kind, friendly, gracious, nice, warmhearted, sympathetic, brotherly, fraternal   unkind, unfriendly, 5. real, genuine, authentic, legitimate, bona fide   fake, 6. benefit, profit, advantage GOODNESS

good-by farewell, so long, adieu hello

goods 1. belongings, property, holdings, possessions, 2. wares, merchandise

good will willingness, agreeability, readiness, friendly relations, harmony

gorge 1. stuff, devour, gulp, gobble (*Slang* — eat like a horse), 2. valley, ravine, gully

gorgeous splendid, beautiful, ravishing, stunning, glorious, divine, brilliant, dazzling hideous

gory bloody

gossamer 1. fine, delicate, dainty coarse, 2. filmy, sheer, transparent

gossip chat, talk, tattle, prattle

gouge dig, scoop, excavate, burrow, chisel, carve

govern rule, control, manage, regulate, influence, determine, head, lead, command, preside over, direct, supervise, minister, guide, conduct, handle, run, boss (*Slang* — mastermind) GOVERNMENT, GOVERNOR

gown dress, robe, garment, frock

grab snatch, seize, grasp, grip, clutch (*Slang* — collar, nab)

grace 1. honor, dignify, distinguish dishonor, 2. beauty, loveliness, attractiveness, 3. charm, elegance, taste, refinement, polish, culture tactlessness, vulgarity, 4. sympathy, clemency, mercy, pardon, excuse, reprieve, 5. favor, 6. thanks, prayer, thanksgiving, blessing GRACEFUL

gracious pleasant, kindly, courteous, good, nice, warmhearted, sympathetic, polite, respectful, cordial, friendly, hospitable, generous rude, unkind

grade 1. arrange, sort, classify, group, rank, rate, mark, place, 2. slope, incline, hill

gradual slow, little by little, easy sudden

graduate finish, pass, succeed, advance fail GRADUATION

graft 1. transplant, join, 2. bribery, corruption (*Slang —* boodle)

grain 1. particle, speck, bit, 2. plant, seed, 3. texture, finish, markings, fiber, 4. character, temper, nature, disposition, tendency GRANARY

grand 1. large, great, considerable, sizable, big small, 2. important, main, outstanding, prominent, distinguished, magnificent, glorious, impressive, majestic, dignified, stately unimportant, insignificant GRANDEUR

grandstand gallery, bleachers

granite rock, stone

grant 1. give, donate, present, bestow, award, allot, give out, deal out, mete out, dole out (*Slang —* hand out, fork out, shell out), 2. allow, permit, let, consent, admit deny

graph diagram, chart, plot, outline, draw up

graphic lifelike, vivid, meaningful, significant, representative, descriptive, pictorial

grapple 1. seize, grip, grab, grasp, clutch, clasp, hold release, 2. struggle, fight

grasp 1. seize, hold, grapple, clutch, clasp, grip, 2. control, possession, hold, command, domination, 3. understanding, comprehension

grate 1. grind, file, scrape, pulverize, 2. scrape, scratch, rasp, 3. annoy, irritate, get on one's nerves, rub the wrong way, 4. iron bars, grillwork GRATING

grateful thankful, appreciative, obliged ungrateful

gratify satisfy, please GRATIFICATION

gratitude thankfulness, gratefulness, appreciation ungratefulness

grave 1. serious, solemn, grim, earnest, thoughtful, sober, somber cheerful, gay, 2. dignified, slow-moving, stately, imposing, majestic, 3. important, vital, essential unimportant, 4. burial place, plot

gravel pebbles, stones, grain

gravitate move toward, incline, lean, tend GRAVITATION, GRAVITY

graze 1. feed, 2. touch lightly, scrape, rub, contact, brush, skim

grease oil, lubrication, fat GREASY

great 1. large, grand, sizable, considerable small, 2. outstanding, prominent, famous, main, distinguished, remarkable, glorious, magnificent, impressive, majestic, stately insignificant, unimportant GREATNESS

greed avarice, piggishness, hoggishness, lust, desire GREEDY

green 1. undeveloped, unripe, immature ripe, 2. untrained, new, inexperienced, ignorant experienced

greenhouse hothouse, plant nursery

greet 1. address, hail, talk to, 2. meet, approach GREETING

grieve hurt, mourn, brood over, lament, sorrow GRIEF

grievance wrong, evil, protest, objection, injury, injustice, complaint (*Slang* — beef, howl, kick, gripe, squawk, bellyaching, grumbling)

grievous 1. severe, outrageous, terrible, deplorable, awful, wretched, contemptible, 2. sorrowful

grill 1. broil, cook, barbecue, 2. question, cross-examine, interrogate, 3. gridiron, grating

grim 1. stern, strict, harsh, fierce, merciless, rough, unyielding, rigid, inflexible, adamant (*Slang* — tough, hard-boiled) relaxed, lenient, 2. horrible, frightful, ghastly, dreadful, terrible pleasant

grimace wry face

grime dirt, soot, smut, mud, slime, filth   GRIMY

grin smile, smirk, beam

grind 1. crush, pulverize, grate, crumble, mash, squash, 2. sharpen, smooth, rub, edge, whet, file, 3. study, work, drudge, plod

grip 1. seize, hold, grasp, clutch, clasp, clench release, 2. suitcase, handbag, valise, 3. control, command, domination, possession, 4. understanding, comprehension

grit 1. grind, rub, grate, 2. gravel, sand, grain, 3. courage, pluck, stamina (*Slang* — spunk, backbone, guts)

groan moan, harsh sound, wail, howl

groom 1. tidy, clean up, tend, preen, 2. newlywed

groove 1. channel, furrow, track, rut, 2. routine

grope feel around, fumble, poke around

gross 1. whole, entire, total, 2. bad, terrible, stupid (*Slang* — dumb), 3. coarse, vulgar, unrefined, crude refined, 4. big, fat, obese, bulky, massive, clumsy petite, delicate, 5. thick, heavy, dense slight

grotesque 1. fantastic, incredible, bizarre, monstrous, ridiculous, absurd, 2. deformed, unnatural, queer, odd, disfigured, ill-shaped, ugly natural, normal

grotto cave, cavern, tunnel, hole

grouch complain, grumble, mutter, mope, sulk, fret (*Slang* — kick, howl, squawk, gripe, crab, bellyache, beef) GROUCHY

ground 1. fix, establish, root, set, 2. surface, soil, sod, dirt, land, base, floor

grounds 1. lawns, garden, real estate, 2. dregs, leftovers, sediment, 3. foundation, basis, reason, cause, premise, motive

group arrange, assemble, cluster, organize, grade, sort, classify, gather, collect, bunch disassemble

grovel crawl, creep, cower

grow 1. increase, mature, become, advance, gain, rise, develop, age, progress shrink, decrease, 2. raise, farm, cultivate GROWN, GROWTH

growl snarl, complain, grumble (*Slang* — kick, howl, grouch, squawk, bellyache)

grub 1. dig, gouge, excavate, scoop out, tunnel, burrow, 2. toil, drudge, plod (*Slang* — plug away), 3. larva, 4. food (*Slang* — eats, chow)

grudge ill will, dislike

grudgingly unwillingly, reluctantly, involuntarily, under protest, against one's will willingly

gruff 1. deep, husky, coarse, harsh, 2. rough, rude, unfriendly, brusque, curt, blunt polite

grumble complain, mutter (*Slang* — kick, grouch, squawk, gripe, crab, bellyache, beef)

grunt snort

guarantee promise, secure, pledge, swear, warrant, assure, certify, sponsor, back, endorse, underwrite, stand for

guard 1. watch, defend, shield, protect, secure, 2. check, restrain, control, curb GUARDIAN

guess think, believe, suppose, assume, imagine, consider, conjecture

guest visitor, caller, company (*Slang* —moocher, freeloader)

guide 1. lead, direct, show, steer, escort, conduct, squire, usher, 2. manage, control, regulate, advise, instruct, govern, rule GUIDANCE

guild   society, union

guile   deceit, cunning, craftiness, sneakiness

guilty   criminal, to blame, at fault, blameworthy, culpable GUILT

guise   1. garb, dress, cover, coat, attire, clothes, apparel, 2. appearance, look, show, form, manner

gulch   valley, gorge, ravine, gully, canyon

gulf   1. separation, break, cut, cleft, crack, crevice, hole, rift, opening, gap, chasm, pit, 2. bay

gullible   easily fooled, naive, deceivable

gully   gorge, valley, ditch, ravine, gulf, gulch

gulp   1. swallow, devour, 2. choke, repress, gasp

gun   1. shoot, fire, discharge, 2. weapon, firearm, pistol, rifle, revolver (*Slang* — shooting iron, gat, rod)

gurgle   bubbling sound

gush   1. rush out, pour, flow, spout, surge, flush, flood, spurt, 2. chatter, babble, prattle

gust   1. wind, blast, 2. outburst, outbreak, eruption, flare-up

gutter   channel, groove, trench, ditch

gymnasium   arena, athletic field, playground, court   GYM

gymnastics   exercises, drill, athletics, calisthenics, sports, acrobatics

gyp   cheat, swindle, defraud (*Slang* — rook, con)

gypsy   nomad

H

habit   1. custom, practice, nature, pattern, trait, 2. religious dress   HABITUAL

habitation   abode, dwelling place, residence, lodging, housing   HABITAT

hack　1. cut, sever, split, cleave, chop, 2. cough

hag　witch, crone (*Slang* — old girl, old battle-axe)

haggard　thin, poor, pale, deathlike, wild-eyed, tired-looking, seedy

hail　1. greet, cheer, welcome, call, shout, 2. sleet

hale　1. drag, haul, pull, tug, tow, 2. strong, mighty, powerful, healthy, sturdy, rugged, strapping, hardy, robust, vigorous, husky weak

hall　1. passageway, corridor, arcade, vestibule, lobby, foyer, 2. large meeting room, assembly, auditorium, 3. building, community center, theater　HALLWAY

halo　1. circle, ring, 2. glory, glamour

halt　stop, come to a standstill, check, arrest, quit, cease, end (*Slang* — lay off, knock off)

halve　divide, dissect, split, share (*Slang* — fifty-fifty) HALF, HALVES

hamlet　village

hammer　1. hit, drive, pound, beat, knock, bang, 2. repeat, drill, 3. mallet

hamper　1. hinder, impede, cramp, obstruct, block, restrain, limit help, 2. basket

hand　1. give, turn over, deliver, transfer, pass, 2. worker, person, laborer, 3. possession, central power, command, grasp, clutches, 4. handwriting, penmanship

handbag　pocketbook, purse

handicap　hindrance, burden, disadvantage, load asset

handle　1. touch, feel, finger, manipulate, use, 2. manage, direct, regulate, carry on, govern, run (*Slang* — mastermind), 3. deal in, trade in

handsome　1. good-looking, attractive ugly, 2. large, considerable, big, generous, liberal meager

handwriting penmanship

handy 1. useful, convenient, nearby, available, ready (*Slang* — on deck) inconvenient, 2. skillful, adept, apt, proficient inept

hang 1. suspend, fasten up, 2. execute, string up, 3. droop, bend down, sag

haphazard chance, random, casual planned

happen 1. take place, occur, come off, pass, 2. chance, turn up HAPPENING

happy contented, glad, joyful, blissful, cheerful, bright, radiant unhappy, sad HAPPILY, HAPPINESS

harass 1. trouble, torment, molest, bother, badger, plague, persecute, haunt, bully, threaten, 2. disturb, worry, vex HARASSMENT

harbor 1. shelter, protect, shield, defend, guard, screen, cover, house, 2. keep in mind, consider, think, entertain the idea, 3. port, dock, wharf, pier

hard 1. firm, solid, stony, rigid soft, 2. stern, unyielding, strict, inflexible easygoing, 3. difficult, rough, rugged, tough (*Slang* — wicked, mean) easy, 4. with effort, with vigor, laboriously, strenuously, 5. unpleasant, harsh, ugly, severe, callous pleasant

hardly barely, just, not quite, scarcely, narrowly, nearly (*Slang* — by the skin of one's teeth)

hardship trouble, ups and downs

hardy 1. strong, healthy, robust, mighty, powerful, sturdy, rugged, hale weak, 2. bold, daring, courageous, valiant, gallant, heroic cowardly

hark listen, heed HARKEN

harm hurt, damage, wrong, injure, impair help, improve HARMFUL, HARMLESS

harmonious 1. agreeing, in accord, congenial, compatible conflicting, 2. musical, in tune, blending
HARMONIZE, HARMONY

harness 1. control, use, 2. saddle, hitch up, yoke, hook up

harp dwell on, elaborate

harrow 1. hurt, wound, pain, afflict, distress, irritate, torment, torture, agonize soothe, 2. rake, plow

harry 1. raid, rob, storm, besiege, invade, 2. trouble, worry, torment, vex, harass

harsh 1. rough, coarse, husky, grating, raspy, gruff smooth, 2. cruel, unfeeling, severe, bitter, sharp, cutting, piercing, gruff, brusque, curt, strict, stern, tough kind

harvest 1. reap, gather, pick, 2. crop, yield, product, proceeds, 3. result, consequences, effect, outcome
HARVESTER

hash 1. mixture, assortment, mix (*Slang* — stew), 2. mess, muddle, jumble, scramble, fiasco

hasty 1. quick, hurried, fast, swift, speedy, rapid, fleet (*Slang* — snappy) slow, 2. rash, reckless, unprepared, sudden, premature, impulsive, impetuous planned, 3. quick-tempered, hotheaded
HASTEN, HASTE, HASTILY

hat cap, headdress, chapeau, millinery

hatch 1. arrange, plan, plot, scheme, intrigue, invent, concoct, make up (*Slang* — cook up), 2. produce, generate, incubate, breed, brood, be born, 3. opening, door, trap

hatchet tomahawk, ax

hate dislike, loathe, detest, abhor, abominate love
HATEFUL, HATRED

haughty arrogant, proud, lofty, scornful (*Slang* — uppish, highfalutin) modest

haul 1. pull, drag, draw, heave, tug, tow, 2. take, catch

haunch hip, side, flank

haunt 1. visit often, frequent, hang around, 2. obsess, torment HAUNTED

have 1. hold, possess, own, 2. must, be forced, should, ought, need, 3. cause, make, compel, require, 4. experience, feel, meet, undergo, endure, 5. permit, tolerate, suffer, put up with, stand for HAS

haven shelter, safety, harbor, refuge, sanctuary

havoc destruction, ruin, devastation, ravage, damage, harm, injury restoration

hawk 1. hunt, chase, 2. peddle, sell, vend buy

hay fodder, feed

hazard risk, chance, gamble, bet, wager HAZARDOUS

hazy 1. misty, smoky, dim, cloudy, overcast, foggy, 2. obscure, indistinct, unclear, indefinite, vague, faint, blurred, fuzzy, uncertain, confused, muddled clear HAZE

head 1. lead, come first, precede, initiate follow, 2. govern, command, lead, direct, manage, supervise, administer, control, rule, dominate, conduct, run (*Slang* — mastermind), 3. proceed, move toward, go, gravitate, 4. pate, crown, top (*Slang* — noodle, noggin, bean), 5. mind, intelligence, understanding, mentality, brain, 6. crisis, conclusion

headfirst hastily, rashly, impetuously, impulsively, recklessly, carelessly cautiously

heading topic, title, subject, issue, question, theme, headline

headquarters main office, base, central station

headstrong obstinate, stubborn, willful, bullheaded

headway progress, advance, improvement setback

heal cure, remedy, correct, mend, repair damage, impair

health well-being, physical condition
HEALTHFUL, HEALTHY

heap pile, gather, fill, stack, load

hear listen, heed (*Slang* — get an earful) HEARD

hearsay gossip, rumor, common talk

heart 1. body pump (*Slang* — ticker), 2. feelings, soul, spirit, temperament, 3. kindness, sympathy, warmth, love, affection, 4. courage, enthusiasm, stamina (*Slang* — spunk, guts) cowardice, 5. middle, center, core, nucleus, hub, 6. substance, main part, meat, 7. valentine

hearten cheer, encourage, inspire, gladden dishearten

heartfelt sincere, genuine, profound, deep insincere

hearth fireplace, fireside, home

heartily sincerely, warmly, devotedly, completely, fervently, ardently indifferently HEARTY, HEARTINESS

heat 1. warm, make hot cool, 2. cook, prepare, 3. excite, move, affect, stir, provoke, arouse, kindle, inflame calm
HEATER

heave 1. lift, raise, hoist, pull, haul, lug, tug, tow, drag, 2. breathe hard, pant, 3. swell, rise, bulge, billow, surge subside

heaven 1. sky, space, 2. paradise, bliss, ecstasy hell
HEAVENLY

heavy weighted, laden, bulky, fat, hefty light, thin
HEAVILY, HEAVINESS

hectic 1. feverish, heated, hot, burning, 2. exciting, stirring, frantic, moving, busy calm

hedge 1. dodge, sidestep, evade questions, duck (*Slang* — pussyfoot), 2. boundary, limit, border, borderline

heed notice, observe, follow, care, mind, attend ignore

height 1. altitude, elevation, tallness, stature, 2. top, summit, highest point, peak, crown, tip, apex, acme bottom HEIGHTEN

hello greetings, salutations, good day (*Slang* — howdy)

helm control, reins, driver's seat

help 1. aid, assist, lend a hand, avail hinder, 2. benefit, relieve, 3. avoid, prevent, deter, keep from HELPFUL, HELPLESS

hem border, edge, rim

hence 1. therefore, consequently, accordingly, because of this, thus, 2. away, elsewhere, 3. later, from now, in future time HENCEFORTH

herald 1. announce, bring news, proclaim, cry out, shout, 2. messenger

herd flock, assemble, join together, drive, shepherd, collect, gather scatter

here 1. this place, this spot there, 2. now, at present, at this time later, 3. present, in attendance absent HEREABOUT, HEREAFTER

hereditary inherited, inborn HEREDITY

heresy misbelief, dissent HERETIC

heritage heredity, birthright

hermit recluse, shut-in

heroic brave, gallant, valiant, stalwart, courageous, bold, chivalrous cowardly HERO, HEROINE, HEROISM

hesitate 1. pause, rest, let up, 2. feel doubtful, be undecided, flounder, falter, waver HESITATION

hew cut, chop, sever, split, cleave

hibernate sleep, slumber, hole up

hide 1. conceal, cover up, screen, cloak, veil, mask expose,
2. skin, pelt HID, HIDDEN

hideous ugly, frightful, horrible, horrid, dreadful, terrible,
repulsive, ghastly (*Slang* — awful) beautiful

high 1. tall, long, lofty, elevated, steep, towering, soaring,
2. great, chief, main, important, eminent, exalted, grand
unimportant, 3. shrill, sharp, piercing, screechy low
HIGHLY

high-strung sensitive, nervous, excitable, edgy, jumpy
(*Slang* — jittery) calm, steady

highway road, thoroughfare, turnpike, expressway, thruway, freeway

hike walk, march, tramp, parade

hilarious merry, gay, joyful, gleeful HILARITY

hill elevation, mound, heap HILLY

hind back, rear front

hinder stop, obstruct, impede, check, curb, retard, restrain,
hold back help HINDRANCE

hinge 1. fasten, clasp, lock separate, 2. depend, rest on,
revolve on

hint suggest, imply, intimate, insinuate

hire 1. employ, engage fire, 2. lease, let, rent, charter

hiss boo, hoot cheer

history record, chronicle, annals
HISTORIAN, HISTORIC, HISTORICAL

hit 1. strike, blow, knock, punch, poke, smack, whack, slug,
bat, crack, swat, sock, clout (*Slang* — clobber, belt, paste,
wallop, clip), 2. meet, find, discover, come upon, reach, arrive
at miss, 3. affect, impress, strike, 4. success (*Slang* —
smash, wow, sensation, killing) failure

hitch 1. fasten, hook, clasp, bind, tie separate, 2. jerk, yank, 3. obstacle, stopping, block, catch, snag, difficulty, drawback

hoard save, store, collect, accumulate, amass, gather use

hoarse rough, gruff, harsh, husky smooth

hoary old, aged, elderly, white, gray young

hobble limp, totter, stagger

hobby avocation, pastime

hobgoblin goblin, imp, elf, ghost

hobo tramp, vagabond, vagrant (*Slang* — bum)

hodgepodge mixture, mess, jumble, scramble

hoe plow, dig, loosen, till

hog 1. pig, swine, 2. glutton, greedy person HOGGISH

hoist raise, lift, elevate, boost lower

hold 1. grasp, keep, grip, cling to, clutch, retain release, 2. contain, support, bear, carry, 3. have, maintain, occupy, 4. apply, be true, stand up (*Slang* — hold water), 5. think, consider, suppose, assume, presume, regard, surmise

holding land, property, possession, ownership, title, claim, stake

hole opening, hollow, pit, gap, chasm, cavity

holiday vacation, leave, furlough

hollow 1. empty, vacant, bare, void, blank, barren occupied, 2. deep, sunken, concave bulging, 3. false, unreal, insincere sincere, 4. hungry, starved, famished, ravenous, empty full

holy sacred, spiritual, pure, religious, godly HOLINESS

homage respect, honor, reverence, regard, esteem, deference, acknowledgment disrespect

home 1. abode, dwelling, residence, hearth, habitat, 2. institution, sanitarium, hospital, asylum HOMELIKE

homeland native land, mother country

homely 1. ugly, plain, unattractive attractive, 2. simple, ordinary, common, 3. homelike, comfortable, cozy, domestic

homestead farm, plantation, house and grounds

homework lesson, task, assignment, exercise, duty

honest fair, upright, truthful, frank, open, genuine, pure, sincere dishonest, insincere HONESTY

honk toot, blast, blare

honor glory, fame, renown, respect, regard, esteem, homage, deference, praise dishonor
HONORABLE, HONORARY

hood cover, lid, veil, cap

hoodlum rowdy, ruffian, thug, tough (*Slang* — bruiser, roughneck, gorilla, hooligan)

hoof foot, paw (*Slang* — kicker)

hook 1. fasten, clasp, bind, clip, snap, latch unhook, 2. catch, snare, trap release, 3. hanger, wire, crook

hoop circle, band, ring

hoot yell, call, cry

hop spring, jump, vault

hope wish for, desire, yearn for, expect
HOPEFUL, HOPELESS

horde crowd, swarm, multitude, throng, mob, force, pack

horizontal level, flat, even, plane

horrible frightful, shocking, terrible, dreadful, outrageous, horrid, ghastly, deplorable, scandalous (*Slang* — awful, atrocious) splendid HORRID, HORRIFY, HORROR

horse   steed, colt, mare, stallion, stud (*Slang* — nag)

horseplay   rowdiness, boisterous fun

hose   1. stockings, socks, 2. tube, pipe   HOSIERY

hospitable   friendly, receptive, welcoming, cordial, amiable, gracious, neighborly, generous   unfriendly
HOSPITALITY

hospital   clinic, sanitarium

host   1. receptionist, proprietor, 2. large number, quantity, multitude, score, flock, army, swarm   HOSTESS

hostel   inn, hotel, tavern, roadhouse

hostile   unfriendly, unfavorable, bitter, antagonistic, aggressive, belligerent, militant   friendly   HOSTILITY

hot   1. torrid, burning, boiling, fiery   cold, 2. spicy, sharp, peppery, nippy, tangy   bland, 3. fresh, new   stale

hotel   inn, tavern, roadhouse, lodging, hostel, motel

hothouse   greenhouse, nursery, conservatory

hound   1. hunt, chase, seek, search, follow, 2. urge, press, insist, 3. dog

house   1. shelter, building, dwelling, lodge, residence, home, 2. audience, congregation   HOUSING

household   family, brood, folks

housekeeper   mistress, homemaker, housewife

hovel   shack, pigsty (*Slang* — dump)

hover   1. float, sail, drift, 2. waver, hesitate, pause, falter

however   1. nevertheless, although, notwithstanding, yet, still, but, 2. whatever, whatsoever

howl   cry, yell, shout, bawl, scream, screech, roar, bellow, bark, yelp, wail

hub   center, middle, nucleus, core

hubbub   noise, uproar, racket, din, clamor, tumult, commotion, fracas, ado, fuss, turmoil, bustle, row, rumpus   calm

huddle   assemble, crowd, gather, flock together, cluster, congregate   scatter

hue   color, tint, shade

huff   1. puff, blow, exhale, 2. fit of anger (*Slang* — stew)

hug   hold, clasp, embrace, press, enfold, squeeze

huge   great, very large, vast, immense, enormous, monumental, gigantic, tremendous (*Slang* — terrific, whopping, whacking)   tiny

hulk   1. ship, boat, 2. oaf, lout, clod (*Slang* — lummox, galoot)   HULKING

hum   1. drone, buzz, murmur, 2. active, busy   quiet, inactive

human   man, person, mortal, being   HUMANITY

humane   kind, good, gracious, warmhearted, brotherly, sympathetic   cruel

humble   modest, meek, plain, simple, homely, unpretentious   vain, showy   HUMBLY, HUMILITY

humbug   cheat, deceive, trick, hoax

humid   moist, damp, wet, muggy   dry   HUMIDITY

humiliate   embarrass, disgrace, shame, mortify, offend, insult, dishonor   honor, dignify   HUMILIATION

humor   1. cater to, give in to, pamper, spoil, coddle, oblige, please, satisfy, 2. wit, pleasantry, comedy, 3. mood, temper, frame of mind, disposition   HUMORIST, HUMOROUS

hump   bump, bulge, ridge, hunch

hunch   1. hump, bump, bulge, 2. feeling, suspicion, impression   HUNCHBACK

hunger   desire, eagerness, appetite, craving
HUNGRILY, HUNGRY

hunk   lump, piece, mass, bulk, wad, gob, chunk

hunt   search, seek, look, pursue, chase
HUNTER, HUNTSMAN

hurdle   1. leap, jump, vault, bound, 2. obstacle, block,
difficulty, hitch, catch, snag, barrier

hurl   throw, fling, sling, pitch, toss, cast, heave, chuck, flip

hurrah   cheer, cry, shout, yell, applause   HURRAY

hurricane   storm, cyclone, blizzard, tornado, squall

hurry   hasten, speed, urge, rush, accelerate, hustle (*Slang* —
step on it, make it snappy)

hurt   injure, bruise, harm, damage, wrong, impair, pain,
wound, distress, grieve, offend   help, benefit, soothe
HURTFUL

hurtle   jostle, collide, clash, strike, bump, crash

husband   1. save, economize, preserve, keep, reserve, scrimp,
skimp, 2. spouse, mate, married man

hush   silence, quiet, mute, muffle, calm

husky   1. strong, sturdy, mighty, powerful, rugged, strapping, well-built, muscular, athletic, hefty, beefy, 2. hoarse,
harsh, rough, coarse, raspy   smooth, 3. Eskimo dog
HUSKINESS

hustle   1. hasten, speed, urge, rush, 2. push, shove, jostle,
prod, bump, jolt, bounce

hut   cabin, shed, shanty, shack

hybrid   mongrel, crossbreed, half-breed

hydrophobia   rabies

hymn   song of praise, psalm, spiritual   HYMNAL

hypnotize   entrance, spellbind, mesmerize
HYPNOTISM, HYPNOTIST

hypocrite   pretender (*Slang* — fake, phony)
HYPOCRISY

hysterical   uncontrollable, frenzied, frantic, delirious, beside oneself, overexcited, upset   calm, composed   HYSTERIA

I

ice   frozen water, sleet

icebox   refrigerator

ice cream   frozen dessert, sherbet

icing   frosting, topping

idea   thought, plan, notion, fancy, opinion

ideal   perfect, faultless, flawless, model   faulty, imperfect

identical   same, alike, exactly like, duplicate   different

identify   recognize, know, place, distinguish, make out, name, tell, label, tag, designate (*Slang* — spot, nail, peg)
IDENTIFICATION, IDENTITY

idiot   simpleton, imbecile, moron, half-wit, fool (*Slang* — nitwit, dimwit, simp)   IDIOTIC

idle   1. inactive, unoccupied, at leisure   busy, 2. lazy, loafing ambitious, 3. useless, vain, futile, worthless   worthwhile, 4. unwarranted, groundless, unfounded   IDLER

idol   1. god, 2. favorite, darling   IDOLIZE

igloo   ice hut, Eskimo hut

ignite   burn, set afire, light, kindle, stoke   IGNITION

ignoble   mean, base, low, without honor, shameful, disgraceful   noble

ignorant   unintelligent, foolish, uninformed, unaware, uneducated (*Slang* — dumb)   smart, knowledgeable
IGNORANCE

ignore   disregard, overlook, snub, slight, avoid   mind, heed

ill   1. sick, ailing, unwell, indisposed, out of sorts, below par, under the weather, rocky   healthy, 2. evil, bad, wrong good   ILLNESS

illegal   unlawful, criminal, illegitimate   legal

illegible   unclear, indistinct, unreadable   legible, clear

illiterate   uneducated, uncultured, unlearned, ignorant learned, educated

ill-natured   cross, disagreeable, bad-tempered   pleasant

illogical   unreasonable, senseless, unsound, unscientific logical

illuminate   1. light, brighten, spotlight, 2. clarify, explain, simplify, show, illustrate   ILLUMINATION

illusion   deception, delusion, trick, misconception

illustrate   1. clarify, explain, show, demonstrate, 2. represent, picture, portray   ILLUSTRATION

illustrious   famous, great, outstanding, splendid, radiant, bright, shining, glorious

image   likeness, representation, picture, reflection, resemblance, vision, appearance

imagine   1. envision, fancy, conceive, dream, 2. suppose, guess, assume, presume, gather
IMAGINABLE, IMAGINARY, IMAGINATION, IMAGINATIVE

imbecile   simpleton, idiot, moron, half-wit, fool (*Slang* — nitwit, dimwit, simp)

imbed   enclose, fix, inset, inlay

imitate   copy, act like, repeat, mirror, reflect, echo, emulate
IMITATION

immaculate   pure, clean, spotless   dirty

immature   undeveloped, unripe, inexperienced, green, childish   mature

immeasurable   great, boundless, endless, unlimited, infinite   limited

immediately   instantly, at once, without delay, now, promptly, straightaway, forthwith, quickly, swiftly, directly (*Slang* — pronto)   later

immense   huge, large, vast, great, stupendous, enormous, monumental, mammoth, gigantic, giant   tiny
IMMENSELY, IMMENSITY

immerse   1. submerge, plunge, sink, dip, inundate, drown, dunk, 2. absorb, engross, occupy, engage, grip, hold, fascinate, enthrall

immigrate   enter, come into   leave
IMMIGRANT, IMMIGRATION

imminent   forthcoming, approaching, nearing, impending (*Slang* — in the cards)

immoral   wrong, wicked, evil, bad, sinful   moral

immortal   everlasting, undying, eternal   IMMORTALITY

immovable   fixed, firm, steadfast, stable, stationary
movable

immune   resistant, exempt, clear, excused, spared, let off
subject to   IMMUNITY, IMMUNIZE

imp   1. pixie, sprite, elf, little devil, gremlin, 2. brat, whippersnapper, mischief-maker (*Slang* — cutup)

impact   collision, crash, bump, clash, shock, brunt

impair   damage, harm, weaken, hurt, make worse, break
improve

impartial fair, neutral, unprejudiced, unbiased, uninfluenced, indifferent prejudiced

impassable unapproachable, inaccessible passable

impassioned emotional, ardent, passionate, fervent, earnest, sincere, serious, excited indifferent

impassive unmoved, unfeeling, unemotional, unresponsive, unsympathetic emotional

impatient restless, anxious, eager, intolerant patient
IMPATIENCE

impeach accuse, charge, indict, arraign, denounce, reproach (*Slang* — pin on, put the finger on, hang something on)

impede hinder, obstruct, curb, inhibit, arrest, check, interrupt, retard, delay, limit, confine, cramp, hamper
facilitate IMPEDIMENT

impel drive, force, cause, push, move, propel, stimulate, compel, make

impenetrable 1. unapproachable, inaccessible, impassable, dense open, passable, 2. obscure, unclear, vague, unintelligible clear

imperative urgent, necessary, compulsory, compelling, pressing, crucial, critical, mandatory unnecessary

imperceptible slight, vague, unclear noticeable

imperfect defective, faulty, incomplete, inadequate, deficient, impaired, blemished, marred perfect
IMPERFECTION

imperial supreme, majestic, magnificent, regal, royal

imperious 1. haughty, arrogant, domineering, overbearing, 2. urgent, necessary, compelling, pressing, crucial, critical, imperative unnecessary

impersonal impartial, neutral, unbiased, detached, unprejudiced biased

impertinence insolence, impudence, rudeness, brazenness, cockiness (*Slang* — brass, freshness, gall, crust, nerve) respectfulness, courtesy IMPERTINENT

impetuous hasty, rash, sudden, abrupt, impulsive, unexpected, reckless restrained, careful, thoughtful

impetus driving force, momentum, thrust, push

implement 1. carry out, get done, bring about, complete neglect, 2. tool, utensil, instrument, apparatus, device, appliance, contraption (*Slang* — gimmick)

implore beg, plead, appeal, entreat, beseech, pray

imply suggest, hint, intimate, infer, insinuate

impolite rude, discourteous, disrespectful, ill-mannered, insolent polite

import 1. bring in, receive, take in, admit, introduce export, 2. meaning, significance, implication, substance, effect, importance IMPORTATION

important meaningful, valuable, influential, significant, substantial, prominent, outstanding unimportant IMPORTANCE

impose put, place, set, charge, levy, tax, burden with, force

imposing impressive, dramatic, spectacular, grand, magnificent, splendid, noble, glorious, proud, stately, majestic, elegant unimpressive

impossible inconceivable, unimaginable, absurd, unthinkable (*Slang* — no go) possible IMPOSSIBILITY

impostor pretender, deceiver, cheat, impersonator, fraud, faker (*Slang* — phony)

impoverish make poor, ruin, break, bankrupt, exhaust, deplete enrich

impractical unfeasible, unworkable, unrealistic practical IMPRACTICABLE

impregnable   resistant, strong, unconquerable, unassailable, invincible   vulnerable

impress   1. affect, strike, 2. fix, establish, root, plant, stamp, 3. mark, imprint, engrave   IMPRESSION, IMPRESSIVE

imprint   mark, engrave, impress, stamp

imprison   jail, confine, lock up   free, release
IMPRISONMENT

improbable   unlikely, doubtful, questionable   probable

improper   1. wrong, incorrect, unsuitable, inappropriate, unfit, bad, 2. indecent, unbecoming   proper

improve   better, perfect, progress, mend, develop, advance
worsen   IMPROVEMENT

improvise   invent, make up, devise, originate, dream up, dash off, ad-lib

imprudent   rash, indiscreet, overconfident, unwise, unsound, unreasonable, unintelligent, ill-advised   careful, prudent
IMPRUDENCE

impudent   forward, bold, immodest, pert, impertinent, rude, disrespectful, brash, saucy (*Slang* — flip, cocky, cheeky, smart, smart-alecky, fresh, crusty, nervy)
polite, courteous   IMPUDENCE

impulse   1. thrust, push, urge, pressure, compulsion, 2. notion, sudden thought, fancy, flash, inspiration
IMPULSIVE

impure   1. dirty, unclean, polluted, contaminated, infected
clean, pure, 2. bad, corrupt, indecent, obscene, foul, filthy, nasty   clean, decent   IMPURITY

inability   incapability, ineptitude, incompetence
ability

inaccessible   unreachable, out-of-the-way, unapproachable, out of reach   accessible

inaccurate   incorrect, inexact   accurate   INACCURACY

inactive   idle, sluggish, motionless, still, calm   active

inadequate   deficient, lacking, wanting, short of, insufficient, unsatisfactory   enough, adequate

inadvisable   unwise, imprudent, ill-advised, ill-considered   wise, advisable

inappropriate   unfitting, unsuitable, improper   appropriate

inattentive   unmindful, heedless, unobserving, distracted, negligent, wandering   attentive

inaugurate   begin, install, introduce, launch, admit, initiate, instate   INAUGURAL

inborn   natural, innate, hereditary, instinctive

incapable   unable, incompetent, unqualified, unfit   capable

incense   1. provoke, anger, annoy, irritate, vex, exasperate, ruffle, pique (*Slang* — aggravate, peeve, miff, rile), 2. fragrance, perfume, aroma, scent

incentive   motive, stimulus, encouragement, inducement

incessant   continual, uninterrupted, unbroken, constant, ceaseless, endless, nonstop, infinite, perpetual, steady   interrupted

incident   happening, event, occurrence, experience, adventure   INCIDENTAL, INCIDENTALLY

incinerator   furnace, burner

incipient   beginning, initial, introductory   final

incite   stir, urge, rouse, agitate, excite, inflame, provoke, instigate

inclement   rough, stormy, cold, harsh, severe, cruel   pleasant

incline   1. tend, be willing, be game, 2. influence, affect, sway, move, induce, persuade, 3. lean, bend, bow, tilt, tip, 4. slope, hill, grade   INCLINATION, INCLINED

include contain, comprise, cover, enclose exclude
INCLUSION, INCLUSIVE

income receipts, returns, profits, earnings, proceeds, wages, payment

incomparable matchless, unequaled comparable

incompetent unable, incapable, unqualified, unfit
competent, able

incomplete unfinished, deficient, wanting, lacking, imperfect, partial complete

incomprehensible unintelligible, hard to understand, difficult, vague, obscure understandable

inconceivable unbelievable, unthinkable, unconvincing, incredible believable

inconsiderate thoughtless, unmindful considerate

inconsistent disagreeing, illogical, unreasonable, senseless, invalid consistent

inconspicuous unseen, unnoticed, unapparent
conspicuous

inconvenient untimely, inappropriate, unfavorable, troublesome, bothersome, awkward convenient, timely
INCONVENIENCE

incorporate join, unite, combine, unify, merge

incorrect wrong, faulty, inaccurate, improper
correct, right

increase enlarge, extend, add to, expand, advance, raise
decrease INCREASINGLY

incredible unbelievable, doubtful, questionable, unconvincing, staggering, preposterous, absurd, ridiculous believable
INCREDIBLY, INCREDULOUS

incur contract, bring on, catch (*Slang* — come down with)

incurable   hopeless, beyond remedy   curable

indebted   owing, obliged, involved

indeed   in fact, in truth, really, absolutely, positively, perfectly, certainly, definitely, surely, of course

indefinite   unclear, vague, indistinct, obscure, confused, hazy, general, broad   definite

indelible   permanent, indestructible, unforgettable, fixed

indent   dent, impress, cut, nick

independent   acting alone, unconnected, unassociated, self-reliant   dependent   INDEPENDENCE

indescribable   unexplainable, extraordinary, exceptional, remarkable   ordinary

index   list, chart, file, table, sign, symbol, guide

indicate   show, point out, exhibit, demonstrate, display, present, express, suggest, hint, imply, signify   INDICATION, INDICATOR

indifferent   unbiased, impartial, detached, disinterested, cool, neutral, impersonal, unconcerned   concerned   INDIFFERENCE, INDIFFERENTLY

indigenous   native, original, natural to   foreign

indignant   angry, irate (*Slang* — mad, sore, worked up, riled up)   INDIGNATION

indignity   insult, affront, offense, injury   respect

indirect   devious, roundabout, out-of-the-way   direct

indiscreet   unwise, imprudent, unsound, unreasonable, ill-advised   careful

indispensable   essential, necessary, needed, required, vital   unnecessary

indisposed   1. ill, sick, ailing (*Slang* — under the weather, out of sorts, rocky)   well,   2. unwilling, forced   willing

indistinct unclear, confused, dim, obscure, vague, cloudy, hazy, blurred clear, distinct

individual 1. single, separate, one, personal, special, 2. human, man, being
INDIVIDUALITY, INDIVIDUALLY

indivisible inseparable, solid divisible

indolent lazy, shiftless, do-nothing, unenterprising, slothful ambitious INDOLENCE

indomitable unconquerable, unyielding, invincible, unbeatable, uncontrollable, unruly, unmanageable yielding, controllable

induce influence, persuade, lead on, cause, elicit, evoke, prompt, move, sway INDUCEMENT

induct introduce, bring in, install, place, inaugurate, enlist, enroll, draft

indulge humor, favor, oblige, please, gratify, satisfy, cater to, pamper, coddle, spoil
INDULGENCE, INDULGENT

industrious hard-working, diligent, energetic, tireless lazy

industry trade, business, manufacture, labor, work, concern, dealings INDUSTRIAL

inedible uneatable edible

ineffectual useless, ineffective, powerless, unsuccessful effective

inefficient unable, incapable, incompetent, unfit, inept, unskillful efficient INEFFICIENCY

inequality unevenness, irregularity, imbalance equality

inert lifeless, slow, sluggish, motionless, inactive, stagnant, listless active

inevitable destined, fated, doomed, unavoidable, sure, certain, inescapable

inexact   vague, indefinite, broad, general, unclear, obscure, inaccurate, incorrect   exact

inexcusable   unpardonable, unforgivable, unjustifiable   excusable

inexhaustible   1. tireless, 2. endless, unlimited, infinite   limited

inexpensive   cheap, low-priced, reasonable   expensive

inexperienced   unpracticed, untried, green, unfamiliar, ignorant, immature, undeveloped   experienced

inexplicable   unexplainable, mysterious   understandable

infallible   reliable, sure, unerring, right   unreliable

infamous   wicked, bad, disgraceful, evil, base, low, shameful, notorious, terrible, scandalous, outrageous
virtuous, good, moral   INFAMY

infancy   beginning, babyhood   maturity
INFANT, INFANTILE

infantry   army, foot soldiers

infect   1. disease, contaminate, communicate, pollute, corrupt, poison, 2. influence   INFECTION, INFECTIOUS

infer   1. conclude, reason, deduce, gather, derive, assume, presume, suppose, expect, reckon, calculate, imagine, 2. indicate, imply, suggest, hint   INFERENCE

inferior   lower, worse, subordinate, secondary, lesser
superior   INFERIORITY

infernal   hellish

infest   overrun, crawl with, plague, beset

infidel   unbeliever, skeptic   believer

infinite   limitless, boundless, endless, immeasurable, perpetual, everlasting, eternal, ceaseless   limited
INFINITELY

infirm weak, feeble, unstable, sickly, unsound, frail
strong, healthy INFIRMITY

inflame 1. excite, stir, move, affect, provoke, arouse, incite,
anger soothe, calm, 2. redden, swell, irritate
INFLAMMABLE, INFLAMMATION

inflate swell, puff out, expand, broaden, enlarge, stretch,
increase, blow up deflate
INFLATION

inflexible stiff, rigid, firm, unbending, unyielding, stubborn,
inelastic flexible

inflict give, cause, impose, effect, produce, bring about,
wreak

influence sway, affect, move, induce, persuade, prejudice
INFLUENTIAL

inform 1. tell, communicate, advise, enlighten, instruct,
notify, report, 2. accuse, tattle, blab, snitch, squeal, betray
INFORMATION

infrequent rare, scarce, sparse, scattered, occasional,
uncommon, irregular frequent

infringe violate, break, trespass, overstep

infuriate enrage, anger, madden, antagonize, provoke,
irritate, incite, agitate soothe, calm

infuse 1. put in, instill, 2. inspire, lift, infect, animate,
3. drench, saturate, bathe

ingenious clever, skillful, proficient, masterful, inventive,
original, creative, imaginative, productive, inspired
unoriginal, dull INGENUITY

ingenuous 1. frank, open, sincere, candid, straightforward
secretive, 2. simple, natural, innocent, plain, unsophisticated
sophisticated

ingredient part, element, factor, component

inhabit   live, dwell, occupy, reside, lodge, stay, room
INHABITANT

inhale   breathe in, gasp, sniff, smell   exhale

inherent   internal, natural, implanted, existing, belonging, instinctive

inherit   receive, come into   INHERITANCE

inhospitable   uncordial, unfriendly, unreceptive, ungracious, unneighborly   friendly, hospitable

inhuman   unfeeling, cruel, brutal, ruthless, uncivilized kind

iniquity   injustice, evil, sin, wrong, crime, outrage   justice

initial   1. first, earliest, beginning, primary, introductory final, 2. letter

initiate   1. start, begin, originate, pioneer, lead, head, institute, introduce, launch, break the ice, 2. admit, receive, take in, install, let in   expel, 3. instruct, introduce, educate INITIATION, INITIATIVE

inject   force into, fill, insert   extract   INJECTION

injure   damage, harm, hurt, wound, wrong, impair   heal, correct   INJURIOUS, INJURY

injustice   inequity, unfairness, unjustness   justice

inkling   hint, suggestion, notion, indication, glimmer, clue, suspicion, impression, idea

inlaid   embedded, inset, lined

inlet   entrance, entry, opening, passageway

inmate   occupant, resident, tenant, inhabitant

inmost   1. deepest, farthest in, 2. private, secret

inn   hotel, tavern, roadhouse, lodge

innocent   1. guiltless, faultless, blameless, sinless   guilty
2. harmless   harmful   INNOCENCE

innovate introduce, change, modernize INNOVATION

innumerable countless, many, infinite, unlimited few

inoculate immunize, vaccinate INOCULATION

inoffensive harmless, unobjectionable offensive

inquire ask, question INQUIRY

inquisitive curious, prying, snooping, meddlesome

inroad raid, attack, invasion, foray

insane crazy, foolish, mad, unbalanced, deranged (*Slang* —
nutty, screwy, wacky, goofy) sane INSANITY

insatiable greedy, unquenchable, covetous

inscribe write, engrave, mark, imprint, impress, stamp
INSCRIPTION

insensible unfeeling, unaware, unconscious, numb, unknowing sensitive, aware INSENSITIVE

inseparable indivisible, solid, joined separable

insert put in, enter, introduce, inject, set in extract
INSERTION

inside 1. in, into, within, 2. interior, innermost

insight wisdom, perception, intuition

insignia emblems, badges, symbols

insignificant unimportant, meaningless, negligible, small,
little, slight significant, meaningful

insincere dishonest, false, superficial, artificial sincere

insinuate hint, suggest, imply, intimate, indicate

insist urge, press, maintain, stress, demand
INSISTENCE, INSISTENT

insolent rude, insulting, impudent, arrogant, haughty, defiant, bold polite INSOLENCE

insoluble unexplainable, unsolvable solvable

inspect examine, observe, study, contemplate
INSPECTION, INSPECTOR

inspire influence, cause, prompt, encourage discourage
INSPIRATION

install 1. admit, establish, let in, inaugurate, instate, receive,
2. place, put in, fix, plant, set INSTALLMENT

instance example, case, occasion, circumstance

instant 1. immediate, pressing, urgent, prompt, quick, 2.
moment, second INSTANTANEOUS, INSTANTLY

instead in place of, rather than, in lieu of

instinct natural feeling, natural tendency
INSTINCTIVE

institute 1. establish, begin, set up, create, organize, form,
launch (*Slang* — start the ball rolling), 2. society, organization, school, establishment, foundation INSTITUTION

instruct 1. teach, educate, show, guide, 2. inform, direct,
tell, command, order, dictate, advise
INSTRUCTION, INSTRUCTIVE, INSTRUCTOR

instrument tool, device, means, implement, utensil, apparatus, gadget, appliance, contraption (*Slang* — gimmick)
INSTRUMENTAL

insufferable unbearable, intolerable tolerable, bearable

insufficient inadequate, not enough, unsatisfactory, deficient enough

insulate isolate, separate INSULATION, INSULATOR

insult offend, affront, humiliate

insure 1. protect, safeguard, defend, shelter, cover, 2.
guarantee, warrant, assure, endorse, certify, sponsor, back,
3. make sure, affirm, vouch, determine INSURANCE

insurgent rebel, rioter, revolter, agitator, ringleader, troublemaker, instigator, rabble-rouser

insurrection revolt, rebellion, mutiny, riot, uprising obedience, compliance

intact untouched, whole, uninjured, undamaged, unchanged, complete

intake 1. input, entry, 2. income, earnings, revenue, receipts, proceeds, profits outgo

intangible untouchable, unsubstantial tangible

integrate 1. equalize, balance, coordinate, proportion, 2. amass, form a whole segregate INTEGRATION

integrity 1. honesty, sincerity, uprightness, honor, respectability dishonesty, 2. wholeness, completeness, entirety, totality incompleteness

intelligent sensible, bright, knowing, understanding, rational, aware, perceptive ignorant
INTELLECT, INTELLECTUAL, INTELLIGENCE, INTELLIGIBLE

intemperate excessive, extreme, unreasonable, unrestrained INTEMPERANCE

intend mean, plan, propose, aim, have in mind, contemplate INTENT, INTENTION, INTENTIONAL

intense 1. great, considerable, extreme, drastic, 2. forceful, strong, dynamic, fierce, severe, rigorous (*Slang* — snappy, zippy, peppy) moderate

inter bury, entomb

intercede go between, interfere, intervene, mediate, negotiate, arbitrate, umpire, referee

intercept interrupt, check, stop, arrest, hold up

interchange exchange, change, switch, trade, substitute

intercourse   1. communication, dealings, 2. sexual relations, copulation

interest   1. concern, curiosity, intrigue   unconcern, apathy, 2. share, portion, part, percentage (*Slang* — divvy, cut), 3. premium, rate, profit, 4. business, affair, matters

interesting   arousing, provocative, inviting, entertaining, thought-provoking, fascinating, absorbing, gripping, engrossing, enthralling, spellbinding, captivating, intriguing, attractive, appealing   uninteresting, dull

interfere   1. intervene, intercede, mediate, arbitrate, umpire, referee, 2. meddle, intrude, encroach, interrupt (*Slang* — barge in, cut in, butt in, horn in, crash)
INTERFERENCE

interior   inside, inner, middle, heart, core, nucleus
exterior, outside

interject   insert, put between, implant, interpose

interlace   weave, intertwine, braid

interlock   join, link, connect, mesh, engage   separate

interlude   intermission, interval, interim, respite, break, pause, recess, interruption

intermediate   in between, intervening, middle

interminable   endless, long, lengthy, infinite, perpetual

intermingle   mix, blend, merge, combine, mingle   separate

intermission   pause, interruption, interlude, interval, interim, respite, break, recess

intermittent   periodic, recurrent, sporadic, irregular, broken, unsteady   regular, continual

internal   inner, inside, interior, innermost   external, outer

interpret   explain, clarify, translate, analyze
INTERPRETATION

interrogate   question, examine, quiz, test, inquire of, grill, cross-examine   INTERROGATION

interrupt   break in, hinder, stop, intrude, interfere INTERRUPTION

intertwine   interlace, weave, braid

interval   interruption, intermission, interlude, interim, respite, break, pause, recess

intervention   interference, intrusion, infringement, meddling INTERVENE

interview   question, interrogate, quiz, test, examine

1. intimate   1. close, familiar, 2. innermost, private, secret

2. intimate   hint, suggest, imply, indicate, insinuate

intimidate   frighten, threaten, menace, cow, browbeat, bully, harass, terrorize

intolerable   unbearable, insufferable   tolerable, bearable

intolerant   impatient, unsympathetic, bigoted, prejudiced tolerant, understanding

intoxicated   1. drunk, inebriated (*Slang*—plastered, pickled, soused, crocked, tight, high)   sober, 2. excited, impassioned, moved, touched, impressed, affected   unmoved INTOXICATE

intrepid   fearless, dauntless, brave, courageous, bold, valiant, heroic   timid, afraid

intricate   complicated, perplexing, entangled, complex, confused, involved   simple

intrigue   1. plot, scheme, conspiracy, 2. love affair, romance, amour

intriguing   fascinating, alluring, captivating, charming, enchanting, enthralling, attractive, interesting, appealing, enticing, inviting, tantalizing, thrilling, tempting, provocative   unappealing, dull

introduce 1. bring in, inaugurate, institute, launch, innovate, 2. present, acquaint with INTRODUCTION

intrude interfere, infringe, encroach, trespass, meddle, overstep (*Slang* — barge in, cut in, butt in, horn in, crash) INTRUSION

inundate flood, overflow, run over, cascade, deluge, drench

invade intrude, overrun, encroach, trespass, advance upon, infringe, raid, attack INVASION

invalid 1. sickly, weak, unhealthy, infirm, frail, debilitated, 2. void, without value, ineffective valid

invaluable priceless, precious, dear, worthwhile worthless

invariable unchanging, constant, permanent, unalterable, uniform, steady, consistent changing

invent originate, make up, devise, develop, contrive, concoct INVENTION, INVENTOR

inventory stock, collection, list

invert turn around, reverse

invest 1. venture, stake, 2. empower, place, provide, endow INVESTMENT, INVESTOR

investigate search, explore, examine, inspect, study, scrutinize, review, probe INVESTIGATION, INVESTIGATOR

invigorating stimulating, exhilarating, energizing, refreshing, bracing debilitating, weakening

invincible unbeatable, unconquerable, invulnerable, impregnable vulnerable

invite 1. ask, request, call, summon, 2. attract, tempt, interest, appeal INVITATION

invoke pray, beseech, entreat, beg, implore, appeal, plead INVOCATION

involuntary 1. unwilling, forced, 2. instinctive, automatic, mechanical, spontaneous, reflex, unconscious, compulsive, unthinking, unintentional voluntary

involve 1. include, concern, affect, entail, implicate, encompass, envelop, 2. complicate, tangle, confuse, confound, 3. occupy, absorb, engross INVOLVEMENT

irate angry, mad, indignant, infuriated

irksome tiresome, tedious, wearisome, troublesome, bothersome, trying, annoying, irritating

irregular 1. unnatural, abnormal, 2. uneven, erratic, distorted, rough regular

irrelevant unfitting, inappropriate, unrelated, far-fetched relevant

irresistible compelling, moving

irresolute hesitating, uncertain, unsure, indecisive, fickle resolute, definite

irreverent disrespectful, discourteous, insolent, impudent, impious respectful

irritable impatient, cross, cranky, irascible, testy pleasant, agreeable

irritate 1. annoy, vex, incite, agitate, stir up, provoke, instigate, foment, infuriate, madden, anger, 2. make sore, pain, hurt, wound, chafe, rub, grate soothe IRRITATION

isolate separate, segregate, set apart, quarantine, seclude ISOLATION

issue 1. cause, principle, campaign, problem, topic, subject, theme, text, question, point, 2. publication, edition, copy

itch 1. prickly feeling, 2. desire, craving

item 1. part, segment, portion, subdivision, component, piece, article, 2. notation, entry

itemize list, sum up, total, summarize

J

jab   poke, push, thrust, nudge, prod

jagged   pointy, ragged, notched, serrated   smooth

jail   imprison, lock up, hold captive, incarcerate

jam   1. crowd, stuff, load, cram, press, squeeze, push, crush, heap, 2. jelly, marmalade, preserve

jar   1. shake, rattle, jolt, bounce, 2. glass container

jaunt   trip, journey, excursion, tour, voyage, outing, expedition (*Slang* — whirl, jump, hop)   JAUNTY

jealous   envious, desirous of, covetous   JEALOUSY

jeer   make fun of, taunt, scoff, mock

jeopardize   risk, endanger, imperil, hazard, expose (*Slang* — put on the spot)   JEOPARDY

jerk   pull suddenly, twist suddenly, jolt, yank

jest   joke, fun, mock, tease (*Slang* — ride, josh, kid, rib, razz)   JESTER

jetty   breakwater, pier, buttress, bulwark

jewel   stone, gem, ornament   JEWELRY

jingle   ring, chime, tinkle

job   work, business, employment, task, assignment, duty, position

jog   run, trot, gait, sprint, lope

join   connect, fasten, clasp, unite, combine, couple, link, put together, attach, annex
separate, part, detach, disconnect, disjoin

joke   jest, quip, banter, tease (*Slang* — ride, josh, rib, kid, razz, wisecrack)   JOKER

jolly   merry, cheerful, pleasant, joyful, jovial, gleeful
sad, solemn, grim, serious, glum

jolt   jerk, jar, shake, startle, jounce

jostle push, shove, thrust, bump

jot write, mark down, note, record

jounce jolt, bounce, bump

journal 1. daily record, account, log, diary, chronicle, 2. newspaper, magazine JOURNALISM, JOURNALIST

journey trip, voyage, tour, expedition, excursion, jaunt, outing, junket

jovial kindly, good-natured, merry, good-hearted, good-humored, joyful, gleeful, jolly sad, solemn, grim, serious, glum

joyful glad, happy, cheerful, blissful, merry, jovial, gleeful sad, solemn, grim, serious, glum JOY, JOYOUS

jubilant rejoicing, exulting, triumphant, overjoyed, gay, delighted, elated dejected JUBILATION, JUBILEE

judge 1. decide, consider, form an opinion, 2. mediate, referee, umpire JUDGMENT, JUDICIAL

judicious wise, sensible, thoughtful, well-advised ignorant

jumble mix, confuse, scramble, muddle (*Slang* — foul up, ball up, snafu) compose, arrange, organize

jumbo big, huge, enormous, immense, colossal, giant, gigantic, mammoth, monstrous, tremendous small, little, dwarf, midget, mini

jump spring, leap, bound, vault, hurdle, hop

junction joining, connection, union, linking, coupling, meeting, hookup, tie-up separation JUNCTURE

junior 1. younger, 2. lower, lesser, secondary, subordinate, minor senior

junk 1. rubbish, trash, scrap, litter, debris, 2. Chinese sailing ship

just 1. exact, precise, 2. only, merely, 3. righteous, fair, proper, good, moral, virtuous corrupt, unjust JUSTICE

jut   stick out, project, stand out, protrude   recess, indent

juvenile   young, youthful   old, mature, aged

K

keen   1. sharp, cutting, fine, acute, 2. quick, exact, smart, bright, clever, sharp-witted (*Slang* — quick on the trigger, sharp as a tack)
dull

keep   have, hold, maintain, preserve, conserve, save, tend, protect, guard   discard, lose
KEEPER, KEEPING, KEPT

kennel   doghouse, pound

key   1. opener, 2. clue, answer, explanation, lead, 3. tone, pitch, note

kid   1. tease, joke, fool, jest (*Slang* — ride, josh, rib, razz), 2. child, tot, 3. young goat

kidnap   snatch, carry off, abduct, shanghai

kill   slay, slaughter, murder, destroy, end, finish, annihilate, execute

kin   family, relatives, relations, folks   KINDRED

kind   1. friendly, gentle, decent, generous, considerate, warm-hearted, tender, sympathetic, thoughtful   mean, cruel, unkind, 2. sort, type, variety, species, nature, make
KINDNESS

kindle   1. set afire, light, ignite   extinguish, 2. arouse, stir up, start, trigger, move, provoke   calm, pacify

king   ruler, sovereign, monarch, chief, potentate

kink   1. curl, twist, 2. complication, 3. quirk, mental twist, queer idea

kiss   touch with lips, osculate, buss (*Slang* — smack, smooch)

kit   equipment, set, outfit, furnishings, gear, rig

knack   skill, talent, art, know-how

knave   rascal, tricky man, rogue, scoundrel, villain
KNAVERY

knead   mix, blend, combine, massage

knife   blade, sword

knit   join, grow together, fasten, connect, unite

knock   hit, strike, punch, jab, pound, beat, hammer, rap, bang (*Slang* — bat, crack, wallop, clout, belt, clobber, bash, paste, clip, swat, sock, conk)

know   understand, comprehend, perceive, recognize, identify, be sure of, be aware   KNOWLEDGE

L

label   name, title, tag

labor   work, toil, employment, industry (*Slang* — grind)
LABORER, LABORIOUS

labyrinth   maze, complex, tangle

lacerate   tear roughly, mangle, wound

lack   want, need, require, fall short

lacquer   varnish, polish, gild

lad   boy, youth   LADDIE

laden   loaded, burdened, weighted

ladle   dipper, scoop

lady   woman, matron

lag   linger, loiter, dawdle, poke, dillydally, delay, tarry

lament   mourn, sorrow, grieve, bewail, bemoan
rejoice, celebrate   LAMENTATION

lance   pierce, cut, puncture, stab, perforate, knife, impale

land 1. ground, soil, sod, shore, surface, earth, 2. descend, arrive, touch down, alight LANDING

landmark point, milestone

lane path, road, narrow way, pass, aisle, alley, avenue, channel, artery

language speech, words, tongue, talk (*Slang* — lingo, patter)

languid weak, drooping, feeble, debilitated, listless, lethargic, dull, sluggish energetic, vigorous LANGUISH

lank slender, thin, lean, skinny, gaunt, scrawny stocky, chunky

lap 1. lick, drink, 2. wrap around, fold over

lapse sink, decline, slump, go down

larceny theft, stealing, robbery

lard fat, grease

large big, sizable, great, grand, huge, vast, immense, enormous, colossal, giant, gigantic, mammoth, massive small, little

lariat rope, lasso

lark fun, fling, joke, spree, celebration, revel

lash strike, blow, beat, hit, whip, flog

lass girl, youth LASSIE

lasso rope, lariat

last latest, end, final, conclusive, ultimate first, beginning

latch hook, clasp, lock, fastener, catch, closing, seal

late behind, slow, tardy

latent hidden, concealed, covered, obscured, underlying

lather soap, foam, suds, froth

latter later, more recent former

laud praise, commend, glorify, compliment, extol
belittle, criticize

laugh giggle, chuckle, smile, grin, titter, snicker, guffaw,
howl, roar (*Slang* — be in stitches)
LAUGHABLE, LAUGHTER

launch start, set afloat, introduce, fire, set going, spring

launder wash, bathe, scour, scrub LAUNDRY

lavatory bathroom, toilet, latrine, washroom

lavish free, abundant, liberal, plentiful, ample, extravagant,
generous, prodigal stingy, sparing, skimpy

law rule, principle, standard, formula, ordinance, regulation, act, decree, proclamation, edict
LAWFUL, LAWYER

lax loose, slack, careless, lenient, vague, lazy rigid, firm
LAXITY

lay put, place, set, rest, deposit, arrange

lazy lax, inactive, indolent active, ambitious

lea meadow, pasture, grassy field

lead come first, head, escort, guide, conduct, direct, run
LEADER, LEADERSHIP

league union, alliance, association, society, federation,
group, band

leak drip, dribble, run out

lean 1. thin, scant, spare, lanky, meager, slight, slim,
slender, narrow, skinny, scrawny bulky, fat, 2. bend, rest,
slope, slant, incline, tip

leap jump, spring, vault, hop, bound, hurdle, dive, plunge,
pounce

learn memorize, gain knowledge, discover, find out

lease   rent, hire, let, charter

leash   strap, chain, rein, collar, shackle

least   fewest, smallest, minimum   most, maximum

leave   go, depart, quit, abandon, withdraw, vacate, exit
arrive, stay

lecture   speech, talk, sermon, address, recitation, discourse,
oration

ledge   shelf, ridge, edge, rim

legal   lawful, legitimate, authorized, permitted, allowed,
admissible, valid, sound, just   illegal

legend   story, fiction, fairy tale, myth, fable, folklore
LEGENDARY

legible   readable, plain, clear   illegible

legion   unit, outfit, regiment, troop, battalion, company,
squad, team, division, army, force

legislation   lawmaking, resolution, regulation, ruling, enactment, decree, ordinance, statute
LEGISLATE, LEGISLATIVE, LEGISLATURE

legitimate   lawful, rightful, allowed, legal, authorized,
permitted, admissible, valid, sound, just   illegitimate

leisure   freedom, spare time

lend   give, loan, advance

length   extent, measure, span, reach, stretch, distance
LENGTHEN

lenient   mild, gentle, merciful, lax, loose, relaxed, unrestrained, soft, easy   harsh, strict

less   smaller, fewer, reduced   more

lesson   teaching, instruction, assignment, exercise, course,
study

let 1. allow, permit, leave, consent, grant, admit deny, 2. rent, lease, hire out, charter, contract

letter 1. alphabet sign, character, symbol, 2. message, note, communication, dispatch

level flat, even, equal, uniform, constant, steady, smooth uneven

liable 1. likely, probable, apt, 2. responsible, accountable, answerable

liar fibber, falsifier, fabricator, perjurer, storyteller

liberal 1. generous, plentiful, abundant, ample, extravagant, lavish, extensive, unselfish stingy, 2. tolerant, broad-minded, freethinking, progressive conservative

liberty freedom, independence, autonomy, emancipation

license permit, warrant, consent, authorization, sanction, approval

lick lap, taste

lid cover, top, cap, stopper

lie 1. fib, falsify, fabricate, exaggerate, 2. recline, repose

life existence, being

lift raise, pick up, elevate, hoist

light 1. bright, clear, open, lucid dark, 2. weightless, airy, delicate heavy

like prefer, care for, be fond of, fancy, enjoy, appreciate (*Slang* — have eyes for, go for, get a kick out of) dislike LIKING

likeness similarity, resemblance difference

likewise similarly, also, moreover, too, as well

limber flexible, bending, pliable, elastic stiff, inflexible

limit end, boundary, restriction, extreme, tip, confine

limp weak, drooping, sagging, flimsy, loose, soft, floppy stiff

limpid clear, transparent, lucid, translucent cloudy

line 1. rope, cord, wire, string, 2. mark, stroke, stripe, streak, dash, 3. edge, boundary, limit, confine, 4. row, arrangement, series, sequence, 5. type, kind, brand, sort, make

lineage race, family, ancestry

linger stay, wait, delay, remain, tarry, loiter, dawdle, dillydally, lag (*Slang* — take one's own sweet time, hang around, hold on, sit tight, stick around, wait a second)

link unite, connect, join, combine, couple, put together, bridge separate

liquid fluid solid

liquor whiskey, drink, alcohol, spirits (*Slang* — booze)

list 1. enumeration, schedule, record, register, inventory, line-up, 2. tilt, tip, slant, slope, lean

listen hear, eavesdrop (*Slang* — be all ears)

listless tired, uninterested, unconcerned, lethargic, apathetic active

literally exactly, actually, really, word-for-word

literate learned, scholarly, cultured, educated illiterate

literature writings, books, publications

lithe bending, supple, elastic, flexible, pliable, plastic, limber stiff

litter clutter, rubbish, trash, scrap, rubble, debris, junk

little small, short, tiny, bit, minimum, slight, miniature, mini, puny, teeny, wee big

live 1. be alive, exist die, 2. reside, occupy, dwell, stay, house, room, inhabit (*Slang* — hang out)

livelihood support, keep, maintenance, sustenance, subsistence LIVING

lively exciting, bright, cheerful, vivid, vigorous, gay, active, energetic, interesting, spirited, animated, vivacious, spry (*Slang* — zippy, snappy, chipper, full of life, peppy) dull LIVELIER, LIVELIEST

livestock cattle, animals

livid 1. pale, grayish, 2. very angry, furious, enraged (*Slang* — sore, riled up, fit to be tied)

load 1. burden, pack, cargo, freight, 2. fill, stuff unload, empty

loaf idle, lounge, loiter, lie around

loan lend, advance, give

loath unwilling, reluctant

loathe hate, dislike, abhor, detest, abominate, despise love

lobby entrance, passageway, vestibule, foyer

local regional, limited, particular, restricted

location position, place, region, area, zone, territory, district, section, neighborhood, spot, site, situation LOCATE, LOCALITY

lock fasten, close, hook, clasp, latch, shut, seal unlock, open

locomotion travel, movement, motion, transit

lodge live, reside, inhabit, occupy, dwell, room, stay LODGER, LODGING

lofty high, grand, dignified, proud, haughty, eminent, prominent, elevated, soaring, towering

log 1. wood, lumber, timber, board, 2. record, register, account, scrapbook, album, catalog, journal

logical   reasonable, sensible, sound, sane, rational
illogical, unreasonable   LOGIC

loiter   linger, idle, stop, dillydally, wait, delay, stay, tarry, dawdle (*Slang* — hang around, stick around)

loll   droop, hang, sprawl, repose, recline, relax (*Slang* — take it easy)

lonely   alone, solitary, isolated, unaccompanied, friendless, desolate   LONE, LONELINESS, LONESOME

long   lengthy, extensive, far-reaching   short

look   1. see, search, hunt, explore, stare, glance, peek, peer, gaze, gape, gawk (*Slang* — gander), 2. seem, appear

loom   appear, emerge, come in sight, show up

loose   1. limp, drooping, slack, unfastened, untied   tight, 2. vague, free, unclear, confused, hazy, inexact   definite

loot   rob, plunder, burglarize (*Slang* — hold up, stick up)

lope   run, sprint, bound, race, gallop

lord   owner, ruler, master, boss, proprietor

lose   1. fail, flop, be unsuccessful, forfeit, sacrifice win, succeed, 2. misplace, mislay   find   LOSS, LOST

lot   1. many, bunch, group, cluster, clump   few, 2. quantity, amount, sum, number, portion, 3. fate, fortune, chance, luck, destiny, end (*Slang* — break), 4. field, plot, tract

lotion   ointment, salve, cream, balm

lottery   raffle, drawing

loud   noisy, thunderous, roaring, resounding   soft, low

lounge   rest, relax, loaf, lie down, repose, laze, sit around, take it easy

love   adore, like, care for, be fond of, fancy, idolize, cherish (*Slang* — have eyes for, be set on, dig, go for, have a case on)

lovely delightful, exquisite, charming, appealing, enchanting, beautiful, pretty, attractive, fetching (*Slang* — out of this world) LOVELINESS

low 1. inferior, lesser, short high, 2. mean, coarse, vulgar, base, wicked, evil, bad, sinful, vile

loyal true, faithful, obedient, dutiful, devoted, trustworthy disloyal LOYALTY

lubricate grease, oil, anoint LUBRICANT

lucid 1. clear, shining, light, transparent, translucent, 2. understandable, plain, distinct, clear-cut, explicit unclear, cloudy

luck chance, fortune, fate, lot, fortuity LUCKY

ludicrous ridiculous, absurd (*Slang* — way-out)

lug drag, pull, haul, tug

luggage baggage, bags, valises

lull quiet, calm, hush, silence, stillness, pause, rest, break, recess, intermission, respite, lapse, letup

lumber timber, logs, wood

luminous light, shining, radiant, beaming, gleaming, glowing, bright, clear

lump swelling, bump, mass, hunk, chunk

lunge thrust, attack, push

lurch sway, topple, tip, rock, roll, toss, tumble, pitch

lure pull, attract, draw on, entice, seduce (*Slang* — give the come-on, rope in)

lurid terrible, sensational, startling, melodramatic

lurk hide, sneak, slink, prowl, creep

luscious delicious, savory, pleasing, tasty

luster   shine, brightness, brilliance, sheen, glow, gleam, gloss
LUSTROUS

lusty   strong, healthy, vigorous, powerful, mighty, sturdy, rugged, strapping, robust, hardy, hale, husky, hefty   weak

luxury   extravagance, frills, prosperity, elegance, comfort, well-being, magnificence, grandeur, splendor, swankiness
poverty   LUXURIOUS

lyrical   musical, poetic   LYRIC

M

mad   1. crazy, insane, wild, foolish, lunatic, daft, demented, deranged, unbalanced, touched (*Slang* — cracked, not all there)   sane, 2. angry, annoyed, irritated, exasperated, disgruntled, enraged, furious, cross, irritable, ornery, raging, disagreeable (*Slang* — sore, riled up, fit to be tied)   peaceful
MADDEN

magazine   journal, periodical, publication

magic   witchcraft, wizardry, sorcery, voodoo
MAGICIAN

magistrate   judge

magnetic   attractive, pulling, drawing, alluring
MAGNET, MAGNETISM

magnificent   splendid, grand, stately, majestic, superb, exquisite, marvelous, wonderful, grandiose, glorious, imposing, elaborate, impressive (*Slang* — divine, terrific, sensational, out of this world, swell)

magnify   exaggerate, increase, intensify, expand, enhance, enlarge, extend, broaden, stretch, inflate (*Slang* — step up, lay it on, talk big, jazz up, boost)   minimize

maid   servant, helper, domestic, housekeeper

mail 1. send, dispatch, post, 2. letters, correspondence

maim cripple, disable, injure, hurt, wound

main chief, most important, principal, foremost, leading, dominant, primary, first secondary MAINLY

maintain keep, uphold, possess, support, bear, sustain, preserve, save, guard, protect, retain MAINTENANCE

majestic grand, stately, noble, great, kingly, dignified, high, prominent, eminent, regal, royal, imperial, sovereign, grandiose, magnificent, impressive, elegant, imposing, proud MAJESTY

major larger, greater, superior, higher, senior minor MAJORITY

make 1. build, form, shape, compose, create, assemble, manufacture, fashion, fabricate, construct, produce, do, execute destroy; 2. cause, force, compel, 3. kind, brand, type, line, sort

malady sickness, illness, disease, ailment, disorder, infirmity

male manly, masculine female

malice spite, ill will, meanness MALICIOUS

malign slur, slander, speak evil of, defame, smear

malignant deadly, harmful, destructive, killing, fatal, mortal, lethal harmless, benign MALIGNANCY

malleable yielding, adaptable, changeable, pliant, flexible, plastic, elastic, bendable, supple stubborn, unyielding, rigid

maltreat abuse, mistreat

mammoth huge, gigantic, immense, vast, enormous, giant, colossal, titanic, monumental (*Slang* — whopping) microscopic, miniature

man   1. human being, person, Homo sapiens, folk, society, mortal, individual, soul, 2. male, fellow, gentleman (*Slang* — chap, guy)   woman   MANKIND

manage   control, conduct, handle, direct, operate, work, regulate, govern, lead, supervise, administer, run (*Slang* — mastermind)   MANAGEMENT, MANAGER

mandate   command, order, dictate, injunction, referendum

maneuver   operate, work, run, conduct, handle, drive, manipulate, engineer, plot, scheme, intrigue, conspire, plan

mangle   cut, tear apart, lacerate, mutilate, maim, injure, hurt, wound

manhood   manliness, maturity, adulthood   youth

mania   craze, insanity, madness, infatuation, enthusiasm, desire (*Slang* — bug)

manifest   apparent, clear, plain, visible, open, exposed, perceptible, discernible, evident, obvious, open-and-shut   hidden, obscure   MANIFESTATION

manifold   many, various, multiple   few

manipulate   handle, manage, touch, feel, operate, work, conduct, maneuver

man-made   artificial, not natural   natural

manner   way, kind, mode, style, fashion, form, nature, character, means, method

manor   estate, land, property, domain, mansion, large house, palace, castle, villa, chateau

manslaughter   killing, homicide, murder, assassination, elimination

mantle   cloak, cover, coat, robe, wrap

manual   1. guidebook, directory, handbook, 2. by hand

manufacture make, invent, create, fashion, construct, build, erect, compose, prepare, devise, fabricate

manuscript writing, copy, composition, work, paper, document

many numerous, various, multitudinous, myriad, several, considerable (*Slang* — zillion) few

map chart

mar damage, injure, blemish, disfigure, scar, deform, spoil, ruin

marathon race, relay, contest

march walk, hike, parade, tramp

margin border, edge, rim, leeway, room

mariner sailor, seaman, navigator, tar, salt

marionette puppet, doll

mark 1. line, sign, evidence, indication, manifestation, 2. grade, rating

marked noticeable, plain, evident, noted, apparent, decided

market store, shop, mart

marriage union, joining, coupling, linking, wedding, matrimony, nuptials MARRY

marshal arrange, lead, conduct, escort, guide, usher, squire

mart market, shop, store

martial militant, warlike, military, combative, belligerent, aggressive, hostile peaceful

martyr sufferer, victim, tortured

marvelous wonderful, extraordinary, miraculous, astounding, superb, magnificent, glorious, divine, exceptional, remarkable MARVEL

masculine manly, strong, vigorous, virile

mash crush, mix, soften, crumble, grind, grate, granulate, pulverize

mask disguise, cover, camouflage

masquerade disguise, pretend, impersonate, pose

mass bulk, lump, quantity, load, amount, measure, volume, accumulation, hunk, chunk, lots, pile, stack, heap, slew, batch (*Slang* — gobs, scads, oodles)

massacre slaughter, killing, butchery, carnage, pogrom

massage rub, knead, stroke

massive big, large, heavy, solid, sturdy, strong, clumsy, ponderous, thick, coarse   little

master director, commander, ruler, head, controller, chief MASTERY

masterly expert, skillful, proficient, adept, handy, clever (*Slang* — crackerjack)

mat rug, cover

match 1. lighter, 2. contest, battle, engagement, encounter, game, sport, play, 3. duplicate, twin, double, companion, mate, fellow, counterpart, complement, equivalent, equal

mate pair, couple, team

material substance, fabric, stuff, matter, composition, goods

maternal motherly   paternal, fatherly

mathematics numbers, measurements, figures, calculation, computations MATHEMATICAL, MATHEMATICIAN

matrimony marriage, wedding, nuptials

matron woman, lady

matter 1. material, substance, composition, content, 2. affair, business, concern, transaction, activity

mature ripe, full-grown, developed, mellow, adult, ready immature MATURITY

maul   bruise, batter, abuse

mausoleum   tomb, vault, crypt, shrine

maxim   proverb, rule, law, code, regulation, principle, adage, saying

maximum   largest, highest, greatest, uppermost, head, chief minimum

may   be able, can, be allowed

maybe   possibly, perhaps, conceivably, perchance

maze   network, complex, tangle, labyrinth, confusion, muddle

meadow   grassland, pasture, range, field

meager   poor, scanty, thin, lean, sparse, skimpy generous, abundant

meal   repast, spread

mean   1. signify, intend, denote, imply, indicate, suggest, connote, 2. petty, unkind, malicious, ill-humored, cross, irritable, testy pleasant, 3. average, medium, normal, middle MEANING

meander   wander, wind, twist, stray

measure   size, grade, rank, compare, assess, appraise, estimate, rate MEASUREMENT

mechanic   machinist, repairman, craftsman, technician MECHANICAL, MECHANISM

medal   award, honor, reward, medallion, prize

meddle   interfere, busybody, intrude, interrupt, intervene, trespass (*Slang* — barge in, butt in, horn in) MEDDLESOME

media   instruments, tools, agents, implements

mediate   make peace, settle, negotiate, intercede, intervene, referee, umpire, arbitrate MEDIATION

medicinal   healing, helping, relieving, remedial, corrective, therapeutic   MEDICAL, MEDICINE

mediocre   average, ordinary, fair, moderate, adequate, satisfactory, acceptable, passable, so-so   MEDIOCRITY

meditate   think, reflect, consider, contemplate, study, ponder, weigh, brood, deliberate   MEDITATION

medium   1. middle, average, mean, halfway, mediocre, fair, 2. instrument, tool, agent, implement

medley   mixture, hodgepodge, conglomeration, assortment, combination

meek   mild, patient, submissive, gentle, tame, subdued, uncomplaining, passive, modest, unassuming, unpretentious aggressive

meet   join, unite, connect, come together, assemble, gather, encounter, converge separate   MEETING

melancholy   sad, gloomy, blue, pensive, wistful, depressing, dismal cheerful

mellow   mature, ripe, developed, full-grown, soft

melody   tune, song   MELODIOUS

melt   dissolve, change, soften, liquefy solidify

member   part, offshoot, branch, organ   MEMBERSHIP

membrane   covering, tissue, layer

memorable   notable, rememberable

memorandum   note, letter, report, reminder, memo

memorize   learn by heart, remember   MEMORY

menace   threat

menagerie   zoo, collection, kennel

mend   repair, improve, fix, service, patch up, heal break, impair

mental   intellectual, thinking, rational   MENTALITY

mention   remark, comment, observe, say, note, state, name, specify, stipulate, designate

menu   list, account, bill of fare, line-up

merchandise   goods, wares, commodities, products
MERCHANT

mercy   kindness, compassion, pity, sympathy, charity
MERCIFUL

merely   simply, only, purely, barely   MERE

merge   absorb, swallow, combine, unite, mix, blend, fuse, join, mingle, scramble separate   MERGER

merit   quality, value, worth, goodness, excellence, fineness

merry   gay, joyful, jolly, jovial, gleeful, mirthful, festive
sad, downcast   MERRILY, MERRIMENT

mesh   net, screen, web, complex

mess   dirty, disfigure, contaminate, pollute, corrupt

message   word, communication, dispatch, letter, epistle, note

mete   distribute, share, give, allot, grant, present, dispense, measure, deal out, dole out, hand out (*Slang* — dish out)

meteoric   swift, flashing, brief, blazing
METEOR, METEORITE

meter   measure, record, gauge

method   system, way, manner, means, mode, fashion, style, procedure, process, form, course, plan, scheme, design, arrangement   METHODICAL

metropolitan   city, civic, urban, municipal
METROPOLIS

mettle   spirit, courage, nerve, stamina, pluck, spunk (*Slang* — backbone, guts)

microscopic   infinitesimal, tiny, minute huge
MICROSCOPE

middle   center, heart, core, nucleus, hub

midget   dwarf, pygmy, runt   giant

mien   manner, way, conduct, behavior, semblance

might   be able, can, be allowed

mighty   strong, powerful, great, grand, potent, powerful, forceful, vigorous, stout, sturdy, rugged, robust, hearty   weak   MIGHT, MIGHTILY

migrant   roving, traveling, wandering, roaming, rambling, meandering, drifting, straying, transient   stationary   MIGRATE, MIGRATION

mild   gentle, kind, calm, warm, temperate, moderate, lenient, good-natured, good-humored   harsh, violent

militant   fighting, warlike, combative, belligerent, aggressive, hostile, antagonistic, contentious, pugnacious, bellicose (*Slang* — scrappy)   peaceful

military   army, troops, soldiers, armed forces, service

mimic   imitate, copy, ape, mock, mime, parrot, copycat (*Slang* — take off on)

mince   chop, shatter, crush, smash, fragment

mind   1. brain, intelligence, mental ability, intellect, 2. obey, heed, regard, comply, listen to   ignore, 3. attend, watch, observe, notice, look after

mine   1. excavate, dig, scoop out, 2. blow up, blast

mingle   mix, associate, blend, combine

miniature   small, tiny, minute

minimum   least, lowest, smallest   maximum

minister   clergyman, spiritual guide, pastor, chaplain

minor   1. smaller, lesser, inferior, secondary, lower   major, 2. underage, immature

minstrel   musician, bard, troubadour

minus less, lacking, without, excepting, missing, absent

1. minute instant, moment, twinkling (*Slang* — jiffy, sec, half a shake)

2. minute small, tiny, miniature, slight, negligible, insignificant large, significant

miraculous wonderful, marvelous, remarkable, extraordinary, phenomenal, incredible, awesome MIRACLE

mire mud, slush, muck, slime

mirror reflect, echo, copy, imitate

mirth fun, laughter, merriment, joy, glee, levity, amusement gloom, sadness

misbehave behave badly, act up (*Slang* — carry on, cut up) behave

miscellaneous mixed, combined, blended, conglomerate, scrambled, jumbled

mischievous naughty, harmful, devilish, impish, playful, prankish, elfish MISCHIEF

miser moneygrubber (*Slang* — scrimp, penny pincher) spendthrift

miserable poor, mean, wretched, unhappy, pitiful, shabby, woeful, sorry happy MISERY

misfortune difficulty, trouble, distress, hardship, ruin, mishap, disaster, catastrophe, calamity, tragedy, accident fortune, good luck

misgiving doubt, suspicion, anxiety, question, skepticism, qualm, concern, uneasiness

mishap misfortune, difficulty, trouble, distress, hardship, ruin, disaster, catastrophe, calamity, tragedy, accident good luck, fortune

misjudge mistake, err, slip up, miscalculate

mislay   lose, miss, misplace   find

mislead   deceive, misdirect, misinform (*Slang* — give a bum steer)

misplace   mislay, lose, miss   find

miss   fail, lose, forfeit, sacrifice   get, succeed

misshapen   deformed, disfigured, grotesque

missile   rocket, projectile

missing   lacking, wanting, lost, absent, nonexistent, vanished, gone

mission   errand, business, purpose, task, work, stint, job, assignment, chore, charge, duty

mist   cloud, fog, vapor, haze, film, dimness, blur   MISTY

mistake   error, blunder, fault, slip, oversight, faux pas (*Slang* — boo-boo, boner)

mistreat   abuse, ill-treat, molest, bruise

mistress   woman, matron, housekeeper

mistrust   doubt, be skeptical, suspect, distrust, question, challenge, dispute   trust

misunderstanding   disagreement, difficulty, difference, misinterpretation, mistake, error   understanding

misuse   mishandle, treat badly

mitt   glove

mix   stir, join, blend, combine, fuse, mingle, merge   separate   MIXTURE

moan   wail, groan, howl, cry, bawl, suffer, agonize, complain

moat   trench, fortification, channel, ditch, entrenchment

mob   crowd, mass, throng, multitude, horde, pack, bunch

mobile   movable, changeable, fluid   immobile

mock   mimic, imitate, ape, ridicule, scoff, jeer, taunt, deride, laugh at (*Slang* — ride, pan, razz)   MOCKERY

mode   manner, way, style, fashion, form, vogue, custom, method

model   copy, shape, design, reproduction, duplicate, replica, standard, prototype, image, likeness

moderate   calm, fair, medium, mild, conservative, temperate, gentle, restrained, lenient   extreme, harsh

modern   contemporary, up-to-date, progressive, forward-looking   archaic

modest   humble, bashful, shy, quiet, unpretentious, plain, simple   showy   MODESTY

modify   change, alter, vary, diversify, qualify, adjust, fix MODIFICATION

moist   wet, damp, humid, dank, watery   dry MOISTEN, MOISTURE

mold   1. shape, form, sculpture, carve, model, 2. decay, rot, spoil, deteriorate, disintegrate, crumble, go bad

molest   trouble, injure, harm, hurt, damage, wrong, disturb, mistreat, annoy, abuse, torment, harass, badger, pester, plague

moment   instant, minute, twinkling (*Slang* — jiffy, sec, half a shake)   MOMENTARILY, MOMENTARY

momentous   important, great, outstanding, considerable, eventful, stirring, influential, powerful, effective unimportant

momentum   force, impetus, thrust, push

monarch   ruler, sovereign, head, emperor, king, queen, chief

money   currency, legal tender, cash, dollars (*Slang* — dough, jack, beans, wampum)

mongrel   crossbreed, hybrid

monitor   1. helper, assistant, 2. recorder, clerk, 3. adviser, informant, counselor, reporter, announcer

monogram   signature, mark, seal, stamp

monopoly   control, corner, possession

monotonous   boring, humdrum, repetitious, tedious, dreary, dull   interesting   MONOTONY

monsoon   rains, storm, winds

monstrous   horrible, dreadful, shocking, grotesque, deformed, disfigured   MONSTER

monument   tower, memorial, shrine, pillar

monumental   important, weighty, great, vast, immense, stupendous, enormous, huge, notable, remarkable, memorable, extraordinary, exceptional, special (*Slang*—tremendous, terrific, whacking, thumping, rousing)   insignificant

mood   feeling, temperament, humor, disposition, nature, frame of mind, phase

moody   gloomy, sullen, glum, mopish, morose, sulky   cheerful

moor   anchor, fasten, secure, dock, tie

mop   wipe, wash, scrub, scour, swab

mope   sulk, grieve, sorrow, brood over, fret   rejoice

moral   right, just, ethical, honorable, reputable, upstanding, respectable, law-abiding, virtuous, good, righteous   immoral   MORALS, MORALITY, MORALLY

morale   spirit, enthusiasm

morass   swamp, marsh, bog, mire

morbid   1. unhealthy, sickly, diseased, unwholesome   healthy, 2. ghastly, horrible, dreadful, awful, shocking, appalling   pleasant

more   greater, further, farther, in addition, extra, another   less

moreover besides, also, furthermore, as well, too

morose gloomy, sullen, sulky, moody, glum cheerful

morsel piece, fragment, particle, bit, crumb, scrap, shred

mortal 1. man, human being, person, soul, individual, body, 2. deadly, fatal, lethal, killing, destructive, malignant

mortify wound, humiliate, shame, embarrass, disgrace MORTIFICATION

most greatest, extreme, maximum, supreme, highest, majority least

mostly mainly, chiefly, almost all, nearly

mother 1. originate, produce, cause, bring about, breed, 2. female parent, mommy, mama, mom father, 3. care for, attend to, look after, watch, mind, foster, nurse, nurture MOTHERHOOD, MOTHERLY

motion 1. movement, stir, activity, proceedings, doings, 2. suggestion, proposal, legislation, resolution, proposition

motive reason, cause, ground, basis, motivation, prompting

motley mixture, varied, assorted, diversified, various, several, many

motor engine, machine

mottled spotted, streaked, dappled, speckled, flecked, piebald

motto saying, maxim, proverb, adage

mound heap, hill, swell, pile, stack

mount 1. rise, get on, ascend, go up, climb, board descend, 2. increase, gain, grow, advance decrease, 3. position, place, fix, set remove

mountain 1. hill, elevation, 2. large amount, quantity, volume, mass, abundance, much (*Slang* — heap, pile, stack, slew, batch, oodles, gobs, scads)

mourn grieve, sorrow, lament, bewail, bemoan rejoice
MOURNFUL

move 1. change, budge, stir, stimulate, impel, motivate, animate, 2. influence, sway, affect, persuade, induce, arouse, prompt, convince MOVABLE, MOVEMENT

mow cut, clip, crop, prune, shear, shave

much quantity, abundance, volume, mass

mucilage glue, adhesive, cement, paste

muck dirt, filth, rot, slime, mire

mud mire, muck, slush, slime, dirt

muddle mess, disorder, confusion, chaos (*Slang* — mix-up, foul-up, snafu, hassle)

muff bungle, blunder, fumble, botch, spoil, mess (*Slang* — foul up, louse up, goof up, gum up)

muffle silence, mute, dull, soften, deaden, cushion, smother, stifle, suppress MUFFLER

muggy warm, damp, close, stuffy, humid, dank, sticky

mulish stubborn, obstinate, willful, headstrong, tenacious, unyielding, inflexible, rigid, adamant

multiply increase, advance, gain, grow, rise, procreate

mum silent, mute, speechless, quiet

mumble mutter, speak indistinctly shout

municipal civic, urban, metropolitan

murder 1. kill, assassinate, eliminate, purge, liquidate, slaughter, massacre, 2. spoil, ruin, botch, muff, mar, butcher, make a mess (*Slang* — foul up, louse up, goof up, gum up)
MURDERER, MURDEROUS

murky dark, gloomy light, cheerful MURK

murmur mutter, whisper shout

muscle strength, brawn (*Slang* — beefiness) MUSCULAR

muse dream, think, envision, ponder, contemplate, reflect, deliberate, consider

musical melodious, tuneful, lyrical, dulcet, harmonious MUSIC, MUSICIAN

muss rumple, mess, disarrange, disorganize, disarray, litter, clutter arrange, fix

must should, ought to, be obliged to, have to, need to, be forced to

muster assemble, gather, collect, summon, cluster, accumulate, amass, group, compile, recruit scatter, disperse

musty moldy, mildewed

mute silent, dumb, voiceless, speechless

mutilate cut, tear, break off, amputate, clip, lacerate

mutiny rebellion, revolt, riot, insurrection, uprising, insurgence MUTINEER, MUTINOUS

mutter mumble, complain, grumble, murmur, whisper

mutual reciprocal, joint, common

muzzle silence, restrain, gag, bind, bridle

myriad many, numerous, multitudinous, considerable (*Slang* — quite some, zillion)

mysterious secret, hidden, profound, mystical, recondite, occult MYSTERY

mystify bewilder, puzzle, perplex, baffle, confound (*Slang* — bamboozle, stick, stump, floor, get, beat, throw, lick)

myth legend, story, fiction, fantasy, fable, fairy tale, falsehood, fabrication truth MYTHICAL, MYTHOLOGY

N

nag 1. pester, annoy, bother, pick on (*Slang* — bug), 2. horse, pony

nail 1. fasten, hold, fix, secure, 2. catch, seize, hook, snare, trap, capture, apprehend (*Slang* — land, rope, collar, grab) release

naked uncovered, exposed, nude, bare, undressed (*Slang* — in the buff, in the altogether, in the raw) covered

name title, label, tag, appellation (*Slang* — moniker, handle)

nap sleep, doze, drowse, siesta (*Slang* — snooze)

narcotics drugs, opiates, tranquilizers, sedatives, barbiturates (*Slang* — dope, junk, pot, goofballs)

narrate tell, relate, recount, report, recite, review, describe NARRATIVE, NARRATOR

narrow slender, close, tight, restricted, cramped, confined, meager, limited wide

nasty unpleasant, revolting, disgusting, repulsive, offensive, foul, vile, sickening, nauseating, filthy, odious, obnoxious, dirty (*Slang* — icky, ugly)

nation country, land, society, community NATIONAL, NATIONALITY

native natural, original, indigenous foreign

natural genuine, typical, real, authentic, legitimate, honest, pure, original, true, characteristic, normal unnatural, false NATURE

naturally of course, plainly, certainly, surely, indeed (*Slang* — you bet, you bet your life, you bet your boots)

naught nothing, zero, nil

naughty bad, disobedient, misbehaving, disorderly, evil, wrong

navigate sail, steer, cruise, guide
NAVIGATION, NAVIGATOR

near close, imminent, at hand far

nearly almost, close to, just about, approximately

neat 1. clean, orderly, trim, tidy, shipshape, well-kept disorderly, sloppy, 2. skillful, clever, apt, adept, proficient, handy, expert, masterful, well-done (*Slang* — cute, crack, crackerjack)

necessary required, compulsory, urgent, important, imperative, obligatory, compelling, needed, essential, exigent unnecessary

need want, lack, require NEEDY

neglect overlook, disregard, ignore, pass over, slight, be inattentive, be careless, be thoughtless, be inconsiderate care

negligent careless, indifferent, neglectful, inattentive, remiss careful NEGLIGENCE

negotiate arrange, talk over, settle, mediate, intervene, umpire, arbitrate, referee (*Slang* — deal)

neighboring near, bordering, next to, adjoining, adjacent, surrounding NEIGHBOR, NEIGHBORHOOD

neighborly friendly, kind, amiable, congenial, cordial, warm, amicable unfriendly

nerve strength, courage, stamina, daring, bravado, mettle (*Slang* — spunk, cheek, backbone, guts, gall, crust)

nervous excited, upset, restless, disturbed, ruffled, shaken, flustered, agitated, perturbed, high-strung, tense, strained, edgy, jittery calm, composed

nestle snuggle, cuddle, hold closely

net 1. trap, snare, 2. lacelike cloth, mesh, web, 3. gain, earn, acquire, get, obtain, secure

nettle irritate, provoke, annoy, vex, anger, disturb

neutral impartial, detached, unprejudiced, cool, independent, indifferent involved

nevertheless however, notwithstanding, although, but, regardless, anyway

new fresh, modern, recent, original, young, unused, firsthand old

news tidings, information, word, story

next following, nearest, closest, succeeding, successive, subsequent

nibble chew, munch

nice pleasing, agreeable, satisfactory, enjoyable, desirable, gratifying, good, fine

niche nook, corner, cranny, recess, alcove

nick notch, cut, dash, indentation

niggardly stingy, cheap, miserly (*Slang* — tight, penny-pinching)

nimble light, quick, active, fast, swift, speedy, agile (*Slang* — quick on the trigger, snappy) slow

nip 1. pinch, bite, squeeze, 2. cold, chill, crispness, 3. small drink, sip (*Slang* — swig)

noble great, grand, majestic, distinguished, lofty, eminent, prominent, important, grandiose, magnificent, stately, dignified, aristocratic common NOBILITY

nocturnal nightly

nod bow, bob, tip, bend, signal

noise sounds, racket, clamor, din, clatter, uproar, tumult, bedlam, hubbub, commotion, ballyhoo, rumpus (*Slang —* ruckus) quiet NOISILY, NOISY

nomad wanderer, traveler, rover, roamer, vagrant, migrant

nomination naming, appointment, selection, choice, designation NOMINATE

nonchalant indifferent, unconcerned, cool, blasé, lackadaisical, easygoing, devil-may-care, casual

nonsense foolishness, ridiculousness, folly, absurdity, stupidity, rubbish, poppycock (*Slang —* bunk, hooey, baloney)

nook corner, niche, cranny, recess, alcove

noose rope, snare, lasso

normal usual, regular, average, standard, ordinary, typical, characteristic, true to form abnormal, unusual

notable striking, important, remarkable, noteworthy, memorable, special, extraordinary, exceptional, rare, famous, distinguished, renowned, celebrated, well-known, prominent, popular, notorious

notch nick, cut, gash, indentation

note 1. write, record, inscribe, list, mark down, jot down, indicate, mark, comment, 2. observe, heed, regard, notice

notice note, observe, heed, regard, see NOTICEABLE

notify announce to, inform, advise, report, tell, instruct, remind, warn (*Slang —* post, tip, tattle, squeal, snitch, blabber)

notion idea, understanding, opinion, view, belief, thought, impression, sentiment

notorious famous, renowned, celebrated, popular, well-known, infamous

nourish feed, nurture, nurse, strengthen, sustain, maintain NOURISHMENT

novel new, original, fresh, unique, firsthand, different, unusual NOVELTY

novice beginner, newcomer, tyro, greenhorn, freshman (*Slang* — rookie)

now 1. at once, immediately, right away later, 2. presently, today, at this time

noxious harmful, poisonous, damaging, detrimental, toxic harmless

nucleus middle, core, heart, kernel, hub, focus

nudge push, prod, shove, poke, jab, prompt

nugget lump, clump, mass, wad, hunk, chunk

nuisance annoyance, pest, bother, trouble, irritation (*Slang* — headache, pain in the neck)

numb dull, unfeeling, deadened, insensitive

number 1. quantity, sum, count, collection, amount, measure, bulk, portion, multitude, 2. numeral, figure, digit, symbol

numeral number, figure, digit, symbol

numerous many, multitudinous, several, abundant, various, myriad, considerable (*Slang* — zillion) few

nurse nurture, nourish, foster, feed, sustain, care for, tend to, mind

nurture rear, bring up, foster, train, care for, raise, feed, tend, mind, nurse, nourish

nutrition food, nourishment NUTRITIOUS

O

oaf lummox, clown, clod, lout, fool, dunce, blockhead (*Slang* — dope, jerk)

oath   promise, pledge, vow, agreement, commitment, bond

obey   yield, submit, comply, mind, heed, listen to
disobey, resist   OBEDIENCE, OBEDIENT

object   1. thing, article, 2. purpose, end, goal, target, intent,
aim

objection   protest, challenge, dissent, disapproval, complaint, criticism (*Slang* — kick, squawk, howl)   approval

obligate   require, oblige, bind, pledge, compel, force
OBLIGATION

obliging   helpful, considerate, thoughtful, accommodating,
well-meaning   discourteous

obliterate   destroy, erase, blot out, wipe out, demolish,
delete

oblivious   unconscious, senseless, preoccupied, forgetful
mindful, aware   OBLIVION

obnoxious   offensive, disagreeable, hateful, nasty, repulsive,
disgusting, loathsome, vile, terrible, dreadful, deplorable,
wretched, abominable, detestable, despicable, contemptible
(*Slang* — awful, atrocious, impossible)   pleasant

obscene   dirty, smutty, filthy, lewd, bawdy, pornographic,
unclean, indecent   decent, clean

obscure   indistinct, unclear, indefinite, faint, dim, vague,
dark, shadowy, blurred, fuzzy, hazy   clear   OBSCURITY

observe   1. see, note, examine, study, perceive, behold,
inspect, scrutinize, contemplate, review, 2. celebrate, commemorate, 3. keep, practice, obey, comply with, heed,
follow   neglect, ignore
OBSERVANCE, OBSERVANT, OBSERVATION

obsolete   extinct, passé, old-fashioned, dated, outmoded,
discontinued, antiquated (*Slang* — old hat, has-been)
recent, stylish

obstacle barrier, obstruction, block, stoppage, hindrance, deterrent, impediment, hitch, snag, catch

obstinate stubborn, willful, headstrong, bullheaded, pigheaded, unyielding, unbending, inflexible, adamant, firm, stiff, rigid flexible

obstruct block, hinder, clog, bar, impede, delay aid, help
OBSTRUCTION

obtain get, acquire, gain, secure, procure, earn, receive lose

obtuse 1. slow, stupid, dense, slow-witted bright, quick, 2. blunt, dull, unsharpened sharp

obvious plain, understandable, apparent, clear, evident, manifest, explicit, distinct hidden

occasionally sometimes, now and then, once in a while, from time to time OCCASION, OCCASIONAL

occupant tenant, resident, lodger, inhabitant, dweller, boarder OCCUPANCY

occupation 1. business, employment, trade, work, activity, affair, matter, concern, interest, capacity, role, function, duty, task, stint, job, 2. possession, holding, ownership
OCCUPY

occur happen, take place, transpire, come about
OCCURRENCE

odd 1. strange, peculiar, queer, unusual, curious, unique, eccentric, weird, bizarre (*Slang* — funny, screwy, nutty, wacky) usual, ordinary, 2. extra, left over, remaining, spare ODDITY, ODDLY

odious hateful, offensive, displeasing, revolting, repulsive, disgusting, vile, foul, obnoxious, horrible, terrible, dreadful, wretched (*Slang* — awful, beastly, impossible, atrocious) pleasant

odor smell, fragrance, scent, essence, aroma

offend displease, hurt, pain, grieve, wound, disgust, sicken, horrify, affront, insult please
OFFENDER, OFFENSE, OFFENSIVE

offer present, propose, suggest, submit, try, attempt
OFFERING

office 1. position, duty, task, job, work, function, capacity, role, post, 2. room, workplace, headquarters, studio, department (*Slang* — shop)

offset balance, cushion, compensate, counteract, soften, neutralize

offshoot addition, branch, byproduct, outgrowth, appendage, supplement, accessory

offspring child, descendant, young (*Slang* — kid)

often repeatedly, many times, frequently seldom

ogre monster, fiend, demon, devil

old 1. aged, ancient, antique, elderly, mature young, new, 2. former, obsolete, abandoned, discontinued, stale, outworn, discarded recent

omen sign, indication, warning, portent

ominous threatening, unfavorable, sinister, menacing

omit neglect, exclude, leave out, bar, miss, skip include
OMISSION

omnipotent almighty, all-powerful, divine

one-sided partial, unfair, prejudiced, biased
neutral, impartial

onlooker spectator, observer, watcher, bystander, witness

only just, merely, simply

onset 1. beginning, commencement, start, opening end, 2. attack, assault, offense, charge, drive, onslaught (*Slang* — push)

onslaught attack, assault, onset, offense, charge, drive, push

onward further, forward, ahead backward

ooze leak, seep, filter, drip, flow

opaque dark, dull, filmy, cloudy, obtuse, murky, obscure, vague, unclear, indistinct clear, transparent

open 1. begin, start, launch, initiate, unfold, establish, originate close, 2. expose, uncover, disclose, reveal, show, bare cover OPENING

openly frankly, sincerely, freely secretly

operate work, run, manage, conduct, carry on, handle, function, perform, act OPERATION, OPERATOR

opinion belief, judgment, estimate, impression, feeling, sentiment, attitude, view, theory, conception, thought, idea, outlook, conviction

opponent enemy, foe, adversary, competitor, rival, combatant, contender ally, friend

opportunity chance, occasion, time, opening, turn, spell

oppose fight, struggle, resist, hinder, contradict, conflict with, counteract, refute, dispute, cross agree OPPOSITE, OPPOSITION

oppressive harsh, severe, unjust, burdensome, overbearing, domineering, dictatorial, tyrannical OPPRESS, OPPRESSION, OPPRESSOR

optical visual, seeing

optimistic cheerful, happy, bright, pleasant, radiant, glad, lighthearted, jaunty, carefree pessimistic

optional voluntary, elective required OPTION

oral spoken, voiced, vocalized, sounded, articulated, verbal, uttered, said ORALLY

orb sphere, globe, ball

orbit path, circuit, circle, revolution, route

orchestra band, ensemble

ordain order, decide, decree, command, dictate, direct, instruct, bid, rule, authorize, sanction ORDINANCE

ordeal experience, test, trial, tribulation

order 1. arrangement, condition, state, manner, mode, way, disposition, formation, system, 2. command, bid, direction, instruction ORDERLY

ordinary 1. usual, common, normal, average, regular, everyday, standard unusual, special, 2. mediocre, inferior, poor, so-so outstanding, exceptional ORDINARILY

organize arrange, classify, systematize, categorize, sort, group, set up, establish, orient ORGANIZATION

origin 1. beginning, start, infancy, birth, inception, 2. source, parentage, derivation, root
ORIGINAL, ORIGINALITY, ORIGINALLY
ORIGINATE

ornament decoration, adornment, embellishment, garnish, trimming ORNAMENTAL, ORNATE

ornery unruly, disobedient, rebellious, contrary, obstinate, stubborn, willful, headstrong, firm, stiff, rigid, adamant, difficult, mean, malicious, disagreeable, cross, irritable, cranky pleasant

orthodox usual, customary, conventional, traditional, accepted, proper, correct unorthodox, different

ostentatious showy, flashy, pretentious, overdone, garish, fancy, swanky (*Slang* — classy, ritzy)

other different, distinct, additional, extra, supplementary, further, fresh, new

ought should, be obliged, must, need to, have to

outbreak revolt, riot, disturbance, uprising, rebellion, eruption, outburst, torrent

outburst eruption, outbreak, torrent, discharge, ejection

outcast homeless, friendless, abandoned, deserted, forlorn, forsaken, derelict, rejected, disowned

outcome result, consequence, effect, upshot, fruit, conclusion

outcry noise, clamor, uproar

outdated old, old-fashioned, outmoded, unfashionable
stylish

outdo surpass, excel, outshine, defeat, beat (*Slang* — lick, whip, trim) OUTDID, OUTDONE

outfit equip, furnish, prepare, rig, fit

outgrowth product, result, effect, consequence, outcome, fruit, upshot, byproduct

outing trip, journey, jaunt, excursion

outlandish odd, queer, peculiar, curious, strange, weird (*Slang* — funny)

outlaw outcast, exile, criminal, convict (*Slang* — crook, gangster)

outlay spending, expense, costs

outline 1. plan, sketch, diagram, chart, draft, pattern, drawing, 2. profile, contour, skeleton

outlook view, attitude, position

outlying remote, external, outer

outnumber exceed

output yield, production, proceeds, crop, harvest

outrageous shocking, insulting, absurd, nonsensical, ridiculous, foolish, crazy, preposterous, bizarre, excessive, extreme, exorbitant, disgraceful, shameful, scandalous, unwarranted   OUTRAGE

outright   altogether, entirely, completely, thoroughly, wholly, fully, totally, quite, freely, openly, downright

outset   start, beginning, commencement, opening

outspoken   frank, unreserved, unrestrained, open, vocal, candid, straightforward, direct, forthright   shy, reserved

outstanding   important, well-known, great, eminent, famous, prominent, distinguished, conspicuous, significant, noticeable, striking, bold   unimportant, insignificant

outwit   outmaneuver, outdo, outsmart

overbearing   masterful, domineering, dictatorial, autocratic, arbitrary, arrogant, bossy   humble

overcast   cloudy, dark, gloomy, dismal, somber, bleak, hazy, misty   clear, bright

overcome   conquer, defeat, upset, overpower, surmount (*Slang* — smear, clobber, shellac)

overdo   exaggerate, stretch, magnify, enlarge, carry too far, go to extremes

overflow   flood, run over, cascade, spill, inundate

overhaul   repair, service, mend, fix, condition

overhead   1. above, high, aloft, 2. costs, expenses

overjoyed   delighted, enchanted, ecstatic, elated, enraptured, jubilant   depressed

overlook   1. neglect, ignore, disregard, pass over, skip, let slip, miss   note, notice, 2. face, view, watch

overpass   bridge, span, viaduct

overpower   master, overwhelm, surmount, defeat, conquer, crush, vanquish (*Slang* — lick, smear, clobber, shellac)

overrun   exceed, spread, infest, beset, abound, flood

oversee   supervise, manage, direct, superintend, administer, preside, boss

oversight   error, slip, negligence, omission

overstep   exceed, go beyond, surpass, transcend, trespass

overthrow   defeat, destroy, overcome, overpower, overturn, upset, unseat, dethrone

overture   1. proposal, offer, bid, 2. prelude, introduction finale

overwhelm   1. crush, overcome, defeat, surmount, conquer, vanquish (*Slang* — lick, smear, clobber, shellac), 2. astonish, surprise, amaze, astound, bewilder, startle, dumbfound, flabbergast

owe   be indebted, be obliged, be liable

own   have, possess, hold, maintain, monopolize OWNER, OWNERSHIP

P

pace   1. rate, speed, 2. stride, gait, step, walk, tread

pacify   quiet, calm, tranquilize, soothe, appease, placate, mollify   anger, provoke   PACIFIC, PACIFICATION

pack   fill, load, stuff, cram, stow, box   unpack, empty PACKAGE

pact   agreement, contract, understanding, bargain, treaty, alliance

pad   1. cushion, pillow, wadding, 2. notebook, tablet, ledger, album

paddle   1. spank, whip, beat, lick, wallop, 2. oar

padlock   bolt, bar, lock

page 1. paper, sheet, leaf, 2. attendant, usher, errand boy, servant

pageant show, spectacle, pomp, display, entertainment, exhibition, presentation, parade, review

pail bucket

pain suffering, hurt, discomfort, distress, ache, pang, soreness, irritation PAINFUL

painstaking careful, particular, thorough, elaborate, diligent, exacting, meticulous, scrupulous, precise, accurate careless

paint 1. coat, color, cover, decorate, trim, garnish, 2. draw, sketch, picture, depict, draft, portray, represent PAINTING

pair set, two, couple, both, twins, mates, team, duo

pal friend, playmate, companion, fellow, comrade, associate, colleague, partner, crony (*Slang* — buddy, chum, sidekick)

palace castle, mansion, villa, chateau

palatable delicious, luscious, delectable, savory, tasty (*Slang* — scrumptious, yummy)

pale dim, colorless, faint, weak, vague, indistinct, lifeless, pallid, wan, sallow, whitish bright, vivid

palpitate tremble, quiver, beat, throb, pulsate, flutter

paltry trifling, petty, worthless, poor, miserable, cheap

pamper humor, favor, indulge, cater to, oblige, coddle, spoil

pamphlet booklet, brochure, leaflet, folder

panel 1. group, forum, board, 2. partition, wall, division, separation, barrier

pang pain, hurt, discomfort, distress, ache, soreness, irritation

panic fear, fright, scare, alarm, dread, awe, terror, phobia

panorama scene, vista, lookout, sight

pant breathe, puff, gasp, wheeze

pants trousers, breeches

par average, normal

parade procession, show, display, review, promenade, march, exhibition, pageant

paradise heaven, bliss, glory, ecstasy, elation, enchantment

paralyze deaden, numb, desensitize, disable, cripple

paramount most important, chief, foremost, principal, main, leading, dominant, primary, top, uppermost, maximum

parcel package, bundle, pack, lot

parched thirsty, dry, dehydrated

pardon forgive, excuse, absolve, exonerate, exculpate, acquit, vindicate

pare peel, trim, skin, strip, scrape

park 1. land, reservation, sanctuary, 2. settle, place, put, set, station

parry avoid, evade, dodge, hedge, ward off, sidestep (*Slang* — duck)

part 1. portion, segment, fraction, share, division, section, component, cut, 2. role

partake share, participate, contribute, join in (*Slang* — get into the act)

partial partly, fractional, fragmentary, limited

participate partake, contribute, take part in, have a hand in, enter into, join in   PARTICIPANT

particular 1. special, unusual, different   ordinary, 2. meticulous, critical, discriminating, fastidious, finicky, exacting, fussy

parting   departure, going away, leaving, exit, withdrawal
arriving

partition   separation, division, wall

partner   companion, mate, collaborator, assistant, participant, comrade, colleague (*Slang* — sidekick)
PARTNERSHIP

party   1. group, company, gang, crew, body, band, faction,
2. person, individual, fellow, 3. festival, fete, affair, ball,
celebration (*Slang* — blowout, jamboree, shindig)

pass   1. succeed, do well   fail, 2. spend, use, employ, 3.
deliver, hand over, transfer, 4. go, travel, move, progress
PASSING

passage   1. corridor, hallway, arcade, entranceway, opening,
lane, channel, artery, passageway, 2. section, paragraph,
chapter, excerpt, selection, extract, 3. voyage, cruise, cross-
ing, trip, trek

passageway   passage, corridor, hallway, arcade, entranceway, opening, lane, channel, artery

passion   1. emotion, strong feeling, fervor, craze, enthusiasm,
2. rage, anger, fury, violence, 3. love, affection, fondness,
ardor, lust, desire   PASSIONATE

passive   inactive, dormant, submissive, unresisting, compliant, yielding, docile, mild, gentle   forceful

past   ended, gone by, former, over, previous, preceding
future

paste   glue, adhesive, cement, mucilage

pastel   pale, soft, light, fair

pastime   recreation, amusement, enjoyment, diversion,
relaxation

pasture   grassland, meadow, range

pat   tap, stroke, rap

patch   mend, repair, fix, service

paternal   fatherly   maternal, motherly

path   route, track, way, trail, road, line

pathetic   pitiful, touching, moving, sad, distressing

patience   tolerance, endurance, indulgence, perseverance, persistence (*Slang* — stick-to-it-iveness)   impatience
PATIENT

patriotic   loyal, nationalistic, chauvinistic
PATRIOT, PATRIOTISM

patrol   watch, guard, protect, keep vigil, police

patronize   1. deal with, trade with, 2. back, sponsor, finance, promote, support   PATRON, PATRONAGE

patter   1. drum, beat, pound, throb, 2. chatter, chat, prattle, babble, jabber, blab

pattern   1. arrangement, design, illustration, picture, print, 2. model, example, standard, prototype, paragon

pauper   poor man

pause   wait, stop, rest, recess, cease (*Slang* — take time out, knock off)

pave   cover, floor   PAVEMENT

pavilion   building, structure, edifice

paw   handle, touch, feel

pawn   pledge, deposit (*Slang* — hock)

pay   give, remunerate, compensate   PAYMENT

peaceful   quiet, calm, still, tranquil, placid, untroubled, pacific, serene, cool   troubled   PEACE, PEACEABLE

peak   top, crest, hilltop, summit, pinnacle, crown, tip, apex, acme, zenith

peal   ring, chime, toll

peculiar   1. strange, odd, unusual, queer, curious   ordinary, 2. special, distinctive, characteristic, typical, representative
PECULIARITY

pedal   drive, push, roll

peddle   vend, sell, hawk   PEDDLER

pedestrian   walker, hiker (*Slang* — hoofer)

peek   glance, glimpse, peep, look slyly

peel   strip, pare, skin

peep   peek, glance, glimpse, look slyly

peer   1. equal, match, equivalent, like, 2. look, peek, peep

peevish   cross, complaining, fretful, petulant

pell-mell   headlong, tumultuous, hastily, hurriedly, quickly, swiftly, speedily

pelt   1. attack, strike, pound, beat, knock, hammer, rap, bang, whip, thrash, wallop, 2. skin, hide, fur

pen   1. write, inscribe, record, 2. enclose, confine, shut in, surround, coop up

penalize   punish, chastise, discipline, castigate   PENALTY

pending   waiting, until, during

penetrate   1. pierce, enter, puncture, bore, perforate, 2. understand, perceive, see through
PENETRATION

penitence   sorrow, repentance, penance

penmanship   handwriting, script, calligraphy

pennant   flag, banner, streamer, ensign, standard, colors

penniless   poor, destitute, down-and-out, bankrupt (*Slang* — broke, busted, flat, strapped)

pension   allowance, aid, assistance, help, subsidy, grant, stipend

pensive thoughtful, contemplative, reflective, meditative, deliberating, absorbed, engrossed, melancholy, serious, wistful

people persons, folks, community, society, public, human beings, men

pep spirit, energy, vim, vigor, verve, punch, dash, drive, animation, life, vivacity apathy

perceive sense, observe, feel, experience, detect, recognize, distinguish, make out PERCEPTION

percentage proportion, part, ratio, rate, quota (*Slang —* cut, divvy)

perch rest, sit, settle, straddle

perchance perhaps, possibly, maybe, conceivably

perennial continuous, constant, perpetual, steady, regular

perfect faultless, flawless, ideal, correct, accurate, right imperfect, faulty PERFECTION

perforate pierce, penetrate, puncture, enter, bore PERFORATION

perform do, act, execute, transact, carry out, accomplish, achieve PERFORMANCE, PERFORMER

perhaps possibly, maybe, conceivably

peril danger, harm, jeopardy, hazard, risk, endangerment PERILOUS

period interval, span, time

periodical magazine, journal, gazette

perish die, decease, succumb, disappear, vanish, decay PERISHABLE

permanent lasting, durable, enduring, long-lasting, unchanging, constant, stable, steady temporary PERMANENCE

permeate   penetrate, spread through, pervade, saturate, soak

permit   allow, consent, let, grant, admit   PERMISSION

pernicious   harmful, hurtful, damaging, injurious, detrimental, malignant, deadly, destructive, fatal, mortal harmless

perpendicular   upright, vertical

perpetrate   commit, effect, achieve (*Slang* — pull off)

perpetual   eternal, lasting, continuous, unceasing, permanent, infinite, endless, incessant, constant   short-lived, brief PERPETUATE

perplex   puzzle, bewilder, baffle, confound, mystify (*Slang* — bamboozle, stump, floor, get, beat, buffalo, throw) PERPLEXITY

persecute   harm, oppress, torment, harass, molest, torture, antagonize, badger

persevere   persist, endure, continue, carry on, keep on PERSEVERANCE

persist   last, stay, continue, endure, prevail, go on, persevere (*Slang* — stick with it)   PERSISTENCE, PERSISTENT

person   individual, soul, somebody, someone

personal   private, special, individual, specific, particular impersonal   PERSONALLY

personality   identity, individuality

perspire   sweat   PERSPIRATION

persuade   convince, convict, convert, win over, induce (*Slang* — sell)   dissuade   PERSUASION, PERSUASIVE

pert   bold, saucy, flippant, forward, impudent, impertinent, brazen, perky, flip, cocky, cheeky (*Slang* — smart-alecky, fresh, crusty, nervy, sassy)   courteous, polite

pertain   belong, relate, be appropriate, be connected, refer, apply, concern   PERTINENT

perturb   disturb, trouble, distress, bother, agitate, upset

peruse   examine, study, inspect, review, read carefully

pervade   fill, permeate, penetrate, overrun

perverse   1. stubborn, contrary, willful, difficult, obstinate, 2. wrong, incorrect, untrue, false, erroneous, 3. wicked, corrupt   PERVERSION

perverted   distorted, twisted, warped, contorted   normal

pessimistic   unhappy, cheerless, joyless, gloomy, cynical   optimistic, cheerful   PESSIMISM, PESSIMIST

pester   annoy, vex, trouble, torment, molest, bother, harass, badger, tease, nag (*Slang* — pick on, ride)   PEST

pestilence   plague, epidemic, disease

pet   stroke, pat, caress, fondle

petite   little, small, slight, tiny   big

petition   request, demand, requisition, appeal, plea

petrify   1. terrify, horrify, shock, appall, frighten, stun, 2. harden, solidify, become stone

petty   1. unimportant, small, trivial, puny, minor, inferior   important, 2. mean, base, low, wretched, miserable, despicable, contemptible

petulant   irritable, peevish, fretful, grouchy

phantom   illusion, fantasy, apparition, specter, ghost, spirit, vision, spook

pharmacist   druggist, chemist   PHARMACY

phase   stage, state, aspect

phenomenal   extraordinary, exceptional, remarkable, wonderful, marvelous, miraculous   PHENOMENON

philanthropic charitable, kindly, benevolent, bighearted, generous, giving, humanitarian selfish, stingy
PHILANTHROPIST, PHILANTHROPY

philosophical wise, reasonable, calm
PHILOSOPHER, PHILOSOPHY

photograph snap, film, take a picture (*Slang* — shoot, mug)
PHOTOGRAPHER, PHOTOGRAPHY

phrase clause, part, section, passage

physician doctor, medic

physique figure, form, shape, build, body, frame

pick choose, select, harvest, gather, cull

picket 1. strike, boycott, revolt, 2. bar, fence, wall, enclose

pickle preserve, marinate

pickpocket rob

picnic feast, outing, festivity

picture represent, illustrate, portray, depict, describe, characterize

piece part, bit, portion, division, segment, section, share (*Slang* — cut)

pier dock, wharf, breakwater

pierce penetrate, puncture, perforate, stab, bore

pigment coloring, shade, stain, dye

pile heap, stack, mound, collection, slew, batch

pilfer steal, thieve, take, filch, rob (*Slang* — lift, cop, pinch)

pilgrimage journey, trip, trek, expedition, crusade
PILGRIM

pillage plunder, rob, loot, burglarize (*Slang* — hold up, stick up)

pillar column, support, shaft, monument, post

pillow   cushion, headrest, bolster

pilot   operator, driver, engineer, conductor

pimple   swelling, bump, boil

pin   clasp, fasten, hook, clip

pinch   squeeze, press, tweak, nip

pinnacle   peak, high point, crest, top, spire, summit, crown, apex, acme, zenith   bottom, base

pioneer   settler, leader, colonist, forerunner

pious   religious, devout, reverent, faithful, believing   atheistic   PIETY

pipe   tube, reed, hose

pique   arouse, stir, incite, instigate, agitate, inflame, invoke, excite, foment, infuriate, exasperate, annoy, anger, disturb, aggravate, peeve, rile   soothe, calm

piracy   stealing, pillaging, plundering, looting, thievery   PIRATE

pistol   gun, firearm, revolver (*Slang* — shooting iron, gat, rod)

pit   hole, cavity, crater, hollow

pitch   1. throw, fling, hurl, toss, sling, cast, heave, 2. sway, fall, topple, flounder, stagger, rock, roll, reel, lurch

pitfall   trap, snare

pity   sympathy, sorrow, compassion, mercy   PITEOUS, PITIABLE, PITIFUL

pivot   turn, swivel, swing, rotate, wheel, gyrate

placard   poster, notice, sign, billboard

place   arrange, fix, compose, put, locate, situate, set, station

placid   calm, peaceful, quiet, still, tranquil, smooth, pacific, untroubled

plague 1. disease, epidemic, pestilence, 2. annoy, vex, bother, torment, molest, trouble, harass, badger, worry, pester, haunt soothe, comfort

plain 1. clear, understandable, simple, distinct, obvious, evident complex, involved, 2. homely, ordinary, unattractive pretty

plan propose, intend, design, mean, aim, think, devise, arrange, plot, scheme, maneuver, project

plane 1. flat, level, horizontal, even, smooth uneven, 2. airplane, aircraft

plank board, wood

plant establish, fix, root, settle, sow

plastic changeable, variable, mobile, fluid, flexible, pliant, supple rigid, fixed

platform 1. stage, rostrum, balcony, 2. policy, program, plan, course

plausible reasonable, logical, sound, sensible, believable unbelievable

playful frisky, sportive, gay, spirited, lively, animated, vivacious, frolicsome, impish, mischievous, devilish serious, solemn PLAY

plaza square

plea 1. request, appeal, petition, asking, 2. excuse, defense PLEAD

pleasant pleasing, enjoyable, likable, desirable, agreeable, gratifying, delightful, charming, appealing, enchanting, cheerful, genial, happy, satisfying unpleasant, displeasing PLEASURE

pleat fold, crease, tuck

pledge promise, vow, oath, assurance, guarantee, word

plentiful ample, enough, abundant, generous, sufficient, lavish scarce, insufficient PLENTY

pliable flexible, supple, plastic, elastic, yielding, limber, suggestible, compliant rigid PLIANT

plight predicament, pinch, complication, muddle, difficulty, dilemma (*Slang* — pickle, spot, jam, hole, hot water, mess, stew)

plod trudge, lumber (*Slang* — plug away, grind)

plot 1. plan, scheme, intrigue, conspire, contrive, maneuver, concoct, 2. outline, sketch, graph, map, chart, blueprint, diagram

plow cultivate, work, till, furrow

pluck pull, pick, jerk, tug, yank

plucky courageous, spirited, brave, bold, valiant, gallant, heroic, resolute, game, mettlesome, spunky, nervy fearful, timid

plug block, clog, stop, obstruct, stuff, jam, congest

plump fat, round, stuffed, stout, obese, fleshy, corpulent, pudgy, chubby, stocky, chunky, tubby thin

plunder rob, steal, loot, pillage, fleece

plunge dive, plummet, drop, fall, swoop down

plush luxurious, sumptuous, elegant, elaborate, grand, magnificent, glorious, impressive, majestic (*Slang* — swell) poor

pocket load, pack, stow, take in, accept, receive, take, get, acquire

poetry verse, rhyme, lyric, ode POEM, POET, POETIC

point direct, aim, show, indicate

poised composed, collected, balanced, confident, assured upset

poisonous toxic, deadly, destructive, noxious, harmful, malignant, venomous POISON

poke thrust, push, shove, ram, jab, goad, spur

pole bar, rod, shaft, post, beam, stick

police guard, watch, patrol, shield

policy plan, program, procedure, course, principles, line, platform

polish shine, burnish, gloss, rub, buff, glaze, wax, furbish

polite refined, courteous, civil, gracious, respectful, well-mannered, tactful rude

poll canvass, survey, vote, questionnaire

pollute contaminate, infect, taint, tarnish, defile, foul, poison POLLUTION

pomp spectacle, display, sight, exhibition, show, pageant, ostentation, magnificence modesty POMPOUS

ponder consider, contemplate, study, reflect, deliberate, meditate, think over, muse, brood

ponderous heavy, clumsy, bulky, massive, weighty, cumbersome, unwieldy light, airy

pool 1. lake, pond, puddle, reservoir, 2. contribute, combine

poor 1. needy, penniless, impoverished, destitute (*Slang* — broke, busted, strapped) rich, 2. pitiful, unfortunate, wretched, miserable fortunate POVERTY

pop shoot, burst, bang, fire, crack, explode, detonate

popular 1. common, usual, regular, customary, ordinary, everyday, prevalent, conventional, traditional unusual, 2. well-liked, dear, beloved, adored, admired, cherished, favorite, pet unpopular, disliked POPULARITY

population inhabitants, people

port   harbor, dock, wharf, pier

portable   movable, transferable, conveyable

portal   door, gate, entrance, threshold

portent   forewarning, omen, sign, premonition

portion   part, share, division, segment, section, fraction, fragment, piece (*Slang* — cut, divvy) whole

portly   1. stout, fat, obese, plump, pudgy, stocky, chubby, heavyset thin, 2. dignified, stately, imposing, grand, noble, majestic

portray   represent, picture, depict, illustrate, characterize, impersonate, describe   PORTRAIT, PORTRAYAL

pose   1. posture, position, bearing, carriage, 2. pretense

position   1. place, location, situation, spot, 2. job, duty, function, role, office, capacity, situation, post

positive   sure, definite, certain, absolute, convinced, assured

possess   own, have, hold, control, maintain, occupy
POSSESSION, POSSESSIVE, POSSESSOR

possible   likely, conceivable, imaginable, feasible, probable, credible, achievable, attainable, plausible impossible
POSSIBILITY, POSSIBLY

post   1. list, schedule, notify, inform, 2. position, situation, office, duty, job

postpone   delay, put off, defer, suspend, hold over, table, shelve, stall, procrastinate

posture   position, carriage, bearing

potent   powerful, strong, forceful, mighty weak, puny

potential   possible, promising, hidden, likely, conceivable

potion   drink, dose (*Slang* — swig)

pouch   sack, bag

pounce jump, swoop, leap, spring, hop, bound, hurdle, vault, plunge, dive

pound beat, strike, knock, hit, hammer, rap, bang, batter, drum

pour drain, flow out, spew, spill, stream

pout sulk, mope, fret, frown, scowl

powder sprinkle, dust, spatter

power strength, might, force, vigor, energy, potency, authority, right, control, influence, command, mastery, dominion POWERFUL

practically 1. usefully, profitably, advantageously, 2. almost, nearly, really, essentially, fundamentally, basically, about PRACTICAL

practice train, drill, exercise, prepare, condition, rehearse, repeat

praise compliment, commend, laud, approve of, extol, glorify, flatter (*Slang* — butter up, soft-soap)

prance stroll, saunter, strut, promenade, bounce, swagger, romp (*Slang* — sashay)

prank mischief, trick, caprice, whim, antic, caper (*Slang* — monkeyshine, shenanigan)

prattle babble, chatter, jabber, blab

pray appeal, plead, petition, beg, entreat, implore, beseech

preach lecture, sermonize, advise, urge, expound PREACHER

precarious dangerous, unsafe, uncertain, hazardous, critical, ticklish, touchy, delicate, unsure, unsound, shaky sure, safe

precaution forewarning, notification

precede lead, head, come first, forerun follow, succeed PRECEDENT, PRECEDING

precept   rule, saying, belief, axiom, principle, proposition

precinct   district, boundary, limit, community, vicinity, neighborhood

precious   valuable, expensive, costly, dear, loved, priceless, adored, cherished, admired, prized, special   cheap

precipice   bluff, cliff, slope, palisade   PRECIPITOUS

precipitation   1. rain, snow, moisture, 2. haste, speed, impetuousness, impulsiveness, rashness   PRECIPITATE

precise   exact, accurate, definite, careful, strict, positive, absolute, meticulous, detailed, explicit, clear-cut
PRECISION

preclude   bar, exclude, prevent, deter, shut out, prohibit, forbid   allow

precocious   advanced, forward, premature

predecessor   leader, forerunner

predicament   mess, complication, plight, embarrassment, pinch, dilemma (*Slang* — pickle, spot, squeeze, jam, hole, hot water, stew)   comfort

predict   foresee, foretell, prophesy, divine, forecast, portend
PREDICTION

predominant   chief, superior, main, principal, leading, foremost

preface   introduction, preamble, foreward, preliminary

prefer   choose, favor, rather, desire, fancy, pick, select
PREFERABLE, PREFERENCE

pregnant   productive, fertile, full

prejudiced   biased, opinionated, partial, influenced
impartial   PREJUDICE

preliminary   prior, preceding

premature   early, advanced, forward, too soon, hasty
late, delayed

premeditated planned, forethought, intended, plotted, calculated, meant, deliberate spontaneous, accidental

prepare ready, fix, arrange, provide, concoct, compose, equip, rig, plan PREPARATION, PREPARATORY

preposterous absurd, senseless, foolish, ridiculous, nonsensical, crazy, outrageous, unreasonable, silly

prescribe order, direct, assign, advise, recommend, suggest, advocate PRESCRIPTION

presence attendance, being, existence, occurrence, appearance PRESENT

present give, offer, tender, submit, extend, donate, bestow, award, grant, deliver, hand over (*Slang* — dish out, slip, shell out, fork over, kick in, come across with)
PRESENTATION

presently shortly, soon, directly, before long

preserve protect, keep, maintain, guard, defend, save, shelter, shield, screen, harbor, uphold, support, reserve, conserve, sustain, retain destroy, neglect
PRESERVATION, PRESERVER

preside direct, administer, officiate, govern
PRESIDENCY, PRESIDENT

press 1. push, force, squeeze, clasp, tighten, 2. urge, insist, coax, goad, prod, stress, 3. iron, smooth

pressing urgent, compelling, crucial, necessary, driving

pressure 1. weight, force, load, burden, 2. influence, power, effect, domination

prestige importance, greatness, distinction, prominence, significance, superiority, mastery, power, influence, authority

presume suppose, assume, surmise, guess, think, imagine, fancy, imply, infer PRESUMABLE, PRESUMPTION

presumptuous daring, bold, arrogant, insolent, brazen (*Slang* — nervy) modest, humble

pretend   make-believe, act, feign, bluff, sham, fake
PRETENSE

pretentious   showy, ostentatious, flashy, fancy, affected
modest

pretext   pretense, excuse, cover, sham

pretty   attractive, lovely, beautiful, handsome, good-looking
(*Slang* — cute)   ugly, homely

prevalent   widespread, common, fashionable, popular,
customary, current, standard, usual, well-known, general,
universal   uncommon
PREVAIL, PREVAILING, PREVALENCE

prevent   prohibit, forbid, deter, keep from, preclude, stop,
block, thwart, inhibit, hinder (*Slang* — foul up, louse up,
gum up)   allow, permit   PREVENTION, PREVENTIVE

previous   prior, earlier, former, one-time, preceding
following, succeeding   PREVIOUSLY

price   cost, value, amount, rate, charge, worth, expense
(*Slang* — tab, damage, score)

priceless   valuable, invaluable, precious, dear, expensive,
costly (*Slang* — stiff, steep)

prickly   sharp, stinging, tingly

pride   self-respect, self-esteem, dignity, vanity, egotism

prim   neat, proper, precise, prudish, overmodest, strait-laced,
puritanical, formal, stiff, stuffy   casual

primary   first, important, chief, main, principal, leading,
dominant, essential, basic, fundamental, foremost, paramount   secondary   PRIME

primitive   1. ancient, original, prehistoric, uncivilized, barbarous, native   modern, 2. simple, basic, fundamental,
elementary, beginning   advanced, sophisticated

principal   chief, main, important, leading, dominant, fore-

most, primary, head, prominent, essential   secondary
PRINCIPALLY

principle   rule, law, standard, belief, dogma, doctrine, truth, proposition, precept

print   1. stamp, impress, mark, etch, engrave, 2. publish, issue, put out, publicize

prior   earlier, before, previous, former   after, later
PRIORITY

prison   jail, penal institution, penitentiary, reformatory (*Slang* — clink, jug, cooler, stir, can)   PRISONER

privacy   secrecy, seclusion, intimacy, retreat, hideaway, sanctum, cloister, withdrawal, isolation, solitude
PRIVATE

privilege   advantage, license, favor, liberty, freedom, grant
PRIVILEGED

prize   1. reward, award, treasure, 2. value, appreciate, hold dear, cherish, adore, idolize, worship, respect, revere

probable   likely, liable, apt, presumable, promising, hopeful improbable   PROBABILITY, PROBABLY

probation   test, trial, try, check

probe   examine, investigate, search, explore

problem   issue, question, mystery, enigma, puzzle, perplexity, conundrum

procedure   process, course, measure, custom, practice, rule, policy, plan, method, way, manner, means

proceed   progress, advance, go forward, go ahead

proceeds   receipts, income, profits, earnings, returns

process   operation, procedure, course, step, act, way, manner, means, mode

proclaim   declare, announce, herald, publicize, voice, advertise   PROCLAMATION

procure   obtain, get, acquire, secure, purchase, buy

prod   poke, jab, goad, stir, thrust, ram, drive, butt

prodigal   wasteful, lavish, extravagant, spendthrift, squandering

prodigious   1. great, huge, vast, immense, stupendous, enormous, colossal, mammoth, gigantic (*Slang* — tremendous, terrific, whopping, whaling, whacking, rousing, roaring, thundering), 2. wonderful, marvelous, miraculous, extraordinary, remarkable, exceptional   ordinary

prodigy   marvel, wonder, miracle, phenomenon, rarity, curiosity, first-rater, genius

productive   fruitful, fertile, yielding, prolific, creative, inventive, gainful, profitable   sterile
PRODUCE, PRODUCT, PRODUCTION

profanity   swearing, cursing   PROFANE

profess   claim, allege, maintain, contend

professional   occupational, vocational   PROFESSION

proficient   skilled, expert, adept, apt, clever, masterful, ingenious, deft, effective, competent, crack
inefficient, clumsy

profit   gain, benefit, advantage, earnings, returns, receipts, proceeds   loss   PROFITABLE

profound   deep, great, extreme, intense, serious   shallow

profuse   lavish, extravagant, abundant, generous, liberal, free, unsparing, bountiful, bighearted, magnanimous, prodigal   scarce   PROFUSION

program   schedule, plan, list, prospectus, bill, calendar, agenda, roster, register, line-up

progress   advance, proceed, go ahead, move
PROGRESSIVE

prohibit forbid, bar, ban, disallow, veto, deny, prevent, deter, thwart, restrict, foil allow PROHIBITION

1. project plan, scheme, proposal, plot, design, intention, undertaking, enterprise, venture

2. project 1. protrude, stick out, bulge recede, 2. show, screen PROJECTION

prolific productive, rich, plentiful, fruitful, creative sterile

prolong extend, stretch, lengthen, elongate, drag out shorten

prominent well-known, important, outstanding, distinguished, great, eminent, famous, popular, celebrated unknown PROMINENCE

promiscuous indiscriminate, uncritical, loose, mixed, combined, scrambled, unorganized, haphazard, random selective

promising hopeful, encouraging, favorable, probable, likely hopeless PROMISE

promotion advancement, forwarding, improvement, lift, rise, betterment, progress PROMOTE

prompt 1. punctual, quick, instant, immediate, ready slow, late, 2. remind, hint, suggest, coach PROMPTLY

prone 1. inclined, liable, willing, ready unwilling, 2. flat, level, horizontal, prostrate, reclining, reposing vertical, standing

pronounce sound, utter, articulate, voice, enunciate, express PRONUNCIATION

pronounced distinct, marked, decided, plain, clear, obvious, evident, definite, clear-cut, visible, downright, absolute, conspicuous, noticeable, prominent, bold, striking, outstanding, flagrant, glaring unnoticeable, vague

prop support, bolster, hold up, brace

propagate produce, increase, breed, multiply, generate, procreate

propel drive, push, shove, move, impel, motivate, stimulate
PROPULSION, PROPELLER

proper correct, right, fitting, decent, respectful, accurate, perfect, faultless, tasteful improper, unsuitable
PROPERLY

property possession, holdings, belongings PROPRIETOR

prophesy predict, foretell, forecast, divine, foresee, soothsay
PROPHECY, PROPHET

proportion ratio, measure, amount, balance, portion, share, interest, part, percentage

proposal plan, scheme, suggestion, offer, intent, project, design, motion PROPOSE, PROPOSITION

prosecute 1. complete, carry out, fulfill, discharge, execute, transact, practice, exercise, pursue, follow, 2. bring suit, take action against PROSECUTION

prospective expected, anticipated, awaited, coming, promised, due, future, eventual PROSPECT

prosperous successful, thriving, fortunate, triumphant, comfortable, flourishing, well-off, wealthy, rich, opulent, affluent unsuccessful, poor PROSPER, PROSPERITY

prostrate 1. helpless, overcome, defenseless, powerless, fallen strong, proud, 2. prone, horizontal, flat, lying, reclining upright, vertical

protect defend, guard, shield, safeguard, shelter, screen, cover, ensure, harbor
PROTECTION, PROTECTIVE, PROTECTOR

protest object, squawk, dispute, challenge, dissent (*Slang* — kick) agree

protrude project, stick out, bulge recede
PROTRUSION

proud 1. boastful, dignified, elated, pleased, satisfied, gratified, delighted, 2. arrogant, haughty, vain, lofty, conceited, bragging (*Slang* — stuck-up, cocky, uppish)
humble, modest

prove show, verify, check, confirm, justify, certify, establish, substantiate, demonstrate, document PROOF

proverb maxim, adage, saying

provide supply, give, furnish PROVISION

province 1. division, department, part, field, sphere, domain, 2. region, area, zone, territory, district, quarter, place, neighborhood, kingdom, empire, principality

provoke anger, vex, excite, stir, irritate, annoy, incense, exasperate, pique, ruffle, enrage, infuriate, antagonize, irk, nettle, disturb, arouse, taunt, aggravate, peeve, rile
pacify, soothe PROVOCATION, PROVOCATIVE

prowess daring, courage, valor, gallantry, heroism, boldness, skill fear, cowardice

prowl sneak, slink, lurk, steal, creep, rove

proxy agent, substitute, deputy, alternate, replacement, representative, surrogate

prudent careful, sensible, discreet, cautious, guarded, judicious careless PRUDENCE

pry 1. meddle, mix, busybody, peek, peep, search, grope, snoop, 2. loosen, jimmy, wrench

public people, populace, society, persons, population, inhabitants

publish divulge, reveal, make known, circulate, broadcast, spread, advertise, print, issue

pucker wrinkle, fold, crumple

puffy swollen, inflated, bloated, distended, dilated
deflated PUFF

pull 1. tug, draw, heave, haul, tow, drag, yank, jerk, strain, stretch push, 2. attract, lure, influence

pulsate beat, throb, palpitate, drum, pound

pulverize crumble, granulate, powder, crush, mash, smash, grind, grate

pummel beat, punch, thrash, flog, strike, pound, hammer, rap, bang, batter, wallop

punch pummel, beat, thrash, flog, strike, pound, hammer, rap, bang, batter, wallop

punctual prompt, quick, immediate, speedy, exact, precise late

puncture pierce, perforate, penetrate, stab, bore, impale

pungent sharp, biting, bitter, acid, stinging, tangy, spicy tasteless, bland

punish discipline, chastise, correct, castigate, penalize
PUNISHMENT

puny 1. weak, meager, slight, little, small, frail, delicate, fragile strong, sturdy, 2. petty, unimportant, trivial important

pupil student, scholar, schoolchild

purchase buy, shop

purify cleanse, clarify, clean, clear, refine, filter soil, pollute
PURE, PURITY

purpose plan, aim, intention, design, object, goal, target, resolution, determination, will
PURPOSEFUL, PURPOSELY

pursue chase, follow, seek, go after, shadow, trail, heel, hunt, quest (*Slang* — tail, tag along, string along)
PURSUIT

push 1. press, thrust, shove, force, drive, propel, nudge pull, 2. urge, encourage, prod, coax, spur, goad discourage

put place, lay, set, arrange, deposit remove

putrid rotten, foul, bad, decayed, spoiled, stinking, smelly, rancid, reeking, awful, atrocious (*Slang* — lousy, punk) clean, pure

puzzle perplexity, quandary, dilemma, confusion, bewilderment, mystery, enigma, problem, conundrum

pygmy dwarf, midget

Q

quack imposter, pretender, charlatan, fake

quaff drink, sip, imbibe, guzzle

quaint odd, curious, old-fashioned

quake shake, tremble, vibrate, quiver, shiver, shudder

qualified competent, fit, capable, efficient, able, suited, eligible unfit, unsuitable QUALIFICATION, QUALIFY

quality nature, kind, characteristic, constitution, trait, feature, mark, type, property

qualm uneasiness, doubt, skepticism, misgiving, question, suspicion, apprehension, anxiety

quandary dilemma, perplexity, predicament, confusion, puzzle, uncertainty (*Slang* — pickle)

quantity amount, number, sum, measure, portion, volume, mass, multitude

quarantine separate, segregate, isolate, confine, seclude

quarrelsome argumentative, cranky, cross, irritable, peevish, belligerent, grouchy (*Slang* — scrappy) peaceful QUARREL

quaver shake, tremble, vibrate, quiver, shiver, quake

queer 1. odd, strange, peculiar, curious, eccentric, weird (*Slang* — funny, screwy, nutty, wacky) normal, 2. homosexual, deviant

quell calm, subdue, quiet, pacify, appease, cool, hush, mollify, lull, smother, crush, reduce, suppress, extinguish, stifle incite

quench stop, extinguish, put out, stifle, suppress, quell, squelch

query question, ask, inquire, demand, interrogate, quiz answer

quest search, hunt, pursue, seek, explore

question inquire, ask, query, demand, interrogate, quiz answer

questionable doubtful, uncertain, dubious, improbable, unlikely, implausible certain, sure

quick 1. fast, swift, hasty, brisk, lively, speedy, rapid, fleet, expeditious (*Slang* — snappy), 2. alert, attentive, smart, bright, keen, sharp
slow QUICKLY

quiet still, silent, hushed, peaceful, serene, tranquil, calm noisy

quip joke, witticism, pleasantry, jibe (*Slang* — wisecrack)

quit stop, leave, cease, discontinue, end, halt, desist, refrain, depart, withdraw, retreat, abandon, resign, vacate (*Slang* — skip, cut, lay off) continue, remain

quite completely, absolutely, entirely, really, truly, rather, very, exceedingly (*Slang* — real, jolly, mighty)

quiver shake, shiver, tremble, vibrate, quake, quaver, shudder

quiz test, examine, interrogate, question, query

quota ratio, share, proportion, percentage, allotment

quote cite, illustrate, refer to, repeat, echo QUOTATION

R

race 1. run, speed, rush, tear, dash, dart, hurry, hasten, scoot, scamper, scurry, sprint, bound, bolt, quicken, accelerate, chase (*Slang* — hotfoot, skedaddle), 2. people, folk, clan, tribe, nation, breed, culture, lineage

rack 1. hurt, torture, pain, torment, agonize, punish, harass, distress, strain soothe, comfort, 2. framework, shelf

racket 1. noise, din, commotion, tumult, uproar, disturbance, hubbub, fracas, ado, fuss, rumpus, stir, row (*Slang* — to-do, ruckus) peace, quiet, 2. fraud, swindle, dishonesty (*Slang* — gyp)

radiant shining, bright, beaming, luminous, gleaming, glowing, lustrous dull, dim RADIANCE, RADIATE

radical extreme, greatest, utmost moderate

radio broadcast, transmit

rage 1. anger, passion, violence, storm, frenzy, furor, fit, delirium, mania, craze, excitement calm, serenity, 2. fad, fashion, style

ragged torn, worn, shabby, shoddy, tattered, frayed, frazzled, seedy neat RAG

raid attack, invade, assault, plunder, pillage, loot, seize

rain precipitate, shower, pour, sprinkle, drizzle

raise 1. lift, increase, elevate, hoist, boost lower, 2. produce, rear, build, create, construct destroy

rally 1. assemble, meet, gather, congregate, collect, throng, crowd, cluster, convene disperse, 2. improve, recover, recuperate, mend, revive

ram strike, push, thrust, shove, press, bear, drive, prod, goad

ramble wander, roam, rove, gad, drift, stray, meander

rampage racket, commotion, hubbub, tumult, uproar, disturbance, fracas, ado, fuss, rumpus, stir, row (*Slang* — to-do, ruckus) peace, quiet

ranch farm, range, plantation, homestead

random haphazard, aimless, irregular, unorganized planned

range limit, extent, distance, reach, length, scope

rank 1. grade, class, position, rate, value, evaluate, gauge, appraise, classify, arrange, group, categorize, 2. offensive, repulsive, disgusting, revolting, foul, vile, odious, repugnant, obnoxious, sickening, nasty, putrid, rotten fresh, wholesome

rankle pain, distress, inflame, irritate, fester, ache, hurt

ransack search, rummage, forage, pillage, plunder, loot, raid, rifle

ransom redeem, reclaim, recover, retrieve, regain

rap knock, tap, hammer, bang

rapid quick, swift, fast, speedy, fleet, hasty, expeditious (*Slang* — snappy) slow

rapture joy, delight, ecstasy, bliss, elation, enchantment, glee, happiness distress, sorrow RAPT

rare scarce, sparse, uncommon, infrequent, peculiar, unusual common, ordinary RARELY, RARITY

rascal rogue, scoundrel, devil, scamp, trickster

rash 1. hasty, careless, reckless, impetuous, impulsive, sudden, imprudent, brash careful, cautious, 2. inflammation, breaking-out

rate grade, classify, position, rank, value, evaluate, appraise, group, categorize, estimate, measure

ratify confirm, approve, validate, certify, support, uphold, authenticate, substantiate, endorse, accept, pass, O.K. veto, refuse RATIFICATION

ratio proportion, comparison, percentage

ration allowance, portion, share, quota, allotment, budget, measure, supply, amount

rational sensible, reasonable, thinking, logical, sound, level-headed irrational, foolish RATIONALIZE

rattle 1. clatter, patter, 2. confuse, disturb, upset, fluster, ruffle, unsettle calm

raucous harsh, hoarse, husky, gruff, coarse melodious, sweet

ravage damage, destroy, devastate, ruin, wreck restore, build

ravenous 1. hungry, starved, famished, empty, 2. greedy, grasping, piggish, hoggish, vulturous, gluttonous satisfied

ravishing enchanting, delightful, lovely, appealing, charming, beautiful, stunning, dazzling, gorgeous, alluring, enticing, fascinating unattractive, plain RAVISH

raw 1. immature, inexperienced, green, undeveloped, callow, crude developed, experienced, 2. cold, wind-swept, nippy, wintry, freezing, piercing, bitter warm, mild, 3. uncooked cooked

ray light, gleam, beam, stream

raze destroy, tear down, level, flatten, demolish build, construct

reach 1. arrive at, come to, approach, land, 2. extend, stretch

react respond, answer REACTION

ready prepared, set, fit unprepared

real actual, true, genuine, authentic, substantial, certain, legitimate, bona fide, sincere, honest, pure untrue, fake REALITY, REALLY

realize understand, grasp, conceive, comprehend, follow, appreciate (*Slang* — catch on, get) REALIZATION

realm   region, range, extent, sphere, field, province, domain

reap   gather, acquire, gain, obtain, get, earn, glean

rear   1. back, hind, posterior front, 2. raise, produce, create, nurse, foster, train

reason   cause, motive, explanation, logic, sense, ground, justification, basis

reasonable   sensible, fair, logical, just, sound, sane, rational, practical, realistic, justifiable   unreasonable

rebel   revolt, rise up, defy, riot, mutiny, disobey, disregard   obey   REBELLION, REBELLIOUS

rebuff   reject, renounce, deny, repudiate, disown, disclaim, spurn, scorn, disdain, snub   accept, welcome

rebuke   scold, disapprove, reprove, reprimand, lecture, correct, chide, berate (*Slang* — tell off, give it to, dress down, bawl out, chew out, give what-for)   praise, approve

recall   1. remember, recollect, review, reminisce   forget, 2. summon, call back

recede   retreat, withdraw, regress   advance

receive   take in, get, gain, admit, accept, obtain, secure   give

recent   new, late, modern, up-to-date   RECENTLY

reception   party, entertainment, social, festivity

recess   1. pause, hesitate, rest, adjourn, 2. indent, notch, set back

recipe   formula, instructions, directions, prescription

recite   narrate, tell, relate, recount, rehearse, review, repeat   RECITAL, RECITATION

reckless   rash, careless, heedless, thoughtless, inconsiderate, hasty, unmindful, impetuous   cautious, careful

reckon   1. think, consider, judge, suppose, hold, regard, deem, imagine, fancy, believe, 2. count, calculate, compute, estimate, figure, evaluate, appraise

recline   lie down, repose, lounge, rest

recluse   hermit, shut-in, isolationist

recognize   1. acknowledge, see, behold, know, 2. realize, appreciate, understand, admit, allow, accept
RECOGNITION

recollect   remember, recall, reminisce, review, reflect
RECOLLECTION

recommend   advise, suggest, advocate, instruct, guide, direct, urge   RECOMMENDATION

recompense   pay, reward, compensate

reconcile   settle, harmonize, bring together, mend, fix up
RECONCILIATION

record   write, inscribe, register, enroll, list, mark down, note, post, enter, log, tabulate, chronicle

recount   recite, narrate, tell, relate, review

recover   1. regain, retrieve, get back, reclaim, rescue   lose, 2. recuperate, get better, rally, revive, heal, improve, come around, make a comeback, get back in shape   RECOVERY

recreation   play, amusement, entertainment, pleasure, enjoyment, diversion, relaxation, pastime, fun, sport
work, toil

recruit   enlist, draft, sign up, enroll, muster

rectify   adjust, remedy, fix, regulate, set right, amend, correct

recur   repeat, return, come again

redeem   fulfill, pay off, deliver, make good, recover, rescue
REDEMPTION

redress   repair, remedy, rectify, correct, right, mend, fix, relieve

reduce   lessen, lower, decrease, diminish, cut, moderate
increase   REDUCTION

reek   smell, stink

reel   1. sway, rock, swing, lurch, roll, wobble, stagger, pitch, flounder, 2. spool, roller

refer   direct, point, recommend, send, allude
REFERENCE

referee   judge, moderator, umpire, arbitrator, mediator

refine   perfect, develop, improve, purify, cultivate, polish

reflect   1. mirror, send back, 2. think, ponder, study, deliberate, consider, contemplate, meditate, muse, mull over
REFLECTION, REFLECTOR

reform   change, improve, convert, revise

refrain   avoid, abstain, forego, shun   indulge

refrigerate   cool, chill   REFRIGERATOR

refuge   shelter, protection, asylum, retreat, haven, port, harbor, sanctuary

refund   repay, reimburse, pay back

1. refuse   decline, reject, say no, rebuff (*Slang* — turn down, not buy)   accept, allow

2. refuse   waste, garbage, rubbish, rubble, trash, litter, junk

refute   argue, dispute, contradict   agree

regal   1. royal, majestic, sovereign, imperial, 2. dignified, stately, splendid, magnificent, imposing

regard   consider, think of, judge

regardless   notwithstanding, despite

region   place, space, area, location, district, zone, territory, section, vicinity

register   record, inscribe, write, enroll, list, post, enter, log, indicate   REGISTRATION

regret   bemoan, bewail, be sorry for, rue

regular 1. usual, customary, steady, habitual, everyday, common, typical, normal, routine, 2. uniform, even, orderly, balanced, symmetrical irregular

regulate 1. manage, govern, handle, direct, rule, control, organize, run, command, 2. adjust, remedy, rectify, correct REGULATION

rehearse practice, repeat, train, drill, exercise, prepare REHEARSAL

reign rule, prevail

reinforce strengthen, fortify, brace, intensify weaken REINFORCEMENT

reiterate repeat, recount, retell, review

reject exclude, bar, eliminate, expel, discard, throw away, dispose of, cast off, refuse, decline (*Slang* — turn down) accept REJECTION

rejoice cheer, gladden, encourage, hearten, inspire, celebrate, glory, delight grieve

relapse return, revert, regress, reverse, slip back advance

relate tell, report, state, declare, recite, narrate, recount

related associated, connected, affiliated, allied, akin RELATIONSHIP, RELATIVE

relax rest, ease up, loosen (*Slang* — knock off, take five) RELAXATION

relay carry, deliver, pass, transfer, hand on, impart

release free, let go, relieve, dismiss, discharge, expel, fire, sack, can, bump, retire, relinquish, liberate hold

relent yield, bend, give, relax, submit, give in

relentless harsh, without pity, merciless, unsympathetic, ruthless, heartless, cruel, strict, firm, rigid, inflexible, unyielding, uncompromising, persevering, persistent, steadfast, hard lenient, sympathetic

relevant   pertinent, applicable, apropos, suitable, connected, fitting   unconnected, irrelevant

reliable   trustworthy, dependable, faithful, steadfast, loyal, true, devoted, safe, sure, stable   undependable, unreliable RELIANCE

relic   memento, remembrance, token, souvenir, trophy, keepsake

relief   1. freedom, ease, alleviation, release, help, assistance, aid, 2. change, substitution, replacement, alternate, proxy (*Slang* — pinch hitter)   RELIEVE

religious   pious, devout, reverent, faithful   RELIGION

relinquish   give up, surrender, yield, waive, forego, abandon, release, sacrifice   hold, keep

relish   enjoy, like, appreciate, savor   dislike

reluctant   unwilling, grudging, disinclined, loath   willing

rely   depend on, trust, confide, count on   RELIABLE

remain   continue, endure, persist, stay, last, keep on leave, depart   REMAINDER

remark   comment, speak, state, say, observe, note, mention

remarkable   unusual, noteworthy, extraordinary, exceptional, wonderful, marvelous, great, striking, notable, special, rare   ordinary

remedy   cure, correct, fix, rectify, heal, treat, doctor

remember   remind, recall, recollect, recognize   forget

remind   prompt, suggest to   REMINDER

remnant   leftover, remains, residue, balance

remorse   regret, sorrow, grief

remote   far, distant, removed, secluded, isolated, hidden near, close

remove take away, withdraw, extract, eject, expel, oust, deduct, subtract, eliminate, dispose of, doff, discard (*Slang* — bounce) keep REMOVAL

render 1. cause, make, do, effect, 2. give, present, grant, allow, allot

rendezvous meeting, appointment, session, get-together

renounce give up, relinquish, surrender, yield, waive, abandon, release, reject, deny, disclaim, discard, spurn, scorn keep

renovate recondition, redo, remake

renowned famous, celebrated, popular, distinguished, notable, notorious, well-known

rent hire, lease, charter, let RENTAL

repair mend, fix, service, overhaul, patch up, restore break, destroy

repast meal, food, refreshment

repeal withdraw, abolish, take back, revoke, recall, cancel, annul, invalidate, rescind, overrule

repeat say again, recite, reiterate, duplicate, echo (*Slang* — come again) REPETITION

repel 1. drive back, rebuff, hold off, 2. repulse, offend, revolt, disgust, nauseate, sicken please

repent regret, be sorry REPENTANCE, REPENTANT

replenish fill again, provide, supply, furnish

replica copy, reproduction, duplicate, double

reply answer, respond, retort, acknowledge, react

report describe, tell, repeat, relate, narrate REPORTER

repose rest, sleep, recline, lounge (*Slang* — take it easy)

represent 1. portray, depict, illustrate, stand for, symbolize,

characterize, express, describe, 2. exhibit, show, demonstrate, display, manifest, present, reveal, disclose
REPRESENTATION, REPRESENTATIVE

repress   keep down, restrain, suppress, quell, crush, squash, smother, stifle, hush up, censor, muffle, squelch (*Slang* — sit on, put the lid on)   REPRESSION

reproach   blame, accuse, denounce, condemn (*Slang* — knock, pan, slam, rap)   absolve

reprove   scold, blame, lecture, reprimand, chide, rebuke (*Slang* — dress down, tell off, jump on, bawl out, chew out, give what-for)   REPROOF

repudiate   reject, renounce, deny, disclaim, disown, discard, spurn, scorn, disdain, exclude

repulsive   ugly, repelling, horrible, hideous, horrid, frightful, disgusting, dreadful, terrible, repugnant, offensive, ghastly, revolting, gruesome (*Slang* — awful)   pleasing
REPULSE

reputable   honorable, respectable, well-thought-of, upstanding, upright, principled, moral, honest   dishonest
REPUTATION, REPUTE

request   ask, requisition, apply for

require   1. need, necessitate, lack, want, 2. demand, order, command, oblige   REQUIREMENT, REQUISITION

rescue   save, free, recover, redeem, salvage, retrieve, release, liberate, extricate

research   investigate, inquire, hunt, explore, look into, search, dig, delve

resemblance   likeness, similarity, sameness   RESEMBLE

resentment   displeasure, irritation, annoyance, vexation, bitterness, wrath, anger, indignation
RESENT, RESENTFUL

reserve   keep, hold, save, store, preserve, put aside
RESERVATION

reside   live, dwell, inhabit, occupy
RESIDENCE, RESIDENT, RESIDENTIAL

residue   remains, leftovers, rest, dregs, sediment, balance

resign   give up, relinquish, surrender, yield, waive, forego,
renounce, abandon, retire, quit, vacate, abdicate
RESIGNATION

resist   oppose, withstand, counteract   comply, yield
RESISTANCE, RESISTANT

resolute   firm, bold, resolved, decided, persevering, obstinate, willful, unyielding, unbending, adamant, game, spirited (*Slang* — nervy, spunky)   wavering   RESOLUTION

resolve   determine, decide, settle

resourceful   skillful, clever, deft, adept, ingenious, smart,
cunning   RESOURCE

respect   admire, regard, esteem, appreciate, value, revere,
honor, idolize, adore   RESPECTABLE, RESPECTFUL

respective   particular, individual, special, specific, personal
RESPECTIVELY

respiration   breathing, inhalation, exhalation
RESPIRATORY

respite   rest, relief, lull, pause, recess, break, interruption,
intermission, breather, reprieve

resplendent   bright, shining, splendid, brilliant, vivid, dazzling, glorious, flamboyant, gorgeous (*Slang* — devastating,
stunning)

respond   answer, reply, retort, acknowledge, react
RESPONSE, RESPONSIVE

responsible   1. accountable, answerable, liable   exempt, 2.
trustworthy, reliable, dependable, faithful, loyal
irresponsible, undependable   RESPONSIBILITY

rest   1. repose, pause, recess, recline, lounge (*Slang* — take it easy), 2. remains, residue, leftovers, balance

restless   uneasy, disturbed, troubled, agitated, excited, disquieted, fidgety, impatient, anxious   calm, composed

restore   put back, replace, reinstate, repair, mend, fix, overhaul, renew, renovate   RESTORATION

restrain   hold back, keep down, control, check, arrest, inhibit, curb, suppress, smother, stifle, retard, impede, limit, confine, restrict (*Slang* — squelch)   RESTRAINT

restrict   confine, limit, restrain, bound, cramp, hamper, impede   free, liberate   RESTRICTION

result   consequence, end, effect, outcome, upshot, fruit, product, conclusion

resume   continue, return to, go on with   RESUMPTION

retain   keep, hold, maintain, preserve, save   relinquish

retaliate   reciprocate, retort, strike back, revenge, avenge (*Slang* — get back at)

retard   delay, hinder, detain, keep back, impede, inhibit, curb, check, arrest (*Slang* — hold up)   accelerate

retire   1. resign, quit, vacate, relinquish, abdicate, 2. withdraw, discharge, dismiss, expel, remove, suspend, 3. retreat, recede, 4. go to bed (*Slang* — turn in, hit the hay)   RETIREMENT

retiring   shy, modest, reserved, timid, bashful, restrained, distant   outgoing, aggressive

retort   reply, answer, respond, retaliate

retract   withdraw, repeal, revoke, rescind, recall, cancel, annul, invalidate

retreat   withdraw, fall back, retire, reverse   advance

retrieve   recover, regain, recoup, get back, reclaim, repossess, retake, salvage, rescue, redeem, save

return 1. go back, come back, revert, revisit, 2. give back, repay, reimburse

reunion gathering, assembly, meeting, get-together, social, reception REUNITE

reveal show, display, open, disclose, expose, manifest, exhibit, demonstrate, present, bare, divulge hide, conceal REVELATION

revenge retaliate, get even with

revenue income, earnings, receipts, profits, returns, proceeds

reverberate echo, resound, reflect

revere love, respect, honor, admire, value, idolize, adore, esteem, cherish, worship, prize despise, scorn REVERENCE, REVERENT

reverse revert, regress, return, back up advance

revert regress, change back, reverse, return

review 1. study, remember, recall, learn, 2. examine, inspect, survey, observe, look at, consider, criticize, size up

revise correct, change, improve, alter, rewrite, amend

revive restore, refresh, bring back, renew, regenerate, resurrect, resuscitate REVIVAL

revoke repeal, cancel, withdraw, rescind, retract, recall, abolish, annul, invalidate, overrule

revolt 1. rebel, mutiny, rise up, riot, revolutionize, 2. offend, repel, sicken, nauseate, disgust, horrify, appall please, delight

revolution 1. change, revolt, overthrow, rebellion, riot, uprising, 2. circle, circuit, cycle, orbit, turning

revolve turn, go around, circle

reward compensate, pay, remunerate, award

rhythm   beat, swing, tempo, meter

rich   1. abounding, fertile, productive, prolific   sterile,   2.
wealthy, affluent, well-to-do, prosperous, opulent, comfortable   poor,   3. valuable, costly, elegant, priceless, expensive
cheap,   4. flavorful   tasteless

rickety   weak, shaky, unsteady   steady

rid   clear, free, do away with

riddle   puzzle, enigma, conundrum

ridicule   mock, deride, laugh at, scoff, jeer, taunt, sneer at
(*Slang* — ride, pan, razz)

ridiculous   nonsensical, foolish, crazy, preposterous, outrageous, bizarre, unbelievable, ludicrous
sensible, believable

rifle   rob, ransack, steal, plunder, loot, pillage

rift   1. split, break, crack, cleft, fracture, fissure, gap, crevice,
2. falling-out, estrangement, difference, parting, breach,
alienation, separation

rig   fit, equip, outfit, furnish, prepare

right   1. good, just, lawful, fitting, suitable, proper, valid,
sound, 2. correct, true, exact, accurate, perfect, faultless
wrong

righteous   virtuous, just, proper, good, moral, pure, worthy
immoral, corrupt

rigid   1. stiff, firm, unbending, unchanging, hard, 2. stubborn, unyielding, adamant, strict, taut, tense
flexible

rigorous   harsh, strict, severe, rigid, relentless, hard
lenient, flimsy   RIGOR

rim   edge, border, margin, fringe

ring   1. sound, peal, toll, chime, tinkle, jingle, clamor, 2.
circle, band

riot   revolt, rebel, rise up, mutiny, brawl   RIOTOUS

rip   tear, break, cut

ripe   developed, ready, mature, full-grown   unripe, green

rise   1. get up, stand   go down, 2. go up, advance, ascend, mount   descend, 3. increase, grow, gain   decrease, 4. originate, begin, start, appear   end, 4. revolt, rebel, riot, mutiny

risk   chance, hazard, gamble, venture, endanger, imperil, jeopardize, expose   RISKY

ritual   ceremony, formality, service, exercise, rite

rival   match, compete with, vie with   RIVALRY

road   path, track, trail, thoroughfare, lane

roam   wander, rove, gad, drift, stray, meander, ramble

roar   thunder, boom, clamor

rob   steal, burglarize, loot, sack, pillage, plunder, thieve, pilfer, filch (*Slang* — hold up, lift, swipe, cop, pinch, stick up)   ROBBERY

robust   strong, sturdy, healthy, mighty, powerful, potent, stalwart, rugged, hardy, vigorous, husky, heavy   weak

rock   1. sway, swing, reel, lurch, roll, bob, flounder, tumble, pitch, toss, 2. stone

rogue   rascal, scamp, scoundrel, mischief-maker, imp, elf, pixie, villain   ROGUISH

role   capacity, character, part, position, function

roll   turn, move, rotate, pivot, swivel, gyrate, wheel

romp   play, frolic, caper, carry on (*Slang* — cut up, horse around)

room   1. space, scope, margin, latitude, leeway, 2. chamber

root   cause, source, origin, derivation

rosy   bright, cheerful, sunny, optimistic, favorable, encouraging

rot   decay, spoil, disintegrate, go bad, crumble   ROTTEN

rotate   spin, turn, gyrate, swivel, pivot   ROTATION

rough   1. coarse, unsmooth, bumpy, choppy, shaggy, broken, uneven, irregular   smooth, 2. harsh, rowdy, severe, fierce, difficult, gruff, brusque, rude, crude, curt, surly, blunt, tough, snippy   gentle

round   circular, globular, rotund, spherical

rouse   stir, excite, arouse, awaken, move, provoke, pique, kindle, inflame, foment, stimulate, agitate, disturb, shake

rout   defeat, conquer, crush, overcome, beat, scatter (*Slang* — lick)

route   course, circuit, path, rounds, itinerary

routine   habit, method, system, arrangement, order

rove   wander, roam, gad, drift, stray, meander, ramble, tramp

1. row   1. line, file, string, train, series, sequence, succession, column, 2. paddle

2. row   quarrel, noise, fracas, brawl, dispute, squabble, rumpus (*Slang* — ruckus, run-in, scrap, rumble, hassle)

rowdy   rough, disorderly, naughty, bad, misbehaving, boisterous, rambunctious   well-mannered

royal   majestic, noble, dignified, stately, grand, regal, imperial, aristocratic   ROYALTY

rub   massage, scrub, scour, buff, stroke

rubbish   1. waste, trash, garbage, refuse, scrap, debris, litter, junk, 2. nonsense, silliness, absurdity, poppycock (*Slang* — baloney, hogwash, malarkey, bunk, hooey)

rude impolite, rough, coarse, discourteous, uncivil, disrespectful, insolent, ill-mannered, ill-behaved, vulgar, boorish, gruff, brusque, curt, blunt, harsh, surly, impudent, impertinent, saucy, crude, crass, flip, cocky, cheeky (*Slang* — smartalecky, fresh, crusty, nervy) polite, well-mannered

rudiment foundation, basis, groundwork, beginning, origin, seed RUDIMENTARY

rue regret, repent, deplore, bemoan, bewail, be sorry for (*Slang* — kick oneself)

ruffian rowdy, rogue, cad, tough, bully, brute, hoodlum (*Slang* — hooligan)

ruffle 1. disturb, annoy, provoke, irk, vex, excite, fluster, upset, shake, trouble, perturb, agitate, rattle, rile, 2. fold, crease, wrinkle, furrow

rug carpet, mat, covering

rugged 1. rough, uneven, jagged, ragged, rocky, snaggy smooth, 2. sturdy, vigorous, strong, powerful, potent, stalwart, hardy, robust, muscular, athletic, brawny, well-built, healthy, hale, husky, hefty, beefy weak, feeble

ruin destroy, spoil, mar, upset, wreck, devastate, ravage, demolish (*Slang* — mess up, foul up, louse up, gum up)

rule 1. govern, control, reign, dominate, regulate, command, head, lead, direct, manage, supervise, administer, decree, dictate, order, instruct, prevail, guide, influence, 2. measure, mark off

rumble roar, thunder, boom, roll

rummage search, ransack, scour, comb

rumor gossip, broadcast, circulate, spread word

rumple crumple, crush, wrinkle, crease, dishevel, muss up

rumpus noise, uproar, disturbance, commotion, hubbub, tumult, racket, fracas, ado, fuss, pandemonium, din, clamor, row (*Slang* — ruckus, rumble)

run 1. hasten, hurry, speed, sprint, bound, flee, bolt, race
(*Slang* — hotfoot, step lively) slow up, 2. go, move, operate, work, 3. stretch, extend, reach, range, lie, spread, 4.
flow, stream, pour, gush, discharge, 5. continue, last, endure,
persist stop, 6. campaign, electioneer, stump, politic, 7.
conduct, manage, direct, regulate, handle, govern, administer, lead, head, guide, steer, pilot, supervise, oversee,
boss (*Slang* — mastermind), 8. tear, ravel, 9. span, period,
time, spell

runway path, track, road

rupture break, burst, fracture, crack

rural countrified, rustic, provincial, bucolic

ruse trick, device, hoax, deception, fraud, subterfuge (*Slang*
— gimmick)

rush 1. speed, hasten, hurry, dash, dart, scurry, race, run,
expedite, accelerate slow up, 2. pressure, push, attack,
charge, besiege, drive, assault, storm

rustic 1. rural, countrified, provincial, bucolic, 2. simple,
plain sophisticated

rusty 1. corroded, eroded, worn, old, 2. unpracticed

rut habit, routine

ruthless cruel, merciless, heartless, cold, unfeeling, brutal,
savage, inhumane kind

S

sack 1. plunder, steal, pillage, loot, rob, fleece, 2. bag, pack

sacred religious, holy, spiritual

sacrifice give up, relinquish, release, surrender, yield, waive,
forego, lose, forfeit

sad sorrowful, unhappy, dejected, depressed, blue, melancholy, downcast, discouraged, gloomy, somber, glum, morose, sullen, grievous, miserable, pathetic, unfortunate, forlorn happy, glad SADNESS

saddle 1. harness, yoke, hitch up, 2. burden, load, encumber, oppress, weigh down relieve

safe secure, unharmed, protected, guarded, sheltered, shielded endangered, unsafe SAFETY

safeguard shield, screen, bulwark, precaution

sag droop, sink, hang, dangle, slump

saga story, tale, yarn, epic, account, anecdote, narrative

sage wise, knowing, learned, profound ignorant, dull SAGACIOUS

sail glide, coast, skim, navigate, cruise, float SAILOR

salary pay, wages, remuneration, compensation

salutary beneficial, healthful, advantageous, wholesome harmful, unhealthful

salutation greeting, hail, hello SALUTE

salvage save, rescue, recover, redeem, retrieve lose SALVATION

salve ointment, lotion, cream, balm, pomade

same identical, alike, equivalent different

sample test, experiment, try

sanction permit, approve, allow, authorize, support, license, accept, O.K. deny

sanctuary refuge, asylum, haven

sand scrape, smooth, file, grind

sane sensible, sound, rational, logical (*Slang* — all there) SANITY

sanguine   hopeful, expectant, confident, cheerful, optimistic
pessimistic

sanitarium   infirmary, hospital, clinic

sanitary   clean, hygienic, sterile, pure, prophylactic, spotless,
healthful   dirty, unsanitary   SANITATION

sap   weaken, debilitate

sarcastic   sneering, cutting, stinging, bitter, sharp, caustic
SARCASM

satisfy   1. please, gratify, content, benefit, suit, appease
deny, 2. convince, persuade, assure, comfort, relieve
SATISFACTION, SATISFACTORY

saturate   fill, load, stuff, pack, cram, gorge, soak, drench
empty

saucy   rude, impudent, impertinent, pert, disrespectful, flippant, cocky, flip, cheeky (*Slang* — smart-alecky, fresh,
nervy, crusty)   polite

saunter   stroll, ramble, wander, meander

savage   uncivilized, barbarous, fierce, cruel, wild, untamed,
ruthless, inhumane   civilized, gentle   SAVAGERY

save   1. store, economize, scrimp, preserve, conserve, keep,
maintain, reserve, accumulate, gather   spend, discard, 2.
rescue, protect, salvage, recover, redeem, retrieve

savor   relish, enjoy, like   SAVORY

say   1. speak, declare, recite, utter, voice, express, tell,
communicate, remark, comment, mention, assert, relate,
2. power, authority, right, prerogative

scald   burn, scorch

scamp   rascal, rogue, scoundrel, devil, mischief-maker

scamper   scurry, rush, tear, dash, dart, run, scoot, race,
hasten, hurry, scuttle, hustle

scan examine, inspect, scrutinize, look at, study, review

scandal disgrace, humiliation, shame, slander (*Slang* — dirt) SCANDALOUS

scanty meager, scarce, sparse, inconsiderable, small, slight, negligible, skimpy

scar blemish, mar, mark, wound, deface

scarce scanty, sparse, rare plentiful SCARCITY

scare frighten, alarm, startle, unnerve, terrify, horrify, appall

scatter disperse, distribute, spread, separate, part, split up, squander, strew gather, collect

scene 1. view, picture, sight, vista, lookout, landscape, setting, 2. act, 3. storm, outburst, explosion, flare-up

scent smell, odor, essence, fragrance

schedule list, index, post, enumerate, slate, program, line-up

scheme plan, plot, intrigue, conspire, connive, contrive

scholar learned man, savant, student

school educate, teach, instruct, enlighten, direct, guide

scoff mock, jeer, taunt, deride

scold blame, reprove, reprimand, chide, lecture, admonish, talk to (*Slang* — tell off, call down, bawl out, chew out, give what-for)

scoop dig, excavate, gouge, ladle

scoot dart, speed, dash, rush, tear, scamper, scurry, race, hasten, hurry, run, sprint

scope extent, degree, measure, range, sphere, space, reach

scorch burn, sear, singe, blister, parch, char

score 1. calculate, compute, figure, tally, 2. gain, earn, get, acquire, attain, win, 3. cut, mark, line, scratch, stroke

scornful mocking, disdainful, contemptuous SCORN

scoundrel villain, rascal, rogue, devil

scour clean, scrub, polish, wash, rub, buff, massage, shine

scourge whip, beat, thrash, spank, flog, lash

scout hunt, search out

scowl frown, look sullen, pout

scramble 1. mix, mingle, blend, combine, jumble, merge, fuse separate, 2. hurry, scoot, scurry, scamper, hasten, rush, tear, dart, hustle, scuttle, bustle

scrap 1. fight, quarrel, struggle, squabble, tiff, spat, bicker, row, 2. small amount, shred, snatch, speck, particle, 3. waste, litter, debris, trash, rubbish, junk

scrape 1. rub, brush, skim, graze, grate, 2. trouble, predicament, plight, pinch, strait, mess, complication, muddle, embarrassment (*Slang* — pickle, spot, jam, hole, hot water, stew)

scratch scrape, mark, cut, graze, score, scar, engrave

scrawl scribble, scratch

scrawny lean, thin, skinny, spare, gaunt, lanky, bony, spindly husky, chubby

scream yell, cry, shout, howl, shriek, screech, wail, squall, bawl, shout

screech shriek, scream, squeal, yell, cry, shout, howl

screen 1. shelter, protect, hide, cover, cloak, veil, shade, safeguard, 2. sift, strain, filter, refine, sort, separate, 3. inspect, analyze, check

screw fasten, tighten, twist, rotate, turn

scribble scrawl, scratch

scrimmage struggle, fight, encounter, battle, fray, clash, tussle, scuffle, melee, hassle (*Slang* — ruckus, scrap)

script writing, penmanship

scrub scour, clean, polish, wash, rub, buff, massage, shine

scrupulous careful, meticulous, exacting, particular, precise, fussy, fastidious (*Slang* — picky) careless

scrutinize inspect, examine, look at, observe, study, contemplate, review SCRUTINY

scuffle struggle, fight, tussle, melee (*Slang* — scrap)

sculpture carve, form, shape, mold, model, chisel

scurry scamper, rush, tear, dash, dart, run, scoot, race, scuttle, hasten, hurry, hustle

scuttle scurry, scamper, rush, tear, dash, dart, run, scoot, race, hasten, hurry, hustle

seal 1. fasten, close, shut, lock open, 2. endorse, sign, mark, stamp, 3. sea lion

sear burn, scorch, singe, char

search seek, look for, hunt, explore

season flavor, spice

secluded concealed, hidden, covered, obscured, secret, private, intimate, undisturbed, withdrawn, isolated, remote accessible, open SECLUSION

secret hidden, mysterious, private, concealed, secluded (*Slang* — hush-hush) open SECRECY

secrete discharge, excrete, eliminate, exude SECRETION

section divide, slice, split, partition, parcel, portion

secure 1. safe, protected, sure, sound, firm, stable unsafe, 2. get, obtain, acquire, 3. close, fasten, shut, lock, seal, fix, attach

seduce tempt, persuade, lure, entice, lead on

seek hunt, search, look for, pursue, quest, explore

seem appear, look

seep ooze, trickle, emit, excrete

seethe burn, fume, simmer, be angry, boil, stew

segment division, section, part, portion, fraction, subdivision

seize clutch, grasp, grab, grip, clasp, snatch   release
SEIZURE

seldom rarely, infrequently, hardly, not often   often

select pick, choose   SELECTION

self-conscious shy, timid, bashful, coy, demure

selfish egotistical, self-centered, possessive   good-natured

sell market, vend, peddle   buy

send dispatch, transmit, forward   receive

senior elder, older   junior

sensational exciting, startling, superb, exquisite, magnificent, marvelous, wonderful, glorious (*Slang* — divine, terrific, super)

sense 1. feel, perceive, understand, realize, comprehend, fathom, follow, grasp, discern, 2. intelligence, mentality, judgment

senseless 1. unconscious, lifeless, inanimate, oblivious, 2. foolish, stupid, asinine, silly, inane, idiotic (*Slang* — dizzy, soft, dumb, screwy, loony, batty, goofy, daffy, nutty) bright, sensible

sensible wise, intelligent, understanding, rational, bright, sound, sane, logical, practical, realistic   senseless

sentimental emotional, tender, affectionate (*Slang* — soft, mushy, sticky)

separate divide, part, segregate, sort, isolate, partition join, unite SEPARATION

sequel continuation, supplement, outcome, follow-up

sequence succession, continuation, series, progression

serene peaceful, calm, tranquil, quiet, untroubled, pacific disturbed, confused SERENITY

serial consecutive, sequential, periodic SERIES

serious 1. thoughtful, grave, reflective, pensive, solemn, engrossed, sincere, earnest, zealous flighty, 2. important, weighty, momentous, profound minor, unimportant

sermon lecture, talk, discourse, recitation

serpent snake, viper

serve 1. supply, furnish, deliver, present, 2. work for, help, assist SERVICE

set place, position, arrange, fix, adjust, regulate

setting scenery, surroundings, background

settle 1. determine, decide, resolve, fix, reconcile, mend, patch up, 2. occupy, inhabit, colonize, locate

sever cut off, split, cleave, chop, detach, part, separate

several some, various, assorted, diversified, many, numerous

severe strict, stern, harsh, rough, stringent, austere (*Slang* — tough, hard-boiled) lenient, easy

shabby worn, ragged, shoddy, tattered, frayed, seedy (*Slang* — tacky)

shack hut, shanty, shed, cabin

shackle tie, bind, chain, manacle, handcuff

shaggy rumpled, tousled, disheveled, mussed up

shake 1. vibrate, tremble, shiver, quiver, quaver, jerk, twitch, 2. jar, bump, bounce, pump, jolt, rock, sway.

shallow 1. featherbrained, simple, slow, empty profound, learned, 2. **not deep** deep

sham fraud, pretense, fake, mock, imitation, hoax (*Slang —* phony)

shambles mess, disorder, chaos

shameful disgraceful, humiliating, scandalous, pitiful, deplorable (*Slang —* awful, atrocious) righteous SHAME

shampoo soap, lather, wash

shanty shack, hut, shed, cabin

shape form, fashion, mold, design, develop, adapt

share divide, proportion, apportion, distribute, allot

sharp 1. pointy, angular dull, 2. severe, biting, caustic, bitter, harsh, curt, gruff, brusque, blunt, snippy charming, 3. keen, bright, smart, clever, shrewd, alert, brainy dull, stupid

shatter destroy, smash, fragment, break

shear cut off, clip, crop

shed 1. cast, throw off, slough, spread, radiate, 2. hut, shanty, shack

sheen luster, shine, brightness, gloss, glow, gleam

sheepish bashful, embarrassed, flushed, blushing, shame-faced, shy, timid

sheer 1. transparent, translucent, clear, thin, diaphanous, 2. simple, plain, pure

shelter protect, shield, hide, guard, defend, screen, cover, harbor expose

shield defend, protect, guard, shelter, hide, screen, cover, cloak, harbor expose

shift change, substitute, alter, vary

shiftless   lazy, inefficient, do-nothing, indolent, laggard
ambitious

shifty   tricky, sneaky, sly, furtive, deceitful, evasive, crafty, foxy, cunning, artful, shrewd, canny (*Slang* — shady, cagey)
honest

shimmer   gleam, shine, glimmer, twinkle, sparkle, glisten

shine   1. glow, gleam, glimmer, twinkle, sparkle, glisten, glare, 2. be smart, be bright

ship   transport, send, dispatch, haul

shirk   slack, avoid, malinger (*Slang* — goof off)

shiver   shake, quiver, quaver, quake, tremble

shock   startle, frighten, terrify, horrify, appall, awe (*Slang* — jar, give a turn, jolt)

shoot   fire, discharge   SHOT

shop   market, buy, purchase

shore   coast, beach, waterfront, bank

short   1. little, small, slight, puny   big, 2. brief, concise, succinct, curt   long

shortage   lack, deficiency, want, need, deficit, absence
abundance

shortcoming   fault, defect, flaw, weakness, failing, imperfection, inadequacy, deficiency

shout   yell, call, cry, scream, shriek, howl, clamor

shove   push, jostle, thrust, ram, bump, prod, goad, nudge

show   1. direct, point, aim, explain, clarify, demonstrate, illustrate, indicate, denote, manifest, guide, 2. display, exhibit, reveal   conceal, hide

showy   flashy, flaunting, ostentatious (*Slang* — jazzy, splashy)   dull

shred   fragment, particle, piece, crumb, scrap

shrewd   keen, clever, sharp, smart, artful, cunning, knowing, crafty, foxy, smooth, canny (*Slang* — slick) dull, dim-witted

shriek   yell, cry, call, shout, howl, scream, screech

shrill   piercing, sharp, screechy, squeaky, harsh, grating soft

shrink   1. shrivel, wither, dwindle, become smaller, 2. withdraw, recoil, pull back, retreat, flinch, cringe

shrivel   wither, shrink, wrinkle

shroud   cover, conceal, veil, cloak, screen reveal, expose

shudder   tremble, quiver, shake, quake

shuffle   1. scrape, drag, scuff, trudge, 2. mix, combine, scramble, jumble

shun   avoid, evade, dodge, snub, slight, ignore (*Slang* — duck, pass up)

shut   close, fasten, seal, lock open

shy   bashful, timid, coy, demure aggressive

sick   ill, ailing, indisposed (*Slang* — under the weather, out of sorts, rocky) healthy, well

sift   sort, separate, divide, screen, filter, refine, strain

sight   vision, view, look, vista, scene, spectacle, display, show

sign   1. mark, endorse, seal, initial, 2. signal, gesture, motion, wave, indicate

signet   seal, insignia, label, tag, stamp, sticker, brand, hallmark

significance   meaning, connotation, implication, drift, substance, gist, effect, importance, consequence unimportance, insignificance SIGNIFICANT, SIGNIFY

silent   quiet, still, noiseless, soundless, hushed noisy
SILENCE

silhouette   outline, contour, profile, configuration, shadow

silly   foolish, ridiculous, inane, senseless, asinine (*Slang —*
screwy, nutty, goofy, daffy, loony, batty, dizzy, wacky)
sensible

similar   alike, like, resembling, same SIMILARITY

simmer   1. boil, stew, cook, 2. seethe, fume, rage, storm,
rant, rave

simple   1. easy, effortless difficult, 2. bare, mere, common,
ordinary, sheer, plain, 3. dull, stupid, half-witted, idiotic,
moronic, ignorant (*Slang —* dumb) bright

sin   wrongdoing, misconduct, crime, vice, offense, evil, error,
indiscretion SINFUL, SINNER

sincere   genuine, real, honest, authentic, legitimate, bona
fide, unaffected (*Slang —* straight) insincere, phony
SINCERITY

sinewy   strong, powerful, tough, athletic, brawny, muscular,
beefy SINEW

sing   vocalize, chant, croon, hum, serenade

singe   burn, scorch, sear, char

sinister   bad, evil, dishonest, wrong, corrupt, fraudulent,
crooked (*Slang —* fishy, shady) righteous

sink   1. fall, go down, decline, slump, settle, lower, submerge,
2. weaken, droop, pine, fade

sip   drink, taste

sire   father, breed, beget, propagate, procreate, reproduce,
produce

siren   alarm, whistle, signal, noisemaker

sit   perch, be seated

site place, location, position, situation, whereabouts

situation 1. place, location, position, whereabouts, 2. circumstances, case, condition, terms

size proportion, measure, extent, scope, dimensions

skillful expert, adept, proficient, apt, handy, clever, masterful, able, capable (*Slang* — crackerjack) unable, awkward
  SKILL

skim glide, coast, sail, slide, graze, brush

skimpy scanty, scarce, sparse, meager generous, abundant

skinny lean, spare, scrawny, lanky, gaunt, bony chubby

skip 1. spring, jump, leap, 2. pass over, omit, bypass
  include

skirmish argument, conflict, clash, scuffle, brush, struggle, encounter, engagement, melee (*Slang* — scrap, run-in)

skirt border, edge, rim, margin, fringe

skulk sneak, hide, lurk, slink, prowl, steal, creep

slack 1. loose, lax, baggy, hanging, droopy tight, 2. slow, dull, lazy, inactive busy

slam close, bang, shut

slander libel, slur, discredit, smear (*Slang* — knock)

slant slope, incline, lean, tip, tilt

slap hit, smack, crack

slash cut, gash, wound, sever

slaughter butchery, massacre, killing, carnage, genocide

slavery bondage, servitude, serfdom freedom SLAVE

slay kill, put to death, exterminate, destroy (*Slang* — croak, bump off)

sleek smooth, glossy, slick, polished

sleep   slumber, doze, drowse, nap, rest, snooze

slender   thin, narrow, svelte, frail, slight   stout

slice   cut, sever, split, carve, slash, slit

slick   1. sleek, smooth, glossy, polished, 2. sly, tricky, cunning, shrewd, shifty, crafty, foxy (*Slang* — cagey)

slide   glide, coast, skim, skid, slip

slight   1. small, petite, puny, tiny   large, gross, 2. slender, frail, delicate, dainty, flimsy, thin, svelte   stout, 3. neglect, disregard, overlook, ignore

slim   slender, thin, svelte, slight, lean   stout

slime   mud, muck, slush, mire

sling   1. throw, cast, hurl, fling, pitch, toss, heave, flip, 2. suspend, hang, 3. bandage, support, splint

slink   sneak, lurk, prowl, steal, creep

slip   1. slide, glide, skid, 2. mistake, error, oversight, blunder

slit   cut, sever, split, cleave, tear

slogan   motto, phrase, expression, cry

slope   slant, incline, tip, lean, tilt

sloppy   1. careless, slovenly, slipshod, negligent, haphazard, messy   neat, 2. wet, slushy   dry

slothful   lazy, sluggish, do-nothing, shiftless, indolent, laggard   ambitious

slovenly   untidy, slipshod, unkempt, shabby, seedy, messy, sloppy   neat

slow   1. lingering, delaying, lackadaisical, leisurely, poking, tarrying, dillydallying   fast, 2. dull, stupid (*Slang* — dimwitted)   quick, bright

slug   1. strike, hit, knock, poke, punch, jab, smack, whack, bat, crack, clout (*Slang* — sock, clobber, paste, wallop, clip, swat), 3. token, coin

sluggish   slow-moving, inactive, lackadaisical, poky, listless, lethargic   quick, fast-moving

slumber   sleep, doze, drowse, nap, rest, snooze

slur   1. skim over, glance at, scan, 2. insult, smear, soil, slander, libel, defame, slight

sly   shrewd, underhanded, artful, cunning, shifty, smooth, crafty, canny, sneaky, clever, tricky (*Slang* — foxy, cagey, slick)

smack   1. hit, slap, crack, strike, whack (*Slang* — clobber, belt, wallop, swat), 2. kiss (*Slang* — smooch)

small   1. little, slight, puny, insignificant   big, 2. unimportant, trivial   important

smart   1. bright, clever, keen, intelligent, quick, shrewd, alert, brainy   stupid, 2. stylish, well-dressed, chic, natty, dapper, fashionable (*Slang* — sharp, nifty), 3. pain, ache, hurt

smash   1. destroy, shatter, ruin, break, crash, fragment, 2. collide, clash, bump, strike, knock, bang

smear   1. stain, mark, soil, tarnish, smudge, spot, 2. spoil, harm, blacken, defile, slander

smell   scent, odor, essence, fragrance

smile   grin, beam, laugh, smirk   frown

smog   fog, smoke, haziness, cloudiness

smooth   1. sleek, slick, glossy, polished, even, level   rough, 2. polite, pleasant, suave, chivalrous, cunning

smother   suffocate, stifle, choke, asphyxiate, muffle, suppress

smudge   smear, mark, soil, blacken, spot, stain

smug   self-satisfied, confident, vain, conceited, arrogant, boastful, egotistical   modest, humble

snag trap, hook, catch, snatch, snare release

snake serpent, viper

snap 1. break, burst, split, crack, 2. snatch, seize release

snare trap, catch, hook

snarl 1. growl, grumble, 2. tangle, mix up, knot

snatch 1. seize, grasp, grab, clutch, hook, snag, snare, trap release, 2. small amount, bit, scrap, shred

sneak lurk, prowl, slink, steal, creep

sneer mock, scoff, jeer, taunt

sniff smell, scent, inhale

snipe shoot at, fire at SNIPER

snobbish haughty, arrogant, priggish (*Slang* — stuck-up, snooty, high-hat) SNOB

snoop pry, meddle, intrude, interfere (*Slang* — butt in, horn in)

snooze sleep, doze, nap

snub slight, ignore, avoid, shun, spurn, rebuff

snug 1. comfortable, warm, sheltered, cozy, homelike (*Slang* — comfy), 2. compact, close, tight roomy

snuggle nestle, cuddle

soak wet, drench, saturate, steep, sop dry

soap lather, shampoo

soar fly, glide, aspire, tower, hover, ascend

sob cry, weep, bawl, blubber, snivel, wail, howl

sober 1. sensible, calm, moderate, temperate, mild, sound, reasonable extreme, 2. unintoxicated, uninebriated drunk

sociable friendly, amiable, congenial, cordial, gregarious unfriendly, unsociable

society 1. people, folks, public, populace, community, world, 2. company, organization, association, alliance, league, union, federation, sect

sock 1. strike, hit, knock, jab, whack, bat, crack (*Slang* — belt, paste, wallop, clip, swat), 2. stocking

sod soil, earth, dirt, ground

soft 1. delicate, tender, flexible, pliable, elastic hard, 2. mild, kind, gentle, tender, pleasant, lenient, easygoing harsh

soggy damp, soaked, saturated, sopping, waterlogged dry

soil 1. dirty, spot, stain, smudge, smear clean, 2. slander, libel, defile, 3. ground, earth, dirt, land

sojourn stay, stopover

solace comfort, relieve, cheer, console, encourage, reassure, hearten

solder cement, bind, weld, fuse, join, mend, fasten

sole only, single, one, individual, unique

solemn serious, grave, gloomy, dismal, somber, dreary, glum happy, cheerful

solicit request, appeal, ask, canvass, beg (*Slang* — mooch, bum, panhandle, touch)

solid 1. hard, firm, rigid, substantial, sturdy, strong, durable flimsy, soft, 2. whole, entire, continuous, complete

solitary single, individual, lone, isolated, unaccompanied

solution 1. explanation, answer, resolution, finding, outcome, result, 2. mixture

solve answer, explain, clear up, work out, figure out, unriddle, decipher, decode

somber dark, gloomy, dismal, dreary, melancholy, bleak, uncheerful, grave, solemn, grim cheerful

soon promptly, quickly, shortly, presently, directly, before long

soothe calm, comfort, quiet, ease, pacify, relieve

sorcery witchcraft, bewitchment, entrancement, spell, magic, wizardry, voodoo SORCERER

sordid dirty, filthy, slovenly, squalid

sore 1. painful, aching, tender, smarting, raw, irritated, inflamed, festering, rankling, throbbing, distressing healed, 2. angry, offended, irate, indignant (*Slang* — mad, riled up)

sorrow grief, sadness, regret, trouble, misfortune, suffering, woe, anguish, misery, agony, remorse happiness

sorry 1. regretful, remorseful, repentant, apologetic, 2. sad, sympathetic, unhappy, miserable, displeased, 3. wretched, poor, pitiful

sort arrange, separate, classify, categorize, group, divide, catalog

sound 1. make noise, utter, pronounce, voice, 2. healthy, wholesome, hearty unhealthy, 3. strong, safe, secure, stable, substantial, firm, solid, solvent weak, 4. correct, right, reasonable, sensible, sane, logical, rational wrong, foolish

sour 1. spoiled, fermented, bitter, rancid fresh, 2. disagreeable, peevish, unpleasant pleasant

source origin, beginning, derivation, root

souvenir remembrance, keepsake, memento, relic, token

sovereign supreme, greatest, regal, royal, imperial, majestic, ruling, reigning, governing

1. sow scatter, spread, disperse, distribute

2. sow female pig

space extent, expanse, measure, dimension, area

spacious vast, roomy, widespread, extensive, sweeping, far-reaching, capacious confining, narrow

span 1. bridge, viaduct, 2. period, interval, spell, 3. distance, extent, reach, stretch, measure, expanse

spank slap, strike, hit, smack (*Slang* — lick, paddle) SPANKING

spar box, fight (*Slang* — scrap)

spare 1. give up, relinquish, dispense with, do without, omit, forego, part with, sacrifice, surrender, yield keep, 2. extra, surplus, remainder, balance, leftover, excess, 3. lean, skinny, thin, scrawny, lanky, bony stout

spark flash, gleam, glimmer

sparkle shine, glitter, flash, glimmer, shimmer, twinkle, glisten

sparse scanty, meager, scattered, scarce, skimpy

spasm twitch, seizure, convulsion, fit

spat quarrel, disagree, differ, dispute, fight, squabble, tiff, bicker, row (*Slang* — scrap)

spatter sprinkle, speckle, dot

speak talk, say, tell, express SPEECH, SPEAKER

spear pierce, stab, puncture, impale, lance, knife

special unusual, exceptional, particular, extraordinary, notable ordinary, usual

species group, class, kind, sort, type, variety

specific definite, precise, particular, special, fixed SPECIFICATION, SPECIFY

specimen sample, representative, type, example

speck tiny bit, particle, iota (*Slang* — dab, smidgen)

speckle spot, mottle, mark

spectacle   sight, show, display, exhibition, pageant

spectacular   dramatic, sensational

speculate   1. guess, theorize, conjecture, 2. gamble, risk, chance, venture, 3. reflect, meditate, consider, contemplate, study, deliberate   SPECULATION

speedy   fast, rapid, quick, swift, hasty, fleet, expeditious (*Slang* — snappy)   SPEED

spell   1. magic power, charm, fascination, trance, 2. time, stretch, shift, period

spellbound   fascinated, enchanted, interested, rapt, enthralled, gripped, engrossed, absorbed, awed, charmed, hypnotized, mesmerized   bored

spend   pay out, lay out, use, consume, finish off, exhaust, expend

sphere   1. ball, globe, 2. extent, realm, expanse, province, field

spice   season, flavor

spike   pierce, stab, puncture, impale, spear

spill   overflow, run over, brim over, cascade, flood, pour

spin   turn, twirl, twist, rotate, pivot, wheel, reel, swirl

spinster   old maid, single woman

spiral   coil, twist, twirl, kink

spirit   1. soul, heart, mind, 2. nature, disposition, temper, 3. courage, vigor, life, vivacity

spiritual   religious, sacred, holy

spit   saliva, drivel, dribble, drool, expectoration

spiteful   annoying, malicious, hostile, vindictive, mean, ornery   SPITE

splash   wet, splatter, sprinkle, spatter

splatter splash, sprinkle, spatter

splendid fine, excellent, brilliant, glorious, magnificent, grand (*Slang* — great, dandy, swell, keen, hot, nifty, hunky-dory)

splendor pomp, glory, magnificence, grandeur, brilliance, brightness, radiance dullness

splice join, bind, tie, connect, attach

split separate, divide, bisect, halve, cleave, partition, sever, break, crack join, connect

spoil damage, injure, destroy, botch, impair, mar, ruin, upset, rot, decay (*Slang* — mess up, foul up, louse up, gum up)

sponsor underwriter, backer, financer, promoter, supporter (*Slang* — angel)

spontaneous instinctive, inherent, natural, automatic planned

spook ghost, specter, apparition, spirit, phantom

sport fun, play, amusement, game, contest

spot 1. stain, mark, discolor, soil, 2. pick out, recognize, know, tell, distinguish, identify, place, discern, spy, sight

spouse mate, husband, wife

spout discharge, expel, spew, eject, pour forth

sprawl spread, extend, stretch out, expand, fan out

spray sprinkle, spatter, splash

spread 1. stretch out, unfold, extend, sprawl, 2. distribute, scatter, disperse

spree gay time, escapade, celebration, fling, whirl, lark

sprig twig, branch, limb, bough, shoot, sprout

sprightly lively, gay, active, animated, spirited, vivacious, spry, energetic, nimble (*Slang* — peppy) dull, lethargic

spring leap, jump, bounce, vault, hop, bound, hurdle

sprinkle spray, spatter, splash

sprite elf, fairy, goblin, pixie, gremlin

sprout grow, develop, shoot up, flourish, thrive, bud, burgeon

spry lively, gay, sprightly, active, animated, spirited, vivacious, energetic, nimble dull, lethargic

spunk courage, pluck, spirit, will power, nerve, grit, mettle, (*Slang* — backbone, guts)

spur urge, goad, prod, provoke (*Slang* — egg on)

spurn scorn, reject, disown, deny, repudiate, disdain, snub, rebuff

spurt flow, gush, spew, expel, erupt, jet, spout, squirt

spy see, detect, view, observe, discern, sight, spot

squabble quarrel, disagree, differ, dispute, fight, tiff, spat, bicker, row (*Slang* — scrap, hassle)

squad group, unit, company, band, gang, crew, outfit, troop, body

squalid filthy, degraded, poor, wretched, shabby, sordid, slummy clean SQUALOR

squall 1. cry, scream, wail, howl, moan, bawl, yell, squeal, 2. gust, gale, blizzard

squander waste, throw away, misspend, dissipate save

square 1. adjust, settle, balance, equalize, 2. just, fair, honest, straight, equitable crooked, 3. old-fashioned, corny, unaware, conventional sophisticated

squash crush, press, mash, suppress, squelch

squat crouch, lie low

squawk complain, grumble, mutter (*Slang* — gripe, crab, bellyache, beef, kick, grouch, howl)

squeak squeal, yelp

squeal 1. cry, squeak, screech, yell, 2. tattle, inform on (*Slang* — blab, snitch)

squeeze press, crush, pinch, cram

squirm wriggle, twist, writhe, wiggle

squirt spew, spout, spurt, expel, pour forth, jet, gush, spray, surge, splash

stab pierce, perforate, puncture, impale, wound

stable 1. steady, firm, unchanging, steadfast, sound, secure, settled, established unsettled, 2. barn

stack pile, heap, load

staff 1. group, committee, personnel, force, crew, gang, 2. stick, pole, rod, scepter

stage 1. arrange, dramatize, present, produce, perform, enact, put on, 2. period, interval, point, time, spell, 3. tier, level, layer, story, 4. platform, podium, rostrum

stagger sway, reel, waver, flounder, tumble, lurch

stagnant still, inactive, sluggish, inert, static, dormant active

staid sensible, level-headed, sober-minded, sedate, serious flighty, unsettled

stain spot, soil, mark, discolor

stake 1. bet, wager, gamble, risk, 2. peg, post

stale old, worn, obsolete, musty new, fresh

stalk 1. pursue, hunt, chase, seek, search, 2. stem

stall 1. delay, procrastinate, dillydally, dawdle, block, hinder hurry, 2. compartment, booth, cell

stalwart 1. strong, robust, firm, potent, rugged, sturdy, powerful weak, 2. brave, courageous, bold, valiant, gallant, heroic cowardly

stammer stutter, falter, stumble

stamp 1. mark, seal, label, brand, engrave, print, 2. trample, pound, crush, tread

stampede flight, rush, panic

stand 1. rise, get up sit, lie down, 2. endure, bear, tolerate, 3. remain, last, continue, stay, persist, 4. pedestal, base, table

standard 1. model, rule, pattern, criterion, ideal, 2. flag, banner, pennant, emblem, symbol, colors

standstill stop, halt, pause, impasse

stanza verse, measure, refrain

staple 1. fasten, clasp, attach, bind, connect, join, link, 2. important, principal, main

star 1. headline, excel, feature, 2. heavenly body

stare gaze, look, gape, glare, gawk

stark complete, entirely, downright, absolute, outright

start 1. begin, commence, set out, 2. move suddenly, jerk, jump

startle frighten, surprise, shock, electrify, upset, alarm, unnerve (*Slang* — jar)

starve hunger, crave food STARVATION

state 1. tell, express, say, pose, declare, assert, relate, recite, report, expound, 2. condition, position, status, situation, circumstance, 3. nation

stately grand, majestic, dignified, imposing, noble, grandiose, magnificent, splendid, impressive

statement account, report, announcement, proclamation, declaration, notice

static 1. still, inactive, sluggish, inert, dormant active, 2. electrical interference

station 1. place, post, 2. position, rank, standing, status, post

stationary fixed, immovable, immobile, firm, inflexible, motionless movable

stationery paper, writing materials

statue figure, sculpture, bust, monument

stature height, loftiness

status 1. standing, position, station, class, division, grade, rank, 2. condition, state

statute law, ordinance, rule, act, regulation, measure, dictate, decree, bill, enactment

staunch loyal, steadfast, devoted, firm, reliable, dependable, trustworthy

stay 1. remain, last, endure, continue, persist leave, 2. dwell, reside, live, occupy, inhabit, 3. delay, detain, retard, stop, hold up proceed

steady constant, fixed, inert, regular, incessant, ceaseless, perpetual changing STEADFAST

steal rob, take, thieve, pilfer, filch (*Slang* — lift, swipe, cop, pinch)

stealthy secret, sly, sneaky, underhanded, shifty open, honest

steam 1. vapor, gas, smoke, 2. power, energy, force, 3. cook, soften, freshen

steed horse, stallion, nag

steep 1. soak, drench, sop, saturate, bathe, 2. high, precipitous

steer 1. guide, direct, drive, manage, regulate, conduct, handle, lead, head, run, 2. cattle

step walk, tread, pace

sterilize clean, sanitize, disinfect, decontaminate STERILE

stern severe, strict, harsh, firm, hard, exacting, austere, stringent (*Slang* — tough, hard-boiled) lenient, easygoing

stew 1. cook, 2. fume, seethe, be angry, rage, rave, rant, storm, fret

stick 1. pierce, stab, perforate, penetrate, puncture, 2. fasten, attach, adhere, cling, 3. continue, keep on, persevere, stop, discontinue

stiff 1. rigid, firm, tense, taut, tight, inflexible, tough flexible 2. formal, unnatural, stilted informal, 3. hard, difficult, tough easy

stifle smother, stop, suppress, suffocate, choke

stigma brand, slur, stain, blemish, disgrace

still 1. quiet, motionless, noiseless, calm, tranquil, peaceful, placid, smooth, untroubled noisy, 2. yet, even, until now, so far

stimulate spur, stir, rouse, energize, invigorate, pep up, activate, motivate, move suppress, stifle STIMULANT, STIMULUS

sting prick, wound, pain, distress, inflame

stingy ungenerous, miserly, cheap, closefisted (*Slang* — tight, penny-pinching) generous, liberal

stink smell, stench, odor

stint task, work, job, chore, duty, assignment, function, role

stir 1. mix, blend, mingle, combine, merge, scramble, jumble, 2. move, budge, mobilize, 3. excite, affect, agitate, disturb, shake, perturb, trouble, disquiet, rouse

stitch sew, fasten, tailor

stock   supply, keep, store up, collect, accumulate, amass, stockpile, gather, hoard

stocky   sturdy, solid, fat, plump, chubby, portly, fleshy, chunky, strapping   lean, thin

stomach   1. bear, endure, take, stand, tolerate, 2. belly, abdomen

stone   rock, pebble, gem

stool   seat, chair

stoop   1. bend forward, crouch, squat, 2. porch, veranda, platform

stop   end, halt, check, stay, cease, block, discontinue, quit, arrest, prevent, conclude, terminate   start

store   1. supply, stock, keep, collect, accumulate, amass, stockpile, gather, hoard, 2. shop, mart, business
STORAGE

storm   1. attack, besiege, beset, raid, charge, assault, assail, 2. rage, be violent, rant, rave, rampage, seethe, boil, fume, 3. tempest, outburst

story   1. tale, account, chronicle, yarn, narrative, anecdote, epic, saga, 2. floor, level, tier

stout   1. fat, large, fleshy, plump, pudgy, chubby, stocky, portly   thin, 2. brave, bold, courageous, valiant, gallant, heroic, chivalrous   meek, cowardly

stow   pack, load, store

straddle   perch

straggle   wander, ramble, roam, rove, drift, stray

straight   1. direct, unswerving   crooked, 2. frank, honest, upright, square, sincere, open

strain   1. stretch, pull, extend, tug, tow, 2. sprain, wrench, injure, hurt, 3. quality, trace, streak, 4. race, descent

strand 1. abandon, desert, leave, 2. thread, string, cord, line

strange unusual, queer, peculiar, unfamiliar, odd, curious, eccentric ordinary, familiar STRANGER

strangle choke, suffocate, smother, asphyxiate

strap 1. fasten, bind, tie, wrap, lash, gird untie, 2. whip, beat, thrash, spank, flog (*Slang* — lick, wallop), 3. belt

strapping tall, strong, healthy, sturdy, rugged, powerful, hardy, robust, vigorous, well-built, athletic, muscular, brawny, beefy weak

strategy planning, management, tactics, manipulation, intrigue, maneuvering STRATEGIC

stray wander, roam, rove, straggle, gad, ramble, drift, meander

streak 1. mark, line, score, striate, stripe, 2. strain, element, vein, nature, quality, characteristic, tendency

stream 1. flow, pour, surge, rush, gush, flood, 2. creek, brook

street road, thoroughfare, avenue

strength power, force, vigor, potency, might, energy, intensity weakness STRENGTHEN

strenuous 1. active, energetic, vigorous, intense inactive, 2. difficult, hard, rough, rugged, arduous, laborious (*Slang* — tough, wicked, mean) easy

stress 1. force, strain, pressure, tension, 2. emphasis, importance, accent, insistence, urgency

stretch extend, draw out, spread, strain, expand, distend, elongate

strew sprinkle, scatter, disperse, distribute

strict 1. harsh, exact, precise, rigorous, severe, exacting, stringent, stern, austere (*Slang* — tough, hard-boiled) lenient, 2. perfect, complete, absolute, literal, exact, real, true

stride step, pace, walk

strife quarreling, fighting, controversy, dispute, squabble peace

strike 1. hit, knock, jab, smack, whack, bat, clout (*Slang* — sock, swat, clip, clobber, belt, bash, paste, wallop), 2. revolt, rebel

striking attractive, noticeable, obvious, conspicuous, prominent, bold, pronounced, outstanding, flagrant, glaring unattractive

string thread, connect, line up, bind, tie

strip remove, uncover, bare, peel, pare cover

stripe line, mark, striate

strive struggle, fight, contend, battle, endeavor, labor

stroke 1. rub, caress, massage, pet, 2. feat, effort, act, deed, undertaking, attempt, 3. attack, seizure, convulsion, spasm

stroll walk, saunter, stride, strut, amble, promenade

strong powerful, vigorous, forceful, potent, mighty, sturdy, hardy, muscular, brawny weak

stronghold fortification, bastion

structure 1. building, construction, house, edifice, 2. form, shape, figure, configuration

struggle 1. endeavor, strive, attempt, try, 2. fight, battle, contend, tussle, scuffle (*Slang* — scrap)

strut swagger, parade

stub end, tip, tail

stubborn obstinate, willful, headstrong, adamant, rigid, unyielding, inflexible yielding, flexible

stubby stocky, chubby, squat, pudgy, chunky *lanky*

student pupil, scholar

studious learned, bookish, educated, scholarly, cultured, profound, erudite, diligent STUDY

stuff 1. fill, load, pack, gorge, saturate *empty,* 2. substance, matter, material

stuffy 1. close, stifling, airless, suffocating, oppressive *airy,* 2. pompous, prim, prudish, strait-laced, unimaginative, dull, staid, stodgy, old-fogyish *casual, regular*

stumble stagger, flounder, tumble, falter

stump 1. baffle, perplex, confound, mystify, puzzle (*Slang* — stick, flaw, get), 2. campaign, electioneer (*Slang* — whistle-stop), 3. remainder, rest, leftovers

stun daze, bewilder, shock, overwhelm, numb, stupefy

stunning 1. attractive, good-looking, beautiful, gorgeous, ravishing, glorious, dazzling, brilliant (*Slang* — devastating) *unattractive,* 2. bewildering, astounding, shocking, astonishing, amazing, surprising

stunt 1. shorten, abbreviate, abridge, condense, 2. feat, act, exploit, performance

stupefy stun, daze, bewilder, shock, numb

stupendous amazing, marvelous, great, huge, enormous, immense, vast, extraordinary, exceptional, remarkable, wonderful

stupid dull, unintelligent, dense, asinine, silly, foolish (*Slang* — dimwitted, dumb, thick) *smart, bright*

stupor unconsciousness, faint, coma, blackout, swoon, lethargy, numbness

sturdy strong, firm, powerful, rugged, hardy, robust, vigorous, well-built, athletic, muscular, brawny, sound, stable, substantial, solid, durable *weak, shaky*

stutter stammer, hem, haw, falter, hesitate

stylish fashionable, modish, voguish, smart, chic, well-dressed, natty, dapper, sporty (*Slang* — swanky, nifty, sharp) drab STYLE

subdue conquer, overcome, crush, vanquish, suppress, quell, put down, squash, squelch

subject topic, issue, problem, theme, text, question, point, plot

sublime noble, majestic, grand, great, distinguished, lofty, prominent, eloquent, exalted

submerge immerse, sink, dip, duck, inundate, dunk

submit yield, surrender, comply, obey, heed, mind SUBMISSION, SUBMISSIVE

subordinate dependent, secondary, inferior superior

subscribe contribute, give to, donate to, support SUBSCRIPTION

subsequent following, later, coming after, succeeding, next preceding

subside decrease, diminish, lessen, decline increase

subsist live, exist, survive SUBSISTENCE

substance matter, material, body, stuff, essence, gist, content

substantial 1. real, actual, true, authentic vague, 2. strong, firm, solid, stable, sound weak, 3. wealthy, well-to-do, rich, affluent, prosperous poor

substitute replace, change, exchange, switch, shift SUBSTITUTION

subtle 1. delicate, thin, fine, faint gross, strong, 2. sly, crafty, tricky, underhanded, shrewd, cunning, foxy, clever (*Slang* — cagey, slick) open, honest

subtract deduct, take away, remove, withdraw, discount
add SUBTRACTION

successful prosperous, fortunate, well-off, thriving, flourishing, victorious, triumphant, winning, providential, booming,
lucky failing, unsuccessful SUCCEED, SUCCESS

succession sequence, order, progression, series
SUCCEED

succulent juicy

succumb 1. yield, give way, submit, comply, acquiesce
conquer, 2. die, decease, expire, perish

suck drink, take in, absorb, draw in SUCTION

sudden unexpected, abrupt, hasty, unforeseen, impulsive,
impetuous planned, deliberate SUDDENLY

sue prosecute, bring action against, litigate

suffer endure, experience, bear, stand, tolerate, undergo

sufficient enough, ample, plenty, satisfactory, adequate
lacking, insufficient SUFFICIENTLY

suffocate smother, stifle, choke, muffle, suppress, asphyxiate

suffrage vote, voice, ballot

suggest hint, imply, intimate, insinuate, propose, advise
SUGGESTION

suit 1. agree with, satisfy, 2. fit, become, 3. costume, dress,
habit, 4. legal action, litigation, case, prosecution

suitable fitting, proper, timely, favorable, adequate, satisfactory unsuitable

sulk mope, fret (*Slang* — grump, grouch)

sullen gloomy, dismal, glum, moody, moping, morose,
sulky cheerful, pleasant

sum total, whole, entirety, quantity, amount

summarize   brief, outline, abridge, capsule expand, elaborate   SUMMARY

summit   top, peak, crest, crown, apex, acme, zenith bottom, base

summon   call, send for, subpoena, conjure

sumptuous   rich, magnificent, costly, grandiose, grand, splendid, imposing, impressive, stately, majestic, elegant, elaborate, luxurious (*Slang* — swell, plush)   poor

sundown   sunset, dusk, evening, nightfall   sunrise

sundry   several, various, diversified, assorted, many

sunken   1. submerged, sunk, 2. hollow, concave

sunny   bright, cheerful, pleasant, radiant   dull

sunrise   dawn, daybreak, morning   sunset

sunset   sundown, dusk, evening, nightfall   sunrise

superb   grand, stately, magnificent, splendid, fine, excellent, exquisite, marvelous, wonderful, grandiose, glorious, imposing, impressive, noble, majestic, sumptuous, elaborate (*Slang* — swell)   inferior

superficial   shallow, surface, cursory   thorough, deep

superintendent   supervisor, manager, director, foreman

superior   better, greater, higher   inferior

supernatural   spiritual, superhuman, ghostly, unknown, mysterious, mystical

supersede   displace, replace, take the place of, supplant

superstition   folklore, tradition, popular belief, old wives' tale   SUPERSTITIOUS

supervise   direct, oversee, govern, regulate, command, head, lead, administer, boss   SUPERVISION, SUPERVISOR

supplant   supersede, replace, displace, take the place of

supple bending, pliable, flexible, plastic, elastic, yielding, limber, lithe stiff, firm

supplement add to, complete, augment, increase, fortify, reinforce subtract

supplication prayer, request, plea, entreaty, appeal SUPPLICATE

supply furnish, provide, stock, store

support help, aid, bolster, sustain, defend, encourage, foster

suppose believe, think, imagine, consider, assume, infer, deduce, presume

suppress restrain, repress, keep down, hold back, inhibit, curb, check, arrest, bridle, squelch, stifle, subdue, squash, restrict, limit, quell foster, encourage SUPPRESSION

supreme highest, greatest, utmost, extreme, uppermost, top, maximum, foremost, chief, paramount SUPREMACY

sure certain, positive, absolute, definite, decided SURELY

surface outside, exterior, face interior

surge wave, gush, flow, mount, whirl, stream, rush, swell, billow

surgery operation SURGEON

surly rude, gruff, bad-tempered, brusque, curt, blunt, harsh, rough, sullen, moody pleasant, affable

surmise guess, judge, consider, regard, suppose, presume, imagine, suspect, infer, gather, conclude, deduce, think

surmount overcome, rise above, triumph over, defeat succumb

surpass excel, exceed, go beyond

surplus excess, extra, superfluous, remaining, leftover, spare, additional, supplementary lack

surprise astonish, amaze, catch unaware, astound, bewilder, awe, dumbfound

surrender give up, yield, relinquish, forego, renounce, submit, capitulate, abandon conquer

surround wrap, envelop, embrace, encircle, enclose, encompass

survey 1. examine, view, inspect, scrutinize, observe, scan, study, contemplate, peruse, review, 2. measure, gauge, assess, estimate, rate, appraise SURVEYOR

survive remain, continue, outlast, outlive SURVIVAL

susceptible pliant, suggestible, yielding, impressionable, open, pliable

suspect 1. think, guess, suppose, assume, imagine, surmise, infer, gather (*Slang* — expect, reckon), 2. doubt, distrust, question, challenge, dispute, mistrust trust

suspend 1. hang, sling, 2. postpone, delay, defer, hold over, shelve, 3. interrupt, break, arrest, halt continue
SUSPENSION

suspense anxiety, fear, concern, apprehension, distress, uneasiness, agitation, disquiet

suspicious suspecting, doubtful, questionable, wary (*Slang* — leery) SUSPICION

sustain keep up, support, bear, endure, maintain, suffer, tolerate, stand, abide succumb

swagger strut, parade

swallow 1. eat, absorb, consume, devour, gulp, ingest, 2. accept, take, believe

swamp 1. sink, overwhelm, flood, 2. marsh, bog

swap trade, deal, exchange, barter, switch

swarm crowd, throng, collect, assemble, meet, gather, cluster disperse, scatter

swat hit, strike, knock, poke, jab, whack (*Slang* — bat, clout, belt, clobber, paste, wallop, clip, sock)

sway 1. swing, reel, rock, lurch, roll, toss, pitch, 2. influence, control, rule, affect, move, persuade, prejudice

swear 1. promise, vow, vouch, 2. curse (*Slang* — cuss)

sweep 1. clean, brush, vacuum, 2. move, glide, coast, skim, slip, slide, 3. stretch, extend, range

sweet 1. sugary, saccharine bitter, 2. pleasant, agreeable, lovely, charming, adorable unpleasant

swell 1. grow bigger, increase, gain, expand, enlarge, broaden amplify, magnify, inflate, stretch, bulge, billow shrink, decrease, 2. good (*Slang* — grand, great, dandy, keen, hot, nifty, bully, ripping, hunkydory)

swelter sweat, perspire, roast

swerve dodge, sidestep, shift, turn (*Slang* — duck)

swift fast, quick, rapid, speedy, hasty, fleet, expeditious, agile, nimble (*Slang* — snappy) slow

swim bathe, float, wade SWIMMER

swindle cheat, defraud, fleece, gyp (*Slang* — beat, crook, stick, shortchange, con, chisel) SWINDLER

swine 1. hogs, pigs, 2. scoundrel, skunk (*Slang* — louse, heel, rat, stinker, bugger)

swing sway, reel, rock, roll, lurch, fluctuate, dangle, hang

swirl twist, whirl, curl, wheel, reel, spin

switch 1. whip, strike, slash, beat, thrash, bang, spank, flog, pummel, lash, strap, club, paddle (*Slang* — lick, wallop), 2. change, turn, shift, exchange, substitute, replace, trade, swap

swoon faint (*Slang* — keel over, pass out)

swoop dive, plunge, plummet, drop, fall, pounce

sword knife, blade

symbolize represent, stand for, typify, illustrate
SYMBOL

symmetrical balanced, even, orderly, regular, uniform,
equal unbalanced, uneven SYMMETRY

sympathy understanding, tolerance, sensitivity, pity, compassion, mercy, commiseration, condolence
SYMPATHETIC, SYMPATHIZE

symphony concert, recital

symptom sign, implication, token, mark, omen, indication

synthetic man-made, artificial, mock, counterfeit, imitation, simulated natural

system plan, scheme, method, design, arrangement, order
SYSTEMATIC

T

table 1. list, chart, index, catalog, schedule, 2. postpone,
delay, put off, shelve

tablet 1. notebook, pad, 2. pill, capsule

tack attach, add, join, affix, fasten, clasp

tackle 1. undertake, get busy, attack, 2. seize, grapple
with, 3. equipment, apparatus, gear, furnishings

tact grace, diplomacy, taste, finesse, sensitivity, sensibility
TACTFUL

tactics procedures, operations, methods, strategy, maneu-
vers

tag 1. label, brand, name, call, designate, 2. follow, shadow, pursue, trail, heel (*Slang* — tail)

tail 1. back, rear, end, tip, 2. follow, pursue, shadow, trail, heel (*Slang* — tag)

taint stain, spot, spoil, discolor, tarnish, mark, soil

take 1. seize, capture, get, receive, gain, obtain, procure give, 2. need, require, involve, entail, implicate, 3. choose, select, pick out, 4. bring, carry, convey, 5. suppose, assume, infer, understand, gather, guess, 6. hire, lease, engage, 7. tolerate, endure, bear, stand, suffer, swallow, stomach

tale 1. story, yarn, account, narrative, epic, saga, 2. falsehood, lie, untruth, fib truth

talent ability, skill, gift, endowment, genius, capability, capacity, forte, aptitude

talk 1. speak, converse, discuss (*Slang* — gab, yap), 2. gossip, rumor, report

tall 1. high, big, long, lengthy short, 2. exaggerated, magnified, enlarged, overstated, excessive, extreme true

tally 1. count, score, calculate, compute, estimate, reckon, figure, list, 2. agree, correspond, coincide, match, check

tame gentle, obedient, temperate, mild, domesticated wild

tamper meddle, pry, busybody, interfere, intrude

tang flavor, taste

tangible 1. real, actual, definite, substantial, concrete vague, 2. touchable

tangle twist, confuse, mess, complicate, knot, snarl, involve

tantalize torment, tease, molest, bother, harass, badger, worry, pester, torture

tantrum fit, outburst, scene, rage, fury, conniption, flare-up

tap 1. rap, pat, 2. faucet, valve, spigot

tape   1. wrap, fasten, bind, tie, bandage, 2. record

taper   lessen, diminish, narrow, contract   increase

tardy   late, overdue, delayed

target   object, goal, aim, end, mark, point

tariff   tax, duty, toll, assessment, levy

tarnish   dull, dim, fade, discolor, stain, soil

tarry   remain, stay, linger, wait, delay, loiter, dawdle, dilly-dally

tart   sour, sharp, bitter, pungent

task   work, duty, job, chore, stint, assignment, function

taste   savor, sample, experiment, test, try, experience, sense, feel

tattered   torn, ragged, shabby, shoddy, frayed, frazzled, seedy, tacky

tattle   gossip, chatter, rumor, report (*Slang* — blab, snitch, squeal)   TATTLETALE

taunt   mock, jeer, reproach, scoff

taut   tight, tense, unrelaxed, firm, rigid, stiff   relaxed

tavern   inn, cabaret, bar, saloon, pub

tax   1. strain, burden, load, encumber, oppress, 2. duty, tariff, levy, toll, assessment

taxi   cab

teach   instruct, educate, show, enlighten, tutor, coach, direct, guide   TEACHER

team   band, company, group, party, gang, crew

tear   cut, sever, split, slash, slice, slit, rip

tearful   weeping, sad, sobbing, crying   TEAR

tease annoy, vex, pester, bother, joke, jest, banter, badger (*Slang* — kid, rib, razz)

tedious dull, dreary, slow, dry, tiring, boring, monotonous, humdrum, wearisome exhilarating, interesting

teem flow, abound, swarm

telecast televise, broadcast

televise telecast, broadcast

tell say, inform, utter, voice, express, communicate, convey, impart, state, declare, assert, relate, recite, remark, comment, note, mention

temerity boldness, rashness, brashness, indiscretion caution

temper disposition, condition, nature, character, constitution, tendency, mood TEMPERAMENT

temperamental moody, sensitive, touchy, thin-skinned

temperate moderate, mild, gentle, calm extreme

tempest storm, violence

temporary passing, momentary, transient, short-lived lasting, permanent TEMPORARILY

tempt invite, attract, interest, appeal, tantalize, titillate, entice, seduce, lure TEMPTATION

tenacious persevering, persistent, continuing, diligent, steadfast, constant, unswerving, untiring, obstinate, stubborn, willful, headstrong lax

tenant dweller, occupant, resident, inhabitant

tend 1. be apt, be likely, incline, lean, 2. attend, administer, care for, look after, mind, watch over, foster, nurse, serve, help

tendency inclination, leaning, bent, proclivity, disposition, aptitude

tender 1. soft, delicate, gentle, kind, affectionate, loving, sensitive harsh, rough, 2. offer, present, submit, extend

tense strained, stretched, tight, rigid, taut relaxed
TENSION

tepid lukewarm, mild

term 1. period, time, duration, 2. condition, premise, 3. name, call, designate, dub, title, label, tag

terminate end, finish, close, conclude, stop, cease, complete begin TERMINAL, TERMINATION

terrible dreadful, horrible, deplorable, outrageous, scandalous, vile, wretched, abominable, detestable, despicable, contemptible, shocking, appalling (*Slang* — awful, atrocious) wonderful, superb

terrific great, superb, magnificent, marvelous, wonderful, colossal, tremendous, glorious, divine, sensational (*Slang* — super)

terrify frighten, horrify, appall, shock, awe, petrify, paralyze, stupefy (*Slang* — scare stiff)
TERROR, TERRORIZE

territory land, region, area, zone, place, country, district, section

terse brief, concise, short, condensed, compressed, curt, succinct, laconic lengthy, long

test 1. examine, question, quiz, interrogate, query, grill, cross-examine, 2. experiment, try, prove, verify

testimony evidence, proof, statement, declaration
TESTIFY

testy impatient, irritated, cross, cranky, irritable, irascible, mean, ornery, ugly pleasant

text subject, topic, theme, issue, point, question, problem, thesis, proposition

textile cloth, material, fabric, goods

GLOBE THEATRE

texture structure, construction, composition, make-up, finish, grain

thankful grateful, appreciative, obliged, indebted
thankless THANKS

thaw melt, defrost freeze

theater 1. playhouse, hall, stadium, 2. arena, battlefield

theft stealing, filching, pilfering (*Slang* — lifting, swiping)
THIEVE

theme 1. subject, topic, text, question, problem, issue, point, proposition, 2. composition, paper, article, treatise, essay, dissertation, discourse, discussion, study, thesis, 3. motif

theory explanation, speculation, supposition, hypothesis, inference, opinion, impression, idea, thought, attitude, view, conception, judgment

therefore hence, consequently, accordingly, for that reason

thick 1. broad, massive, bulky, coarse narrow, 2. numerous, swarming, teeming, crowded empty, 3. stupid, dense, asinine, dull (*Slang* — dumb, numskulled) bright

thief robber, pilferer, filcher, burglar, crook THIEVE

thin 1. slender, lean, slim, svelte, slight, frail, skinny, gaunt, lanky fat, 2. scanty, sparse, meager plentiful

think 1. believe, expect, imagine, deem, fancy, presume, gather, deduce, judge, conclude, guess, suppose, assume, suspect, infer, understand, 2. consider, contemplate, reflect, study, ponder, deliberate, meditate, reason, concentrate, muse, theorize

thirsty 1. dry, arid, parched, dehydrated, 2. desirous, craving, hungering for (*Slang* — crazy for) satisfied
THIRST

thorough complete, intensive, sweeping, all-out, full
shallow, incomplete

thoroughfare   passage, road, highway, street, avenue, boulevard, turnpike, expressway, thruway, freeway

though   however, in any case, nevertheless, notwithstanding

thought   1. thinking, idea, notion, contemplation, reflection, consideration, reasoning, deliberation, meditation, 2. care, attention, regard, concern, indulgence   thoughtlessness   THOUGHTFUL, THOUGHTLESS

thrash   1. beat, pound, knock, rap, batter, spank, whip, lash (*Slang* — wallop, lick), 2. toss, move violently, flounder, tumble, pitch, rock, roll, reel, wallow

threaten   1. warn, caution, advise, admonish, alert, forebode, 2. menace, intimidate, bully, terrorize, harass, browbeat, bulldoze (*Slang* — buffalo)   THREAT

threshold   doorway, portal, gateway

thrifty   economical, saving, frugal, prudent, careful, economizing, sparing   wasteful   THRIFT

thrill   tingle, excite, titillate, delight, enrapture, enthrall, enchant, charm   bore

thrive   prosper, grow, develop, increase, sprout, flourish, mushroom, boom, bloom   shrivel, fade, fail

throb   beat, pulsate, palpitate, pound, thump

throng   crowd, cluster, congregate, gather, assemble, collect, meet

throw   toss, cast, furl, fling, pitch, heave, chuck, flip, sling

thrust   push, shove, press, bear, ram, drive, prod, goad, propel

thump   strike, blow, pound, beat, knock, hit, jab, poke, punch, rap, bang, bat, clout (*Slang* — slug, belt, bash, sock, paste, swat, wallop)

thunderstruck astonished, amazed, surprised, astounded, bewildered, dumbfounded, aghast, awed, spellbound, flabbergasted

thus therefore, hence, consequently, accordingly, so

thwart frustrate, foil, oppose, defeat, balk, spoil, ruin, hinder, inhibit, obstruct, hamper, impede, prevent, prohibit, forbid, deter (*Slang* — foul up, gum up, louse up) help, assist, encourage

ticket 1. label, stamp, sticker, seal, tag, 2. pass, certificate, token, credential, voucher, 3. ballot, slate, 4. summons, subpoena, citation

tickle amuse, delight, titillate, entertain, charm, thrill, excite

tidings news, information, word, advice

tidy 1. neat, orderly, trim, well-kept, shipshape sloppy, 2. considerable, large, sizable, grand, big, goodly, substantial TIDINESS

tie fasten, bind, lash, wrap, strap untie, open

tier row, line, layer, level, story, deck

tight 1. firm, rigid, stiff, taut, tense relaxed, 2. snug, compact, close loose, 3. scarce, hard to get, sparse, rare, skimpy plentiful, 4. stingy, ungenerous, closefisted, miserly (*Slang* — penny-pinching) generous

till 1. cultivate, plow, work, 2. money drawer, cash register, moneybox, vault, safe, depository

tilt tip, slope, slant, incline, lean, list

timber wood, lumber, logs

time 1. duration, period, interval, spell, term, age, generation, era, epoch (*Slang* — hitch, stretch), 2. occasion, opportunity, chance, opening, 3. rhythm, tempo, meter, measure

timepiece clock, watch

timetable schedule, list, program

timid shy, bashful, coy, demure, reserved, restrained, retiring, meek, sheepish, fearful, cowardly, shrinking bold
TIMIDITY

tinge color, tint, stain, dye

tingle sting, prickle

tinker mend, repair, fix, service, condition, patch up

tinkle ring, sound, toll, peal, chime, jingle

tint color, tinge, dye, stain, shade

tiny small, minute, undersized, little, slight, puny, wee
large

tip 1. end, extremity, limit, tail, point, 2. slope, slant, tilt,
list, leaning, inclination, 3. gratuity, premium, bonus, 4.
advice, warning, information, pointer

tiptop excellent, first-rate, superior, high-class, topnotch
inferior

tired weary, exhausted, fatigued, weak, run-down rested
TIRE, TIRELESS, TIRESOME

title name, label, tag, designation, caption, headline

toast drink to

together collectively, simultaneously, concurrently, jointly,
cooperatively alone

toil labor, work

token 1. proof, sign, indication, evidence, clue, mark, symptom, 2. memento, remembrance, trophy, souvenir, keepsake,
relic, 3. ticket, certificate, voucher, coupon, check

tolerate allow, permit, bear, endure, suffer, stand, abide,
accept prohibit, forbid
TOLERABLE, TOLERANCE, TOLERANT

toll 1. ring, peal, chime, tinkle, jingle, 2. charge, fee, due, dues, fare, tax, duty, tariff, assessment, revenue, levy, tithe

tomb grave, vault, crypt, shrine, mausoleum

tone 1. sound, pitch, key, note, intonation, 2. spirit, character, style, nature, quality, mood, 3. condition, vigor, shape, 4. color, shade, hue, tint, tinge, stain, complexion

tongue language, speech, talk

tonic medicine, stimulant, bracer

too 1. also, besides, additionally, as well, furthermore, 2. very, exceedingly, overly, excessively

tool implement, instrument, utensil, apparatus, device, gadget, appliance

top head, highest, summit, peak, crown, tip, apex, acme, zenith, maximum bottom

topic subject, theme, text, question, problem, issue, point, plot

topmost highest, uppermost, maximum, head, supreme

topple tumble, fall, overturn, sprawl, stumble

topsy-turvy upside-down, inverted, reversed, confused, jumbled, chaotic, mixed up (*Slang* — fouled up, haywire, snafu, balled up, screwed up) orderly

torch light, lantern, lamp

torment pain, distress, torture, agonize, harrow, irritate, inflame, persecute, harass, molest, bother, trouble, harry, heckle, badger, pester, worry, tease, plague (*Slang* — pick on, ride)

tornado whirlwind, windstorm, tempest, blizzard, squall, gale, hurricane

torrent flood, burst, eruption, stream, outbreak, deluge

torrid hot, sweltering, burning, scorching, blistering, roasting, broiling, scalding, seething, sizzling cold

torture pain, distress, torment, agonize, harrow, inflame, persecute, plague

toss throw, cast, fling, pitch, hurl, sling, heave, chuck, flip (*Slang* — peg, fire)

tot child, little one (*Slang* — kid)

total 1. whole, entire, complete partial, 2. add, sum up, figure up, count

touch 1. feel, contact, finger, handle, manipulate, 2. graze, brush, reach, scrape, skim, 3. affect, move, stir, impress, strike, 4. borrow, ask for, beg (*Slang* — mooch, bum, panhandle, hit up)

touching tender, provoking, affecting, moving, pathetic

tough 1. hardy, strong, firm, sturdy, durable weak, 2. hard, difficult, complicated, obscure, unclear, vague easy

tour journey, travel, voyage TOURIST

tournament contest, tourney, game, sport, play

tow pull, heave, haul, tug, draw, drag

towering huge, lofty, high, elevated, soaring, immense, monumental, gigantic TOWER

town metropolis, city, municipality

toxic poisonous, venomous, noxious, deadly, malignant

toy plaything, trinket, bauble

trace 1. copy, reproduce, duplicate, transcribe, draw, sketch, outline, delineate, 2. seek, track, trail, follow, smell out, 3. bit, small amount, touch, dash

track 1. path, trail, road, 2. mark, trace, sign, clue, evidence

tract area, field, sphere, expanse, space, extent, measure, dimension

traction friction, pulling, drawing, tugging, hauling

trade 1. exchange, barter, bargain, deal, switch, reciprocate, traffic, swap, 2. vocation, occupation, business, work, line, calling, profession, practice, pursuit, career, craft

tradition custom, long usage, folklore TRADITIONAL

traffic 1. buy or sell, exchange, trade, bargain, barter, deal, 2. vehicle movement

tragic disastrous, dreadful, sad, catastrophic, grievous TRAGEDY

trail 1. follow, pursue, go after, shadow, heel, tail, tag along, 2. track, hunt, trace, run down, 3. path, road, line

train 1. teach, rear, bring up, direct, drill, exercise, practice, prepare, condition, cultivate, discipline, nurture, foster, educate, groom, 2. series, succession, line, sequence, file, string, row, procession, column, 3. railroad cars

trait characteristic, feature, peculiarity, earmark, type, quality, property, attribute, idiosyncracy, habit, pattern

traitor betrayer, informer, tattler, blab, spy, undercover man (*Slang* — squealer, stool pigeon, rat, double-crosser, snitch, stoolie, fink) TRAITOROUS

tramp 1. march, parade, hike, 2. vagabond, vagrant, hobo (*Slang* — bum)

trance spell, ecstasy, rapture, hypnosis

tranquil calm, peaceful, quiet, serene, untroubled noisy, tumultuous TRANQUILIZE, TRANQUILITY

transact execute, perform, discharge, dispatch, enact, carry out TRANSACTION

transfer hand over, deliver, pass, sign over, change hands

transform change, convert, alter TRANSFORMATION

transgress overstep, trespass, encroach, infringe TRANSGRESSION

transient fleeting, passing, migratory, vagrant, straying, drifting, wandering, roaming, roving, rambling, meandering, temporary, transitory, short-lived permanent

transition change, conversion, transformation, transfer TRANSIT

translate interpret TRANSLATION

transmit send over, pass along, dispatch, forward, transfer TRANSMISSION

transplant transfer, transpose, shift, change, move, reset

transportation conveyance, carrying, carriage TRANSPORT

trap catch, snare, hook

trash rubbish, rubble, scrap, debris, litter, junk

travel journey, go, proceed, move, pass, progress, traverse

treacherous deceiving, unreliable, two-faced, fraudulent, shifty, tricky, underhanded, insidious, shady TREACHERY

tread walk, step, pace

treason betrayal, double-dealing (*Slang* — double-cross, sellout)

treasure 1. cherish, value highly, hold dear, adore, idolize, worship, prize, appreciate, 2. store, assets, accumulation, collection, funds, resources, abundance, fortune, wealth

treat 1. deal with, think of, consider, regard, handle, behave toward, 2. doctor, minister to, attend, nurse, 3. delight, pleasure, thrill, enjoyment

treatise study, thesis, article, paper, essay, dissertation, discourse, discussion

treaty agreement, compact, alliance, settlement, arrangement, truce, armistice

trek travel, journey, voyage, migration

tremble shake, quake, vibrate, shiver, quiver, quaver, shudder

tremendous 1. enormous, great, huge, immense, vast, titanic, colossal, gigantic, giant small, minute, 2. superb, exquisite, magnificent, marvelous, glorious, divine, terrific, sensational awful

tremor trembling, shaking, quiver, quake, shiver

trench ditch, moat, dugout, foxhole, channel

trend direction, course, tendency, drift, current, movement

trespass intrude, transgress, encroach, infringe, overstep

trial 1. test, experiment, tryout (*Slang* — workout), 2. trouble, hardship, tribulation, ordeal, 3. court case

tribe group, class, set, kind, people, family, sect, breed, clan, folk, culture TRIBAL

tribunal court, forum, board, council

tribute 1. contribution, donation, subscription, 2. compliment, praise, glorification, eulogy, laudation

trick deceive, cheat, hoax, dupe, delude, betray, fool, hoodwink (*Slang* — kid, spoof) TRICKY

trickle leak, drip, dribble, drop

tried tested, proved

trifle small amount, little bit abundance, lots TRIFLING

trigger begin, start, touch off, spark, fire, kindle conclude

trim 1. cut, shave, pare, reduce, lower, 2. decorate, ornament, adorn, dress, garnish, deck, beautify, embellish, furbish, tidy, straighten up, clean, fix up, spruce up

trinket trifle, bauble, knickknack, toy, plaything

trip 1. stumble, tumble, topple, fall, 2. journey, voyage, trek, tour, expedition, pilgrimage, excursion, jaunt, junket, outing

triumph victory, success, conquest, winning defeat
TRIUMPHANT

trivial unimportant, petty, trifling, slight, superficial, shallow, frivolous, light, foolish, silly, inane important

troop group, band, unit, company, party, gang, crew, body, bunch, crowd, mob

trophy prize, award, laurels, reward, memento, souvenir, remembrance, keepsake

trot run, sprint, bound, trip

trouble distress, worry, disturb, agitate, perturb, disquiet, stir, bother, upset, discomfort, vex, plague calm, soothe
TROUBLESOME

troupe band, company, group, party, gang, crew

truant absentee

truce pause, rest, respite, break, recess, intermission, interruption, interval, armistice, peace

trudge plod, lumber

true real, actual, unmistaken, veritable, certain, valid, genuine, authentic, natural, legitimate, bona fide, right, proper, correct, exact, accurate false TRULY, TRUTH

trust believe, credit, accept, rely on, depend on distrust
TRUSTWORTHY

try 1. attempt, test, experiment, prove, verify, essay, undertake (*Slang* — take a fling at, have a go at, give it a whirl, make a stab at), 2. judge, prosecute, hear

trying annoying, distressing, difficult, troublesome, bothersome, burdensome

tube pipe, hose, reed

tuck   fold, crease, bend, gather

tuft   clump, bunch, cluster, group

tug   pull, jerk, wrench, draw, tow, haul, yank

tuition   teaching, instruction, education, schooling

tumble   fall, toss, sprawl, topple, stumble, wallow, flounder, pitch, plunge, lurch

tumult   noise, uproar, disorder, disturbance, commotion, turmoil, hubbub, racket, fracas, fuss, pandemonium, turbulence, excitement, rumpus, to-do, row   quiet, peace TUMULTUOUS

tune   melody, music, harmony, song

tunnel   underground passage, cave, grotto, cavern

turbulent   violent, disorderly, unruly, tumultuous, storming, frenzied, wild, blustering, furious, frantic, excited, riotous   calm, peaceful

turf   grass, sod

turmoil   commotion, disturbance, tumult, noise, uproar, disorder, hubbub, racket, fracas, fuss, pandemonium, turbulence, excitement, rumpus, to-do, row   quiet, peace

turn   1. rotate, pivot, swivel, wheel, twist, gyrate, go around, shift, swerve, veer, curve, circle, 2. change, alter, vary, 3. spoil, sour

tussle   struggle, wrestle, scuffle, contend, fight, battle (*Slang* — scrap)

tutor   teach, instruct, coach, prime, educate, school, enlighten, direct, guide, show, train, drill, prepare, condition

twig   branch, limb, sprig, sprout, shoot

twine   rope, cord, string

twinge   pain, pang

twinkle   sparkle, gleam, glitter, glisten, glimmer, shimmer, blink, shine

twirl   spin, rotate, whirl, turn, wind, swivel, wheel, pivot, gyrate

twist   1. turn, wind, curve, rotate, swivel, pivot, wheel, gyrate, circle, 2. change, falsify, misrepresent, distort, color, disguise, camouflage, alter

twitch   jerk, jiggle, fidget

type   kind, class, group, sort, ilk, variety, species, nature, make, brand, character, genus

typhoon   storm, hurricane, whirlwind, cyclone, tornado, twister

typical   representative, symbolic, characteristic, distinctive

tyrant   dictator, slave driver, despot, oppressor, martinet, taskmaster, disciplinarian   TYRANNICAL, TYRANNY

U

ugly   1. unattractive, unsightly, homely, plain, hideous pretty, 2. cross, cranky, bad-tempered, disagreeable, unpleasant, quarrelsome, irritable, testy, perverse, mean, ornery   pleasant

ultimate   last, final, terminal, conclusive, eventual

umpire   judge, referee, moderator, arbitrator, mediator

unable   incapable, incompetent, unfit, unqualified   able

unaccountable   unexplainable, inexplicable

unaccustomed   unusual, unfamiliar, strange, unused to accustomed, used to

unanimous   agreed, solid, concurrent, in complete accord

unarmed unprotected, defenseless, unshielded, unequipped armed

unassuming modest, meek, humble, unpretentious, natural, genuine, sincere, honest boastful, arrogant

unattended alone, unaccompanied

unavoidable inevitable, certain, sure, inescapable uncertain

unaware ignorant, unknowing, unconscious, unmindful, unsuspecting aware

unbearable intolerable, insufferable tolerable

unbecoming inappropriate, inapt, unfit, unsuitable, improper, indecent suitable, proper

unbelievable incredible, doubtful, questionable, unconvincing, suspicious believable

unbend straighten, relax, loosen, slacken, let up, ease up bend

unbiased impartial, fair, unprejudiced prejudiced

unbounded free, unconfined, unrestricted, wide-open

unbroken continuous, uninterrupted, constant, even, regular, steady, perpetual, whole broken

uncanny strange, mysterious, weird, creepy, eerie

unceasing continual, constant, incessant, endless, interminable, perpetual, everlasting

uncertain doubtful, unsure, speculative, changeable, unpredictable, insecure, precarious certain, sure

unchain free, release, unshackle, extricate chain, bind

unchanged same, permanent, unaltered, regular, constant, steady changed, irregular

uncivilized barbarous, savage, bestial, wild, brutal, unrefined, uncouth, uncultured civilized, refined

unclean 1. dirty, filthy, soiled, grimy, smutty, slimy, polluted, contaminated, infected, 2. evil, obscene, lewd, foul, pornographic, indecent
clean

uncomfortable distressing, painful, disturbed, bothered, troubled, upset, uneasy comfortable

uncommon rare, unusual, unique, novel, different, original, infrequent, scarce common

uncompromising firm, unyielding, obstinate, stiff, rigid, adamant, unbending, inflexible, strict, relentless
compromising, flexible

unconcerned uninterested, indifferent, blasé, nonchalant, apathetic, easygoing concerned, interested

unconditional unqualified, absolute, unlimited, positive, complete, total, perfect, entire, utter, explicit, express
conditional, limited

unconscious 1. senseless, out cold, 2. unaware, unintentional, unthinking, preoccupied, absent-minded, oblivious
conscious, aware

unconstitutional illegal, unlawful, illegitimate, unauthorized legal

uncouth awkward, clumsy, crude, ungainly, vulgar, coarse, gross, rude, crass, boorish, unrefined, unpolished, uncultured, uncivilized, barbarous, common, base
genteel, courteous, suave

uncover reveal, expose, disclose, open, unmask
cover, conceal

uncultivated wild, undeveloped, rough, crude, fallow
cultivated, refined

undaunted fearless, unafraid, daring, bold, brave, courageous, confident, persevering, untiring meek, fearful

undecided uncertain, unsettled, pending, vague, indefinite, undetermined certain, settled

under below, beneath, lower above

underfed undernourished, starved

undergo experience, go through, meet, have, feel, encounter, endure, suffer

underhanded secret, sly, shifty, surreptitious, deceitful, dishonest, fraudulent, crooked, unscrupulous (*Slang* — shady) open, honest

undermine weaken, sabotage, destroy

underneath below, beneath, under above

underrate minimize, underestimate, belittle overrate

understand comprehend, follow, grasp, conceive, realize, know, appreciate

undertake 1. try, attempt, essay, pursue (*Slang* — have a go at), 2. promise, contract, agree UNDERTAKING

undertone murmur, whisper

undesirable objectionable, disagreeable, unpleasant, distasteful, offensive, repulsive, intolerable, loathsome, unsatisfactory, unacceptable, unsuitable desirable

undisputed unquestioned, uncontested, doubtless, accepted, believed questionable

undisturbed untroubled, calm, tranquil disturbed

undo 1. unfasten, untie, disassemble, take apart, dismantle assemble, 2. destroy, spoil, abolish, wreck build

undress disrobe, unclothe, strip dress

undying eternal, immortal, unfading, imperishable, everlasting, indestructible fading, perishable

unearth dig up, discover, extract, withdraw, remove, uncover, disclose, turn up bury, hide

unearthly strange, weird, ghostly, wild, supernatural, odd, queer, peculiar, spooky, uncanny, eerie

uneasy   restless, disturbed, anxious, uncomfortable, fidgety, impatient, distressed, troubled, bothered, agitated, perturbed (*Slang* — in a stew)   calm, comfortable
UNEASINESS

unemployed   idle, jobless, unoccupied, out of work
employed   UNEMPLOYMENT

unending   continuous, endless, uninterrupted, ceaseless, incessant, interminable, perpetual, infinite, everlasting, permanent

unequal   uneven, irregular, disparate   equal

uneven   unequal, irregular, disparate   even

unexpected   unforeseen, unanticipated, chance, accidental, sudden   foreseen, expected

unfailing   faithful, loyal, sure, true, constant, reliable, dependable, sound, firm, secure, stable, substantial, steadfast   undependable, unreliable

unfair   unjust   fair

unfaithful   untrue, unloyal, false, fickle   faithful

unfamiliar   unusual, strange, uncommon, rare, unique, novel, new, different   familiar, common

unfasten   undo, loosen, open, untie, unhook   fasten, close

unfavorable   unsatisfactory, harmful, detrimental, adverse, contrary, uncomplimentary, disapproving   favorable

unfeeling   hard-hearted, cruel, heartless, cold, callous
sensitive, compassionate

unfinished   incomplete, rough, undone, crude
finished, completed

unfit   unsuitable, inappropriate, incapable, incompetent, unqualified   fit, suitable

unfold   1. reveal, show, open, disclose, uncover, unmask, spread, unfurl hide, conceal, 2. explain, show, clarify, demonstrate, illuminate

unforeseen unexpected, unanticipated, sudden expected

unforgettable memorable, notable, noteworthy, remarkable, extraordinary, exceptional ordinary

unfortunate unlucky, ill-fated (*Slang* — jinxed) lucky, fortunate

unfriendly unsociable, aloof, standoffish, distant, remote, cool, uncordial, inhospitable friendly

ungainly awkward, clumsy, bungling, unhandy, ungraceful, gawky graceful

ungracious impolite, rude, discourteous, uncivil, ungallant, unkind gracious, polite

ungrateful unappreciative, unthankful grateful, thankful

unguarded unprotected, defenseless, unshielded, unsheltered guarded, protected

unhappy sad, sorrowful, uncheerful, displeased, discontented, wretched, miserable, dejected, depressed, downcast, disheartened, despondent, melancholy, blue, wistful, unsatisfied happy, cheerful

unhealthy sickly, infirm, unwholesome, unsound, weak, feeble, frail, run-down, ill, ailing, unwell, indisposed healthy

unheeded disregarded, unnoticed, unobserved, unseen heeded

uniform 1. even, alike, unvaried, constant, steady, regular, consistent, symmetrical, balanced uneven, irregular, 2. outfit, costume

unify combine, unite, consolidate, join, mix, merge, blend, fuse separate UNITE, UNITY

unimportant insignificant, trifling, inconsequential, trivial, petty important

uninhabited unoccupied, deserted, abandoned, vacant occupied

unnecessary needless, uncalled-for, unessential, super-fluous, excess necessary, essential

unnerve upset, frighten, scare, alarm, startle

unnoticed unobserved, unheeded, unseen noticed, seen

unobserved unnoticed, unheeded, unseen noticed, seen

unoccupied vacant, idle, deserted, open, available, unin-habited occupied

unpack unload, discharge, dump pack

unpaid owing, due, outstanding paid

unparalleled unequaled, matchless, unsurpassed, unex-celled, unbeatable, incomparable, extraordinary, exception-al, remarkable

unpleasant disagreeable, distasteful, unsavory, undesirable, unlikable, offensive, odious, repulsive, repugnant, obnoxious pleasant

unpopular unappreciated, unloved, unwanted, unlikable, unwelcome, disliked popular, well-liked

unprecedented unduplicated, uncopied, unimitated, extra-ordinary, exceptional

unprepared unready, unwary ready

unprincipled dishonest, crooked, corrupt, criminal, fraud-ulent, unscrupulous (*Slang* — shady, fishy) honest

unprofitable unrewarding, fruitless profitable, rewarding

unquestionable certain, positive, undeniable, indisputable, questionable, dubious

unravel 1. unsnarl, untwist, disentangle tangle, 2. solve, explain, answer, resolve, figure out, unriddle, decipher, decode, crack

unreal 1. imaginary, fanciful, fictitious, 2. counterfeit, make-believe, false, mock, imitation, simulated, ungenuine, unauthentic, artificial, synthetic, pseudo, fake (*Slang* — phony) real

unreasonable extreme, excessive, outrageous, preposterous, extravagant, impractical, illogical, senseless, inconsistent, irrational, unsound reasonable, moderate
UNREASONABLY

unrest restlessness, agitation, disquiet, stir, disturbance, commotion, turmoil, tumult, excitement
calm, peacefulness

unrestrained unchecked, free, uncurbed, uncontrolled restrained

unrivaled unmatched, unequaled, incomparable

unruly disorderly, riotous, wild, rampant, lawless orderly

unsafe dangerous, unsound, precarious, imperiled, risky, perilous, hazardous safe

unsatisfactory ungratifying, inadequate, insufficient, inferior, second-rate, low-grade satisfactory

unscramble solve, explain, resolve, clear up, figure out, decipher, decode, crack scramble, confuse

unscrupulous dishonest, unprincipled, unethical, corrupt, crooked, criminal, fraudulent honest, moral

unseat displace, dislodge, depose, remove, dismiss, overthrow

unseemly improper, unsuitable, vulgar, indecent, offensive, coarse, crude, objectionable, wrong, unbecoming
proper, suitable

unselfish generous, liberal, free, unsparing, lavish, open-handed, bighearted, magnanimous selfish

unsettle disturb, shake, upset, startle, shock (*Slang* — jar, jolt)

unshaken   firm, resolute, staunch, solid, fixed, unyielding, steady   shaken

unsightly   ugly, unattractive, homely, plain pretty, attractive

unskilled   untrained, untalented, inexperienced, raw, green, amateurish   skilled, talented

unsophisticated   simple, natural, artless, naive, green sophisticated

unsound   unwise, ill-advised, unreasonable, illogical, unreliable, hazardous, risky, unsafe, unsure   sound, reliable

unstable   unsteady, weak, unsound, unreliable, unsure, unsafe   stable, reliable

unsteady   unstable, weak, unsound, unreliable, unsure, unsafe   steady, reliable

unsuccessful   failing, unfortunate, abortive, fruitless successful

unsuitable   unfit, inappropriate, unbecoming, improper, unsatisfactory, objectionable, unacceptable   suitable, proper

unthinkable   unbelievable, incredible, impossible, inconceivable, absurd, ridiculous, preposterous, outlandish, unheard-of   believable

untidy   neglected, slovenly, shabby, frowzy, messy, sloppy, seedy (*Slang* — mussy)   tidy, neat

untie   loosen, unfasten, undo   tie

untrained   unskilled, unprepared, untalented, inexperienced, amateurish, raw, green   trained, skilled

untried   new, unused, untouched, unproved   tried, tested

untrue   1. false, wrong, faulty, erroneous, fallacious   true, right,   2. unfaithful, disloyal, fickle   faithful, loyal

unused   1. new, fresh, firsthand, original, untouched   used, 2. unaccustomed, unfamiliar with   used to

unusual uncommon, rare, unique, out of the ordinary, novel, queer, odd, different usual, ordinary

unveil uncover, disclose, reveal, show, expose, open, unmask, divulge cover, hide

unwelcome unwanted, uninvited welcome

unwell ailing, ill, sick, indisposed well, healthy

unwholesome unhealthy, unsound wholesome

unwieldy unmanageable, unhandy, awkward, clumsy, cumbersome, bulky manageable

unwilling reluctant, forced, involuntary, disinclined willing

unwise foolish, unreasonable, unsound, senseless, irrational wise

unwittingly unknowingly, unconsciously, unintentionally, unmindfully aware

unyielding firm, stubborn, immovable, inflexible, unpliable, unbending, adamant, rigid flexible

upbraid reprove, blame, reprimand, scold, rebuke, chide, lecture (*Slang* — dress down, tell off, bawl out, chew out)

uphold support, confirm, sustain, maintain, bolster, substantiate, corroborate UPHELD

upkeep maintenance, support, backing, provision

uplift raise, elevate, erect, lift, hoist, improve lower

upper higher, superior, greater lower UPPERMOST

upright 1. standing, erect, vertical prone, 2. honorable, upstanding, reputable, respectable, moral, law-abiding

uprising revolt, rebellion, mutiny, insurrection, riot, revolution

uproar noise, disturbance, commotion, hubbub, tumult, clamor, turmoil, racket, fracas, ado, fuss, pandemonium, rumpus, to-do, row peace, quiet

uproot   extract, withdraw, remove, pull out

upset   1. overturn, tip over, unsettle, capsize, 2. disturb, perturb, trouble, agitate, confuse, shake, fluster, ruffle, bother, unnerve   soothe, calm, 3. overthrow, defeat, revolution, overwhelm

upshot   conclusion, result, effect, consequence, outcome, fruit, development

up-to-date   modern, contemporary, advanced, current, fashionable   old-fashioned, outdated

urban   metropolitan, civic, municipal, citified   suburban

urge   push, force, drive, plead, advise, incite, press, pressure, coax, goad, prod, spur, agitate, provoke, prompt   discourage

urgent   pressing, important, imperative, compelling, crucial, essential, vital, necessary, moving, motivating, driving   unimportant

usage   method, practice, way, use, procedure, treatment, handling

use   1. utilize, employ, practice, exercise, handle, manage, 2. exploit, take advantage of

useful   helpful, beneficial, profitable, serviceable, advantageous, practical, functional, handy, valuable   useless

useless   worthless, ineffectual, fruitless   useful

usher   escort, conduct, guide, lead, squire, chaperon, accompany, attend

usual   customary, ordinary, normal, regular, common, everyday, typical   unusual   USUALLY

usurp   take command, take charge, take over, assume control, overthrow, seize command

utensil   implement, tool, instrument, apparatus, device, appliance

utilize use, employ

utmost greatest, farthest, highest, extreme, most

utter 1. complete, total, absolute, thorough, downright, outright, pure, plain, sheer, unqualified, positive partial, 2. speak, express, say, voice, sound

V

vacant unoccupied, empty, void, barren, desolate occupied, filled VACANCY

vacation rest, holiday, leave, recess, furlough, liberty, sabbatical

vaccinate inoculate, immunize VACCINE

vacuum 1. void, 2. sweep, clean

vagabond wanderer, tramp, vagrant, hobo (*Slang* — bum)

vague unclear, indistinct, indefinite, dim, faint, shadowy, obscure, blurred, fuzzy, hazy, misty clear, definite

vain 1. unsuccessful, ineffectual, futile, fruitless successful, 2. proud, conceited, boastful, egotistical, egocentric, haughty, lofty, self-centered (*Slang* — stuck-up, cocky, uppish) humble

valiant brave, courageous, bold, gallant, heroic, chivalrous, daring, unafraid, dauntless cowardly

valid sound, true, good, effective, proven, established, well-grounded, cogent, legal, lawful, adequate, authorized invalid, false

valor bravery, courage, boldness, gallantry, prowess, heroism cowardice

value worth, excellence, usefulness, importance, significance, weight, merit, quality VALUABLE

vandal destroyer, wrecker, demolisher VANDALIZE

vanish   disappear, fade, go away, perish, cease to be   appear

vanquish   conquer, defeat, overcome, subdue, crush

vapor   steam, fog, mist, gas, fume, smoke

various   different, several, many, diverse

varnish   1. paint, coat, lacquer, shellac, 2. distort, falsify, misrepresent, color, disguise, camouflage

vary   change, differ, alter, deviate
VARIABLE, VARIATION, VARIED, VARIETY

vast   large, immense, great, enormous, huge, stupendous, colossal, monumental, mammoth, gigantic   tiny

vault   1. jump, leap, spring, hop, bound, hurdle, 2. storehouse, compartment, depository, safe, coffer, 3. burial place, crypt, tomb

veer   shift, turn, swerve, change

vegetation   plants, flora, growth

vehement   forceful, violent, fierce, furious, severe, intense, ardent, zealous   VEHEMENCE

vehicle   conveyance, carriage

veil   cover, screen, hide, conceal, cloak, mask, disguise, camouflage, eclipse, obscure   unveil, uncover

velocity   speed, swiftness, quickness

vend   sell, peddle   buy   VENDOR

venerable   revered, dignified, stately, grand, majestic, imposing, honorable, important

vengeance   revenge, retaliation, reprisal, avengement

venom   1. spite, malice, animosity, bitterness, rancor, 2. poison   VENOMOUS

vent   hole, opening, outlet, passage, duct

ventilate 1. air, aerate, refresh, cool, 2. discuss, reason, talk over, deliberate, consider, treat, examine, study
VENTILATION

venture undertaking, enterprise, project, attempt, adventure, experiment

verbal oral, spoken, uttered, said, vocalized, voiced, pronounced, sounded, articulated, enunciated written

verdict decision, judgment, finding, determination, decree, ruling, pronouncement

verge 1. tend, incline, lean, border, 2. edge, rim, brink, border

verify confirm, prove, certify, validate, substantiate, authenticate, corroborate, support, document, double-check

versatile skilled, talented, competent, capable, many-sided, adaptable, all-around

verse 1. poetry, rhyme, jingle, 2. section, chapter, passage, part, division, measure

versed experienced, practiced, skilled, educated

version rendition, account, interpretation

vertical standing, upright, perpendicular, erect

very greatly, extremely, much, exceedingly, quite, pretty, intensely

vessel 1. container, receptacle, 2. ship, boat

veteran 1. experienced, practiced, worldly-wise, sophisticated, 2. ex-soldier

veto refuse, deny (*Slang* — kill) accept

vex annoy, disturb, trouble, provoke, irk, irritate, aggravate

viaduct bridge, span

vibrate shake, quiver, quake, tremble, quaver, wobble, bob, bounce

vice   fault, bad habit, weakness, failing, foible, shortcoming, wrongdoing, malpractice, sin, crime

vicinity   1. region, area, zone, territory, place, district, quarter, section, neighborhood, 2. nearness, closeness, proximity

vicious   evil, wicked, spiteful, malicious, bad, naughty, wrong, sinful, base, low, vile, cruel, ruthless, brutal, barbarous, savage, ferocious, inhumane   kind, good

victim   prey, dupe, loser, underdog, sufferer (*Slang* — sucker, sap, pigeon, pushover, butt, goat, easy mark)

victory   success, triumph, conquest, winning, win, knockout   defeat   VICTOR, VICTORIOUS

vie   compete, rival, compare with, match

view   1. see, sight, look at, behold, observe, perceive, watch, regard, 2. opinion, belief, attitude, sentiment, feeling, impression, notion, idea, thought, conception, theory, judgment, outlook

vigilant   watchful, alert, wide-awake, cautious, careful   VIGIL, VIGILANCE

vigorous   strong, energetic, potent, powerful, mighty, forceful, rugged, hearty, robust, dynamic, intense, active, lively, animated, spirited, vivacious   weak   VIGOR

vile   foul, disgusting, bad, terrible, dreadful, horrible, deplorable, outrageous, wretched, base, odious, obnoxious, abominable, detestable, despicable, contemptible (*Slang* — awful, atrocious)

villain   rascal, scoundrel, rogue, knave, scamp, devil

vim   force, energy, vigor, verve, punch, dash, drive, snap, push (*Slang* — pep, kick, zip)

vindicate   justify, uphold, defend successfully, pardon, excuse, forgive, acquit   VINDICATION

vindictive   revengeful, avenging

violate   break, trespass, infringe   VIOLATION

violence   anger, rage, passion, fury, force, intensity, vehe-mence   VIOLENT

virgin   pure, spotless, unused, new, firsthand, original, fresh, green   used, old

virtual   real, actual, basic, essential, fundamental VIRTUALLY

virtuous   good, moral, righteous, angelic, saintly, chaste, pure, innocent, faultless, sinless   sinful, wicked   VIRTUE

visible   apparent, manifest, noticeable, open, exposed, per-ceptible, evident, obvious, plain, clear   concealed

vision   1. sight, perception, 2. apparition, image, illusion, phantom, fantasy, dream, specter, ghost   VISUAL

visit   attend, go to, call on, drop in   VISITOR

vista   view, scene, sight, outlook, perspective, scenery

vital   1. necessary, important, essential, fundamental, needed, required   unimportant,   2. living, alive, animate

vitality   strength, vigor, might, potency, power, energy, stamina (*Slang* — guts)

vivacious   lively, sprightly, animated, gay, spirited, exuber-ant, active, spry, brisk, dynamic, energetic (*Slang* — snappy, peppy)   lethargic, dull

vivid   bright, brilliant, strong, clear, distinct, splendid, flam-boyant, glaring, dazzling, rich, colorful   dull

vocal   spoken, uttered, said, voiced, pronounced, sounded, oral, verbal, articulated, enunciated

vocation   occupation, business, profession, trade, work, line, calling, craft

vociferous   noisy, loud, shouting, clamoring, boisterous, blatant   quiet, hushed

vogue fashion, style, mode, popularity

voice express, utter, verbalize, say, articulate, enunciate, pronounce, communicate, tell

void 1. empty, vacant, bare, blank, barren, desolate, unoccupied, deserted, open, available filled, 2. invalid valid

volume 1. amount, quantity, capacity, content, proportion, measure, extent, 2. book, publication, writing, work

voluminous generous, ample, extensive, bulky skimpy, slight

volunteer offer, come forward VOLUNTARY

vomit retch, heave, regurgitate, spew, throw up (*Slang* — upchuck, puke)

voracious ravenous, greedy, piggish, hoggish, gluttonous

vote ballot, choice, voice, poll, referendum, designation, selection, decision, determination

vouch testify, bear witness, swear, promise, assure, guarantee, vow, pledge

vow swear, promise, assure, guarantee, vouch, pledge

voyage journey, travel, sail, cruise, navigate VOYAGER

vulgar coarse, common, unrefined, indecent, improper, offensive, crude, crass, obscene, uncouth, foul, filthy, nasty refined VULGARITY

vulnerable sensitive, exposed, open, susceptible, unprotected, defenseless

vying competitive, rival

W

wad lump, mass, hunk, chunk

wag wave, flap, flutter, wobble, bob, sway, swing

wage   1. pay, payment, salary, remuneration, compensation, 2. pursue, conduct, carry on, practice, exercise, follow, engage in

wager   bet, gamble, hazard, stake

wagon   carriage, vehicle

waif   stray, vagabond, gamin

wail   cry, screech, shriek, scream, squeal, howl, bawl, moan

wait   delay, postpone, defer, put off, shelve, table, procrastinate, stay, tarry, linger

wake   awake, arise, get up, rouse, arouse, stir (*Slang* — rise and shine, roll out)

walk   step, tread, pace, ambulate, stroll, hike

wallet   billfold, purse

wallop   hit, thrash, beat, strike, knock, jab, smack, whack, slug, rap, whip, spank, flog, bat, crack, clout, lick (*Slang* — belt, clobber, paste, clip, swat, sock)

wallow   roll, flounder, rock, reel, toss, tumble, pitch, lurch, swing, sway

wan   pale, faint, weak, pallid, sallow, pasty, ashen, haggard, ghastly   ruddy, robust

wand   rod, staff, scepter

wander   stray, meander, roam, rove, gad, drift, ramble
WANDERER

wane   decrease, diminish, lessen, decline, subside, recede increase, wax

want   1. desire, wish for, like, long for, fancy, 2. need, lack, require

wanton   1. reckless, careless, hasty, impetuous, wild careful, 2. erratic, whimsical, uncontrolled, unreasonable steady, 3. immoral, unchaste, wayward, loose   moral

war fight, conflict, strife, battle, combat, engagement, encounter, clash, struggle, hostilities, campaign WARFARE

warehouse storehouse, depository, depot

warm 1. hot, tepid, 2. friendly, enthusiastic, cordial, congenial cold WARMTH

warn 1. inform, give notice, notify, caution, forebode, advise, alert, 2. threaten, menace WARNING

warp bend, twist, distort, contort

warrant 1. authority, right, sanction, authorization, certificate, justification, reason, voucher, writ, mandate, 2. guarantee, pledge, promise, vow, word, assurance, oath

warrior soldier, fighter

wary cautious, careful, guarded, suspicious, distrustful (*Slang* — cagey, leery) WARILY, WARINESS

wash clean, scrub, launder, bathe, rinse, scour

waste 1. spend, squander, consume, use up, exhaust save, 2. garbage, refuse, scraps, dregs, rubbish

watch 1. look at, view, observe, regard, 2. guard, protect, mind, tend, shield, care for

waterway channel, river, canal, passageway

wave 1. sway, move, flap, flutter, swing, 2. signal, gesture

wax 1. increase, gain, grow, rise, swell, heighten, intensify, enlarge, develop, sprout, flourish decrease, wane, 2. polish, burnish, furbish, glaze, shine

way 1. manner, style, custom, mode, fashion, usage, practice, 2. means, method, procedure, process, 3. point, feature, detail, respect, 4. direction, line, course, 5. distance, reach, remoteness, length, extent, 6. will, nature, character, constitution, temperament, disposition, mood, humor

waylay ambush, attack, lie in wait

wayward 1. disobedient, lawless, undisciplined, troublesome, loose, immoral, difficult, perverse, contrary, wanton obedient, 2. irregular, unsteady, changeable, unsettled, erratic, wavering steady, settled

weak feeble, powerless, impotent, debilitated, fragile strong, sturdy WEAKEN, WEAKLING

wealth riches, affluence, prosperity, abundance, opulence, possessions, fortune, treasure, resources, assets poverty WEALTHY

wean cure, break of, turn away from

weapon arms, munition

wear 1. dress in, have on, don (*Slang* — sport), 2. deteriorate, corrode, decay

weary tired, fatigued, weak, faint, listless, lethargic, sluggish lively, energetic WEARILY, WEARINESS, WEARISOME

weather climate, the elements

weave braid, intertwine, lace

wed marry, join, unite (*Slang* — get hitched) WEDDING

wedge jam, push, lodge, squeeze

wedlock marriage, matrimony

weep cry, shed tears, sob, bawl, blubber, snivel

weigh measure, gauge, assess, estimate, rate, appraise, size up WEIGHT

weighty 1. heavy, hefty light, 2. burdensome, oppressive, onerous, 3. important, influential, powerful, effective, serious trivial

weird strange, mysterious, odd, fantastic, queer, creepy, peculiar, spooky, eerie, ghostly normal

welcome   greet, receive

weld   join, unite, cement, bind, solder

welfare   well-being, good, benefit, interest, advantage, behalf, prosperity, success, comfort

welt   sore, swelling

whack   strike, blow, hit, jab, smack, slug, bat, crack, clout, lick (*Slang* — belt, clobber, paste, clip, swat, sock, wallop)

wharf   pier, dock, port, harbor

wheedle   coax, persuade, urge, press, goad, prod

whet   sharpen, edge, intensify, stimulate

whether   if, provided, on condition

whiff   odor, smell, scent, fume

whim   fancy, notion, caprice, fad, phase   WHIMSICAL

whimper   cry, whine

whine   cry, whimper

whip   strike, beat, thrash, spank, flog, pummel, lash, lace, strap, paddle (*Slang* — lick, wallop)

whirl   spin, turn, wheel, twirl, reel, swirl, rotate, pivot, swivel, gyrate

whisk   1. sweep, brush, 2. rush, speed, hurry, hasten

whisper   murmur, mutter, mumble

whole   complete, total, entire, one, solid, undivided   partial WHOLLY

wholehearted   earnest, sincere, hearty, cordial, gracious insincere

wholesome   healthful, beneficial, salutary, sound

wicked   1. bad, evil, sinful, vicious, naughty, wrong, base, low, vile good, saintly, 2. difficult, rough, hard, unpleasant, severe, rugged, tough easy, pleasant

wide broad, extensive, expansive, roomy, ample, spacious, far-reaching narrow WIDTH

wield hold, wave, handle, manipulate, use, employ, manage, control

wife spouse, mate, married woman

wig hairpiece, toupee

wiggle wriggle, squirm, writhe, twist, fidget, jerk, twitch, toss

wild 1. untamed, uncivilized, savage, unchecked, unrestrained, violent, barbarous, brutal, rampant, fierce, ferocious, bestial tame, 2. rash, crazy, reckless, impetuous, furious, mad, wanton, frantic, frenzied, rabid, delirious, hysterical, overwrought calm

wilderness wasteland

will 1. wish, desire, pleasure, fancy, hope, urge, inclination, volition, 2. resolution, determination, decision, resolve, purpose, choice, selection, election, intention, design, plan, contemplation, 3. bequest, legacy, testament

willful 1. stubborn, obstinate, headstrong, bullheaded, firm, adamant, uncompromising, 2. intended, intentional, designed, meant, deliberate, conscious, calculated, voluntary, purposeful involuntary, chance

willing ready, consenting, agreeable, inclined, compliant, eager (*Slang* — game) unwilling

wilt wither, deteriorate, pine, droop, fade, shrivel, dry up, languish flourish

wily tricky, cunning, crafty, sly, artful, shifty, smooth, slippery, foxy, canny, shrewd, clever (*Slang* — cagey, slick)

win gain, capture, carry, succeed, triumph, be victorious, prevail lose WINNER

wince   recoil, draw back, flinch, shrink, cringe

1. wind   1. air, draft, breeze, gust, 2. breath, respiration

2. wind   turn, bend, twist, roll, coil, spiral, pivot, swivel

wink   blink, squint

winning   charming, attractive, alluring, fascinating, captivating, lovely, enchanting, enthralling, intriguing,
bewitching, interesting, delightful, appealing, enticing, inviting, tantalizing, provocative, fetching (*Slang* — come-
hither) repulsive

wipe   rub, stroke

wire   1. telegraph, cable, 2. fasten, tie, bind, 3. electrify

wiry   1. lean, stringy stout, 2. strong, tough, muscular,
athletic, brawny weak

wise   bright, smart, knowledgeable, sage, knowing, learned,
profound, educated, cultured, scholarly dull, uneducated
WISDOM

wish   want, desire, long for, like, fancy, request

wistful   longing, yearning, desirous, pining, hankering,
nostalgic, homesick, melancholy, pensive

wit   humor, intelligence, understanding, sense

witch   hag, vixen, shrew, sorceress

withdraw   1. retreat, recede, retire, fall back, reverse, quit,
vacate, abandon advance, 2. remove, subtract, deduct,
extract deposit WITHDRAWAL

wither   fade, shrivel, dry up, shrink, wane, deteriorate,
droop, wilt, languish, pine flourish

withhold   1. reserve, keep, save, preserve spend, 2. refuse,
deny, disallow give

within   inside, in outside

without   lacking, wanting, needing, missing, short of, minus,
less with

withstand   endure, resist, oppose, repel   succumb, give in

witness   1. testify, vouch, swear, 2. see, observe, behold, view, perceive, discern, glimpse, spy, sight

witty   clever, amusing, humorous, funny, whimsical, droll dull

wizard   1. sorcerer, conjuror, 2. expert, master, genius (*Slang* — champ)

wobbly   unsteady, shaky, wavering, rickety, trembling steady

woe   grief, trouble, distress, misery, anguish, agony, heartache, desolation, oppression, sorrow   happiness WOEFUL

woman   female, lady, matron

wonder   1. marvel, gape, stare, 2. doubt, question, be uncertain, not know

wonderful   marvelous, remarkable, striking, astonishing, incredible, extraordinary, exceptional, superb, magnificent, miraculous, splendid, fabulous   ordinary, plain

woo   court, pursue, bid for

woods   forest, bush

word   phrase, say, express, put, voice, tell, communicate WORDING

work   1. labor, toil, accomplish, achieve, effect, make, busy, occupy, engage, employ, 2. operate, run, manage, conduct, handle, manipulate, maneuver

workout   1. exercise, practice, drill, 2. trial, test, rehearsal, dry run, tryout

world   universe, earth, globe

worn   1. damaged, old, secondhand, used, impaired, ragged new, 2. tired, wearied, fatigued, weak, faint   energetic

worry   bother, trouble, torment, molest, harass, harry, badger, plague, vex   soothe, console

worse   deteriorated, impaired, aggravated

worship   respect, honor, idolize, adore, revere, admire, cherish

worth   merit, usefulness, importance, value, benefit, significance, weight   WORTHLESS

wound   1. harm, hurt, injure, damage, pruise   heal, 2. irritate, provoke, sting, infuriate, madden, pain, grieve, offend   soothe

wrangle   argue, quarrel, dispute, bicker, contend, disagree, spat, differ, squabble, row (*Slang* — hassle)

wrap   cover, envelop, sheathe, surround, encompass, bind uncover

wrath   anger, rage, ire   WRATHFUL

wreath   garland, coronet, festoon

wreck   destroy, ruin, devastate, ravage, demolish, dismantle, disassemble

wrench   1. pull, twist, jerk, tear from, wrest, yank, 2. sprain, injure, hurt, strain

wrestle   struggle, battle, fight, tussle   WRESTLER

wretch   1. beggar, sufferer, poor devil, derelict, 2. scoundrel, villain, knave, rogue, shrew

wriggle   twist, turn, wiggle, squirm, writhe

wring   twist, squeeze, press out, wrest

wrinkle   1. fold, ridge, crease, corrugate, furrow, pucker, crinkle, 2. age, grow old, decrease, decline

writ   notice, order, warrant

write   record, inscribe, mark, note, post, pen, scribe WRITER, WRITING

writhe 1. twist, turn, squirm, wiggle, 2. suffer, hurt, ache, wince, anguish, moan, agonize

wrong 1. incorrect, improper, unfit, unsuitable, untrue, false, mistaken right, 2. bad, evil, ill good

wry twisted, crooked, askew, contorted, distorted

X

x-ray photograph

Y

yacht boat

yank jerk, pull, wrench, wrest, tug, draw, heave, haul (*Slang* — lug)

yap bark, yelp, howl

yard 1. court, pen, enclosure, confine, 2. three feet

yarn 1. thread, wool, 2. story, tale, account, narrative, anecdote, spiel

yearn desire, long for, wish for, hope for, pine for, crave YEARNING

yell shout, cry out, call, howl, scream, shriek, whoop, roar, bellow, wail, squall, bawl (*Slang* — holler)

yelp bark, yap, howl

yield 1. produce, give, grant, bear, provide, supply, furnish, 2. surrender, give up, relinquish, waive, forego, part with, sacrifice keep, retain

yoke harness, shackle, bridle

young   youthful, juvenile   old

youngster   child, minor, youth, kid

youthful   young, fresh, juvenile, childish, kiddish, callow
mature, old   YOUTH

yowl   cry, howl, yell, whoop, shriek, scream, wail

Z

zany   foolish, clownish, scatterbrained, comical, silly, crazy

zeal   enthusiasm, eagerness, sincerity, ardor, fervor, passion
indifference, apathy   ZEALOUS

zenith   peak, summit, crown, top, tip, crest, apex, acme,
pinnacle   bottom, base

zero   nothing, naught, nil, none

zest   relish, enjoyment, gusto, savor, delight, eagerness,
pleasure, satisfaction

zone   region, area, territory, place, district, quarter, section,
division, part, department, compartment, vicinity,
neighborhood

zoo   menagerie, animal enclosure

zoom   speed, zip, whiz, fly

REFERENCE